INNOVATIVE INFORMATION SYSTEMS MODELLING TECHNIQUES

Edited by **Christos Kalloniatis**

Innovative Information Systems Modelling Techniques
Edited by Christos Kalloniatis

Published by InTech
Janeza Trdine 9, 51000 Rijeka, Croatia

Publishing Process Manager Romina Skomersic

Technical Editor Teodora Smiljanic

Cover Designer InTech Design Team

Additional hard copies can be obtained from orders@intechopen.com

Innovative Information Systems Modelling Techniques, Edited by Christos Kalloniatis
p. cm.
ISBN 978-953-51-0644-9

For EU product safety concerns:
IN TECH d.o.o., Prolaz Marije Krucifikse Kozulić 3, 51000 Rijeka, Croatia, info@intechopen.com or visit our website at intechopen.com.

Meet the editor

Dr Christos Kalloniatis holds a B.Sc. in Informatics from the Department of Informatics of the Technological Educational Institute of Athens, an M.Sc. in Computer Science from the Department of Computer Science of the University of Essex, UK ,and a Ph.D. in Informatics from the Department of Cultural Technology and Communication of the University of the Aegean. Currently, he is a lecturer at the Department of Cultural Technology and Communication of the University of the Aegean. His current research interests include: Security and privacy in Information Systems, software engineering models and tools and cloud computing. He is an author of several refereed papers in international scientific journals and conference proceedings. He is a member of several program committees of national and international conferences related to Information Security and Privacy and software engineering and is also a reviewer in several scientific journals. He is a member of the Greek Computer Society and has served as a member on the ACM and the IEEE. He is married and lives in Mytilene, the capital of Lesvos Island, in Greece.

Contents

Preface

Information Systems are the software and hardware systems that support data-intensive applications. One of the most critical stages of an Information System development cycle is the System Design stage. During this stage the architecture, components, modules, interfaces and system data are defined and modeled in order to fulfill the respective requirements that the developed Information System should meet. For accomplishing this task a number of requirement engineering methodologies have been proposed and presented in the respective literature aiming on the elicitation, analysis and modeling of the system requirements.

Along with the respective requirement engineering methods a number of modeling techniques have been developed in order to assist analysts and designers to conceptualise and construct the respective models leading to the successful implementation of the Information System. A number of models exist for supporting designers and analysts in various actions taking place during design phase like capturing the right concepts, assisting the analysis and design of the Information System, system simulation as well as for constructing modeling languages for specific systems. The main types of modeling presented are the agent-based modeling, the data modeling and the mathematical modeling.

However, the rapid development of new Information Infrastructure combined with the increased user needs in specific areas of Information Technology (mostly related to Web applications) has created the need for designing new modeling techniques more innovative and targeted on specific areas of Information Systems in order to successfully model the rapidly changed environment, along with the newly introduced concepts and user requirements.

Therefore, this book aims to introduce readers to a number of innovative Information modeling techniques, it is titled "Innovative Information Systems Modelling Techniques" and includes 9 chapters. The focus is on the exploration and coverage of the innovations of recently presented modeling techniques and their applicability on the Information Systems' modeling.

Christos Kalloniatis
Department of Cultural Technology and Communication, University of the Aegean, Greece

1

Information Systems: From the Requirements to the Integrated Solution

José Francisco Zelasco and Judith Donayo
Facultad de Ingeniería, Universidad de Buenos Aires
Argentina

1. Introduction

Database integrity of an information system from its beginning to the end of its life cycle is an important issue of concern among specialists (Melton & Simon, 2002) (Guoqi Feng et al, 2009), (Post & Gagan, 2001) (Eastman C. et al, 1997) (An Lu & Wilfred Ng, 2009). The proposal solution, concerning all the aspects of an information system project, is introduced here with the aim of ensuring the integrity of the database throughout the development of the system. The general aim of this chapter is to propose a method derived from MERISE (Tardieu et al, 1985), consisting of an interconnected set of tools and those heuristics to improve the requirements engineering issues, facilitating the design of specifications, allowing alternatives of organization in terms of workstation, tasks, etc. Establish the requirements for the development of a computer system involves collecting information and expectations from users of various levels of responsibility and belonging to areas that may have, if not conflicting, at least different interests. However, the demands of different users, should reconciled into a set of specifications that will be acceptable, in a concerted way, for all of them. It is essential, to fix up the final solution, to present the proposed options in an understandable way to all users (Zelasco & Donayo, 2011).

Consequently, the information produced must be stricter and simpler, and should facilitate, in terms of design, the use of tools such as those proposed by the Unified Modeling Language (UML) and the Unified Process (UP) (Zelasco et al, 2007). In this presentation we will lay special emphasis on those tools that are related to data structuring and that make their monitoring easier during the optimization and the distribution of data on the physical level, while protecting their consistency.

As an introduction to the process of conception, we will introduce a diagram called sun (Figure 1) (Tardieu et al, 1985) in which we can see the stage of creation articulated in three levels of abstraction:

1. Conceptual level: what the company does, as a whole, to answer the external actor stimuli.
2. Organizational or logical level: (namely, involving internal actors), who does what, where (workstation) and when.
3. Operational or Physical level: how it is done and with what equipment. There is a distinction here between the tasks performed by men known as men's tasks, which give

rise to the user's manual and the tasks performed by machines known as machine tasks, leading to the information system (programs) Design and Development.

These diagrams goes from bottom left to bottom right like the movement of the sun, passing in the middle through the upper level, i.e., the conceptual one. The entire line can be covered by iterating twice.

The first iteration occurs after the selection of elements that due to their volume (data) and frequency (events) are of greater importance. This selection is, thus, known as a representative subset and corresponds to a preliminary study of the project. The second one comprises the field of study as a whole, so it corresponds to a complete and detailed study of the system.

The line (fig. 1) from the beginning to the current conceptual level corresponds to the inverse engineering, which involves the scenarios of the system in its current state: it is the way the system is working.

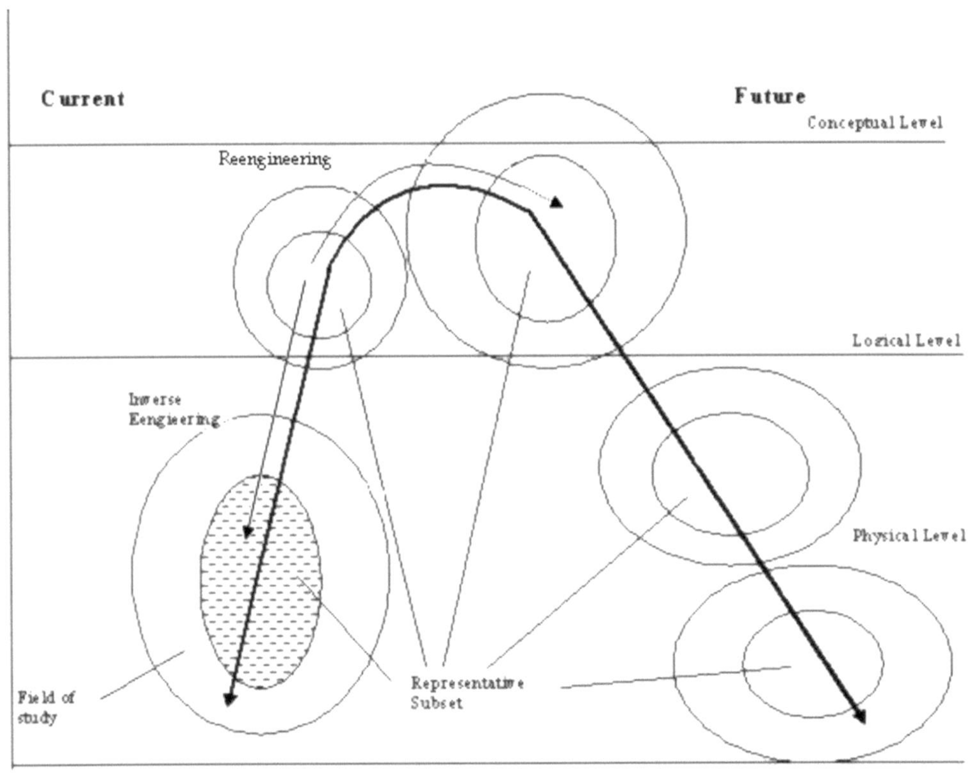

Fig. 1. Diagram of the sun

The reengineering phase involves the transition from the current state to the future state. Some of the factors taken into account for this passage are: the aim of the company, the external actors that affect it (competition, legislation, etc.) factors that could eventually have incidence in the conduct of the organization, all the Board decisions (the company's corporate rules, policies, strategies, objectives, and available resources), fields of activity, the different duties that arise from the organization chart, etc. The direction will fix up in one hand the updated management rules, involving what the company should do as a response to external requirements (stimuli); and in the other hand, the updated data integrity constraints and restrictions, will determine the data structure and functional dependencies. In the lexicon used by this method, the data integrity constraints and restrictions concern the data structure; management rules concern to the data-treatment: process and procedures - some authors use the terms Business Rules for integrity constraints and/or Management Rules together; to avoid confusion, we will not use it-. This updated information determines the passage from present state to future state, which corrects and enriches the results of the current conceptual model. The results of the current model, obtained by means of the inverse engineering, are the starting point, followed by the gathering of information about the context and definitions of the Board (reengineering) to obtain the future model.

It supported the hypothesis that there is greater invariance in the data, related to properties and classes or entities, integrity constrains and restrictions than in the treatments, concerning events and management rules. From now on, we will try to describe how to determine:

1. 1. The minimal data model that includes all the information of a distributed system, in terms of properties, entities, relations, integrity constrains and restrictions, and which will be stored in the physical database to be reached through different transitions, mechanisms and optimizations.
2. 2. Integrity verification. From the system analysis we pass on to the design, and once the relevant objects are created, the consistency between the persistent properties and the minimal established scheme is verified. This is to be done by updating and querying each one of the corresponding entities/properties. This heuristic ensures that the minimal data scheme meets the needs of each subsystem, but the main advantage of this mechanism is to ensure that each subsystem provides all the elements required by the other subsystems. In this way the modifications of the previous subsystems are to be minimized when the following ones are developed according to the priorities established by the Board.
3. 3. The treatments model based on Petri nets (Wu et al, 2005) (Chu et al, 1993) are executed by subsystem. A first scheme describes the Process itself, i.e., what the company is to do as a response to each external requirement, to initial events of processes and to those which derive from them. This brings about a concatenated series of operations, an ongoing activity, per Process. The operations contain tasks expressed in terms of management rules. Next, that same scheme is enlarged in the Procedure, replacing each operation in one or many phases, corresponding to the uninterrupted activity of a specific workstation. This brings about different organization options i.e., scenario options that, in this level, could be evaluated comparatively by the company's Board and other users, and so, to choose the most convenient one. The scheme describes the future scenarios and use cases. The following level is the operational level, in which each job position distributes the tasks according to the human's activity and the information systems activity. The tasks performed by a person will lead to the user's manual and those automated correspond to the system analysis. The tasks derived from management rules are expressed less colloquially and eventually more formally.

2. Conceptual data model

The minimal and complete conceptual data model allows an overall view of the information system data. This overall view of the memory shared by all the actors of the system (all the subsystems) is the mechanism that allows a truly systemic approach of the project. The database administrator transfers this minimal and complete conceptual model without redundancy, to its physical form through passages and optimizations.

To create the minimal conceptual data modeling, that allows for a global view of the information system, we do not proceed as in object creation, i.e., the starting point are the fields of activity from which the relevant properties are gathered and classified, trying not to confuse or relate classes to objects. This yields greater objectivity to the integrity verification, as the person who executes the data scheme is not usually the one who creates the objects of each subsystem.

During the preliminary study, (first iteration) the most important data are chosen, taking into account the volume and the most frequent processes. It is important to determine a representative subset which will allow a good articulation between the Conceptual Data Model, and all of the subsystems. This can be done iteratively, since at the stage of detailed study (second iteration including the complete set of data) such model will have all the properties with no redundancy that have to be stored in the physical base.

A list of integrity constraints and restrictions should be created to give rise to functional dependencies, relations between entities, etc. From the current model and taking into consideration the modifications that result from reengineering, we pass on to the future model, as we have mentioned above.

To avoid property redundancy, this scheme requires the existing relationships to be expressed without being transformed into binaries. Although the *look here* approach (MERISE proposal) (Tardieu et al, 1985) (Tardieu et al, 1987) (Mounyol) and the *look across* one (Chen, 1976) could simplify the representation of options in ternary relationships, it is useless to discuss their advantages because both of them are complementary. In fact, one chosen approach should have to be enriched in a simple way, to allows the representation of all the functional dependencies that both complementary approaches represent.

There are certain points to take into account to reach this minimal model. Some are rather elementary, others are more subtle:

1. Each property appears only once in the scheme, as a class (entity) or relation attribute.
2. The scheme should respect the second normal rule (Batini et al, 1991) (Ullman et al, 1997) (Yourdon, 1993).
3. If a property depends on the identifiers of two or more classes, it is a property of the relation that links such classes (third normal rule). (Batini et al, 1991) (Ullman et al, 1997) (Yourdon, 1993) (Ullman et al, 1988).
4. Only one value can be assigned to each property.
5. An arc that links a class with a relation cannot be optional, i.e., when there is a relation occurrence, it should be linked with an occurrence of each class. If this is not the case, it is because there are two different relations that have to be separated because conceptually it is not the same, even though in the physical level this will not be respected.

6. Only one occurrence of each class converges to each relation occurrence and reciprocally only one relation occurrence converges to each set of occurrences of each class. If this does not happen it is because the indispensable class that avoids this ambiguity has been omitted.
7. It should be verified that each class has a set of occurrences, so as not to confuse unique objects (company's Board) with data classes, which is a frequent mistake among beginners.

It should be pointed out that this minimal scheme can be the basis for a conceptual object-oriented database model scheme using simple generalization (Zelasco et al, 1998), and evaluating multiple inheritance.

3. Integrity verification or consistency

Integrity Verification or consistency allows us to ensure data integrity and the harmonic development of subsystems by reducing costs and the redundancies derived from the modifications of previous subsystems developed in order to satisfy the subsequent ones. The verification process consists of contrasting the object persistent properties of each system with the minimal and complete conceptual data model. With this minimal model we can verify all the updating and queries of each and every persistent data of each application or subsystem object; this is the "verification of the integrity" (fig. 2).

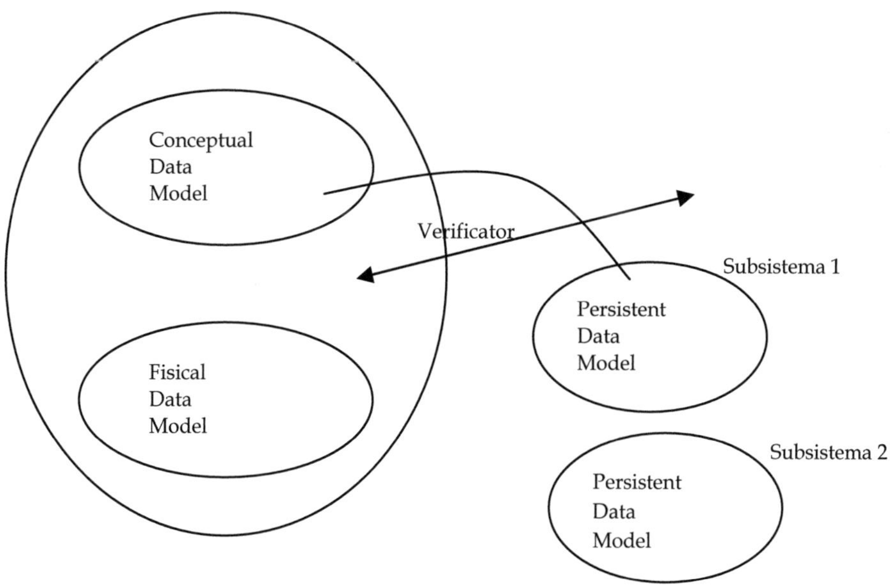

Fig. 2. Integrity verification

When analyzing the object persistent properties in previous subsystems, it is assumed that some anomalies may occur. However, in the minimal conceptual model these anomalies would be considered as a sub product of the verification process. Since verification mainly aims to ensure that each subsystem yields the essential information to the proper functioning of other subsystems. This interaction is fundamental when the information is distributed.

Some applications are developed before others for some priority reasons. In this case, the verification process guarantees that the cost of the modifications of the previously designed applications is minimum or inappreciable.

This objective is achieved by verifying that the persistent properties of each subsystem can be updated and accessed. It is neither necessary nor possible that data structure from the minimal conceptual model resembles that from the object models. However, there must be identifiers (or access paths) that allow for the updating of classes and relation occurrences as well as of particular properties.

From there on, the database administrator may choose between an object-oriented database and a relational database (Ceri et al, 1997). He will progressively simplify and include optimizations with the corresponding redundancy that will be documented to allow inverse engineering to be done without difficulty whenever necessary. This permits to control redundancy since reference is always made to the same minimal model. Indeed, whenever a modification to the database is required, (inverse engineering) that modification must be expressed in the minimum scheme so that it affects the entire distributed database to ensure data consistency. Thus, it will be enough to bring down the optimizations tree and transformations from the minimum model to the database. It should be taken into account that the optimizations must respect, if possible, the search for the minimum storage cost function and process time cost (holding cost) and it must also be well documented; thus facilitating such drop. Besides, the information will be distributed and correctly documented at the corresponding level. Relying on the documented tracing of the simplification, the optimization, and the distribution at its different levels are not irrelevant factors to guarantee integrity and the consequent minimization of the cost of development and maintenance of the project.

4. Processing model

We shall present the tools and the way to proceed with the treatments at different levels.

We suggest tools derived from Petri's nets to develop the Conceptual Model of Treatments (CMT) as well as the Organizational Model of Treatments (OrMT) (Zhang et al, 1994); (Chu et al, 1993). The richness of the proposed diagrams is superior to that of the sequence or activity diagrams and therefore more appropriate to model these levels of abstraction. As it was said, the users dispose of several options of solutions, where he can evaluate advantages and disadvantages. However, we should note that the tools supplied by UML (Larman Craig, 2001) are very useful as long as they are applied in the corresponding level.

Treatment schemes at different levels are made by considering the domains of activity the company develops and for each function which can be extracted, for example, from its organization chart. These subsystems proposed by the users and corroborated by the specialist will lead to different applications and possibly will prioritize stages of development. The activity of the company, both at the conceptual and the organizational level is reflected from the management rules, in other words, what the company should do in response to external requests (stimuli), in terms of events. Management rules of the current model are obtained as a result of reverse engineering, observing which response is given to each request of an outsider to the organization (event).

The model presented to the users is fundamental for -through reengineering, passing from the current conceptual model to the future conceptual model-, enabling the users to see in a very concise way, the changes that involve considering the new circumstances.

4.1 Conceptual model of treatments

The Conceptual Model of Treatments describes the processes that initiate from primary events which are generally external or assimilable to external ones; that is to say **what** to do.

These processes are divided into operations which have a set of management rules. The events as well as such management rules (not business rules) (Ceri et al, 1997) come from the criteria mentioned in the introduction. Management rules describe each action that the company should accomplish to satisfy events, not only the initial ones but also those arising during the process. The operations involve a series of ongoing or uninterrupted actions. The necessity of a new operation arises from an interruption, as a result of a response event from an external actor. The organization thus waits for another external event to restart the following operation. In terms of events, there is no distinction between response and events, that is to say the response is, in itself, a new event.

These events are linked to the activity sector of the organization; the events that will give rise to a particular response won't be equal in the case of a hospital or a bank or an insurance company. So it is necessary have detected all external events (or assimilable to external) that affect the organization in matter, sorted by subsystem or software application, both linked, as we said at the organizational chart. Management rules are the answers that will give the organization to each of these events. Setting these rules is a critical task because from it depend the future of the system. The management agreement is essential. It is noteworthy that different options of conceptual model of treatments, allows comparison in options of management rules and to choose one of these models implies opting for certain management rules. Management rules are codified to facilitate their use in the diagrams. The elements of process diagrams (CMT) are events, synchronization, operation or transaction with any eventual output condition and responses (see the figures in example below). The operations correspond to the performance of one or more management rules and, in a whole, will lead to response events. We insist to notice that the management rules describe each of the actions that the company must take to satisfy events, both initial and those which arise during the process that will involve an operation or a chain of operations. The operations engage a series of uninterrupted actions. The need of a new operation occurs due to an interruption, as a result of an event-response to an external actor, remaining waiting for another external event to reset the next operation. No distinction is made in terms of events between response and event, i.e. the answer is, at the same time, a new event.

It is noteworthy that at this level (CMT), it ignores who does what, when and where in the organization of the company. The responses to events are made by the company as a whole. This allows in the subsequent level, propose, analyze and evaluate different options of organization having previously set the response of the company as a whole in front of each of the external events. In this CMT is observed the synchronization, prior to each transaction, the synchronization uses the logical operators of conjunction and disjunction (and and or) (Fig. 2.5). This allows representing the different sets of events (or a single event) that trigger the operation. In the case of response events, there can also be an indication of the output conditions in which they are produced. Within the operation or transaction, which must be identified with a name, it is placed the code of management rules that apply. The acronyms of the corresponding management rules are inscribed in the operation which must have a name. These acronyms are in correspondence with the list of rules where the actions involved are described.

4.2 Organizational model of treatments

The Organizational Model of Treatments (OrMT) describes the characteristics of the treatments that have not been expressed in the conceptual model of treatment, expanding, in terms of workstations, the conceptual model of the company's organization; that is to say, workstation (who do what, where and when), in other words, time, human resources, places, etc..

The conceptual model of treatments describes the flow of events, mainly those between the organization of the company and the environment (**what**).

The OrMT adds to the conceptual model the company's flow of events among the different workstations (Chu et al, 1993).

A process in the CMT expands in a procedure in the OrMT and operations of each process will result in different phases of the work stations of each procedure. The CMT describes the flow of events, essentially between the organization (the company) and the environment. The uninterrupted or ongoing activity at the procedure level is called phase. The OrMT adds for the CMT the flow of events within the company among the different phases of the work stations (see the figures in example below).

The study of a company's organizational problem, usually, belongs to other experts, so computer specialists are frequently restricted to taking that model as the working base for the system development (Dey et al, 1999). Different organization options, other than the one imposed, show improvements in the information system. This methodological proposal not only prevents this inconvenience and the waste of money and time but also proposes a study of the company's organization options setting, possibly in question, the solution proposed by other experts. When a computer specialist takes part in contributing with this formal tool, based on Petri nets (He et al, 2003), the advantages of one option over the other one become obvious, particularly from the automatization point of view. The decision about the company's organization results, then, in an agreement, and so the computer specialist faces a more solid and robust option. Besides, this OrMT contributes to a more accurate elaboration of the user's manual and to the analysis prior to design.

A chart is used to describe the procedure. The first column or the first set of consecutive columns corresponds to the external actor/actors related to such process. The subsequent columns correspond to the workstations to which the procedures are expanded. The phase structure is identical to the operation structure of the conceptual model of treatments. The phase has the possibility of synchronizing events by means of logical operators of conjunction and disjunction (and and or). It has an identification name, the acronyms of the management rules which correspond to the actions that a workstation must carry out during that phase and the output conditions of the response events. It is important to highlight that response events may be directed to both external actors and internal actors (other workstation phases). From the foregoing, it can be said that one or more phases correspond to each operation and that in the case the operation is divided into various phases, the management rules contained in the operation will be distributed among the respective phases.

Finally, in case the phase has rules capable of automatization, the operations that will be done by the person in that workstation and those operations to be automated will be established. These actions are called "men's tasks" and "machine tasks". This classification corresponds to the called Operational Treatments Model (OpTM) and gives rise to the user's manual and the systems analysis at the level of each use case.

For the OpMT it can establish an analogue diagram between man tasks and machine tasks, which can facilitate the development of the using manual and the pre-programming analysis, however, is not necessary to discuss this scheme with the user as it is an appropriate tool for the specialist.

The progressive detail grade of these three levels shows that they are three different levels of abstraction and that they are useful for a better information system definition. In this way the representation of use cases and scenarios options is facilitated.

5. Examples

This section develops a case study that focuses on the subsystem for admitting patients to an attention centre just with the purpose of presenting the development of treatment paradigms. This is not a real case, but an example that brings out the versatility of the proposed heuristics.

To be able to realize the process for the CMT identifies the events that stimulate and initiate this process and management rules, which indicate how the organization should respond to these events (Fig. 2).

5.1 Description of the admitting process

The admission process begins when a patient arrives at the center of attention. A patient that request an appointment can reach the center of attention in two conditions, as patient with health insurance in which case he pays a supplementary amount (reduced) or as a patient without insurance, in which case he pays the full benefit.

And from the solution 1 they are proposed two options of solution for the OrMT: the diagram a (Fig. 3) and diagram b (Fig. 4).

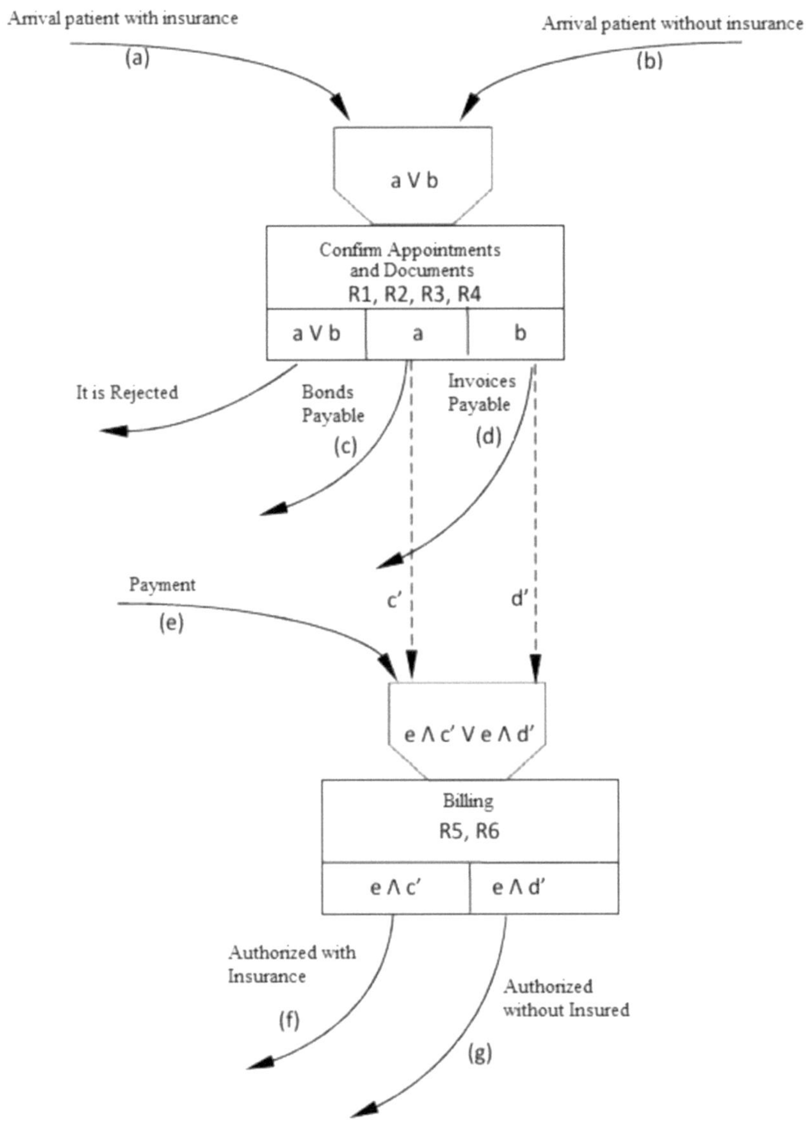

Fig. 3. Conceptual Model of Solution 1 of the example of admission of patients.

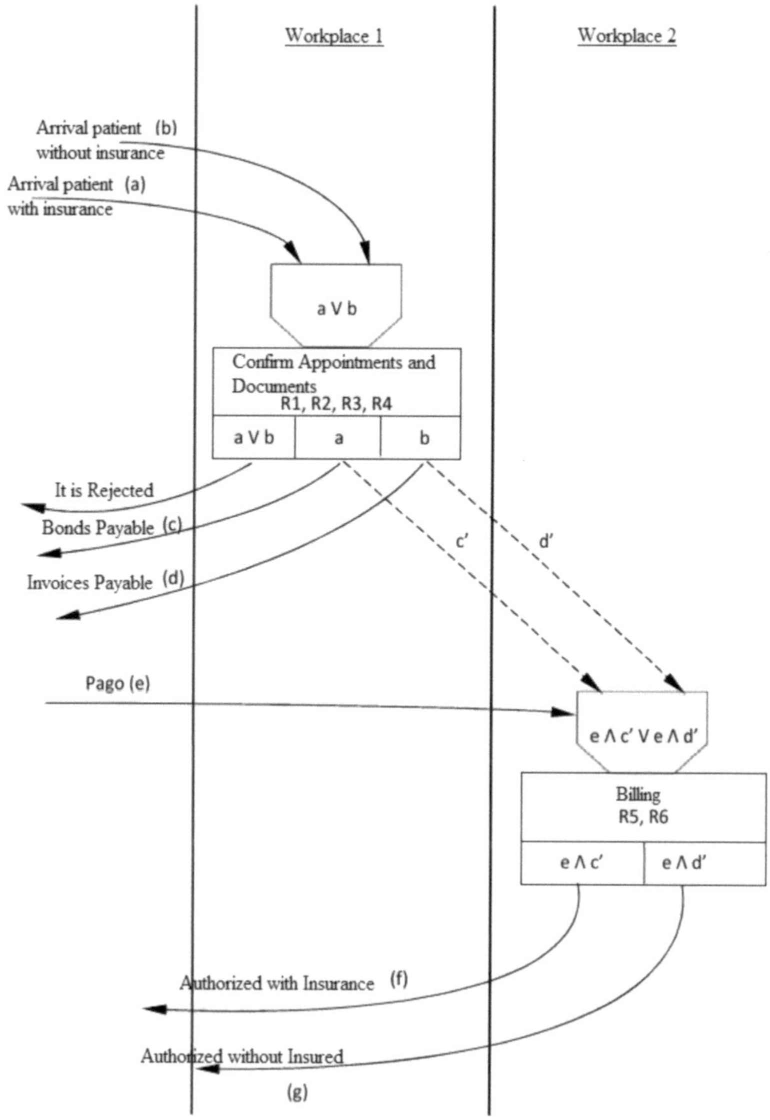

Fig. 4. Organizational Model of Solution 1 of the example of admission of patients to a health centre.

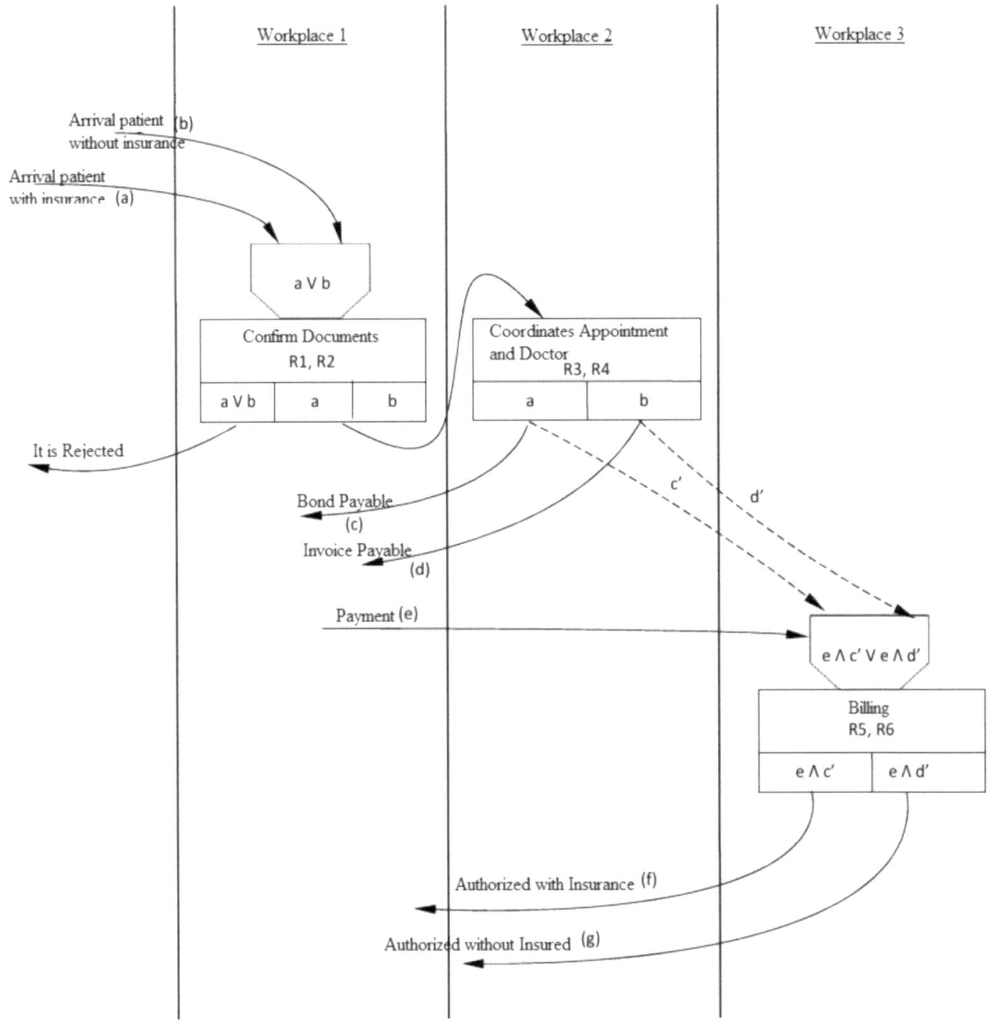

Fig. 5. Another Organizational Model of Solution 1 of the example of admission of patients to a health centre.

5.1.1 CMT Solution 1

Next, we present the external events and the management rules corresponding to the process of the solution 1:

Events:

a. Arrival a patient with insurance.
b. Arrival a patient without insurance.
c. Effectuation of payment.

Rules:

R1: Identification verification otherwise is rejected.

R2: Identify specialty and schedule an appointment with the doctor.

R3: With the appointment scheduled concerted, if the patient has insurance, the bond is issued.

R4: With the appointment scheduled concerted, if the patient hasn't insurance, the invoice is issued.

R5: Verified the bonus payment, a permit is issued to the patient with insurance, to make an appointment scheduled.

R6: Verified the invoice payment, a permit is issued to a patient without insurance, to make an appointment scheduled.

Note that the operation is interrupted because the payment can be made later, not at the same time as the application of turn.

5.1.2 CMT Solution 2

Next, we present the external events and the management rules corresponding to the process of solution 2:

Events:

a. Arrival a patient with insurance.
b. Arrival a patient without insurance.
c. Effectuation of payment.

Rules:

R1: Identification verification otherwise is rejected.

R2: Payment according to condition.

R3: Verified the payment, it proceeds to the specialty identification and it coordinates appointment scheduled, doctor and emission of authorization of corresponding consult.

It is noted that the operation is not interrupted, because the payment it has to be done at the same moment than the appointment solicitation. In this case, because the process is reduced to only one operation, the reader will be able to elaborate this process, including all the rules in the only operation.

5.1.3 Organizational models of treatments corresponding to solution1

Supposed being selected the solution 1 (Fig. 2) they are analyzed the two solution options proposed for OrMT: diagram a (Fig. 3), diagram b (Fig. 4).

In diagram a (Fig. 3), the first operation (Validation of appointments scheduled and documents) of the CMT is performed in the phase validation of appointments scheduled and documents on the first work station, and the second operation (Billing) is done in invoicing phase on the second workplace.

In the diagram b (Fig. 4) the first operation (Validation of appointments scheduled and documents) from the CMT is unfolded in the phase of "document validation" on the first work station, and the phase "coordinating of appointment and doctor" on the second work station; and the second operation (invoicing) is held in the Invoicing phase on the third workplace.

The diagram b would be selected by an organization that prefers to separate a checkpoint (security) from assigning appointments scheduled and doctors.

It is noted that the same workplace can do several phases, what happens if the procedure is more complex.

When the operational level of treatment to a certain stage of a workplace, analyzes the management rules, naturally are being established both the instruction manual corresponding to operator tasks such as system analysis derived from update tasks that should make interacting with the operator.

6. Conclusions

Preserving the minimal conceptual model along the system life preserves from inconsistencies

The minimal conceptual data model provides a systemic global view.

The current model of data and treatments, achieved by inverse engineering, guarantees a higher stability of the system.

And finally, the consistency verification assures minimal modification in previous developed subsystems.

The overall view through the minimal model permits us also to control redundancies and to avoid problems of integrity.

Applying this mechanism and consequently reducing the entropy leads to a more balanced and tolerant system to the changes in the context in which the organization is immersed and to the requirement modifications.

The application of these tools and heuristics ensures the stability of the database, provides a reduction of the number of iterations in the development thus contributing to diminish the system entropy whose cost may be inappreciable mainly at the beginning of the maintenance phase.

In the other hand, the application of this mechanism based on Petri diagrams, and respecting the indicated heuristic, is of great interest as a tool of engineering of requirements. These tools used in abstraction levels superior than usual, lead to relevant advantages. First allows better interaction between users and the specialist to formalize the requirements. The user through these schemes, of reading relatively simple, can select the most convenient solution and will compare management options when it is about CMT and organization in the OrMT. This advantage is accentuated because the proposed mechanism is performed in an iterative fashion by focusing on a representative subset in the preliminary study and taking into consideration the entire field of study in the detailed study. The development of the solution results more robust as it facilitates the visual comparison of the current model (reverse engineering), both of management and organization with different options of the future model (reengineering). The result is greater clarity in the proposed solution which gives greater rigor in the development of the specifications. In addition, from the diagrams adopted derive both the user manuals as analysis and design necessary to the development, and from comparing the diagrams of the current state with the adopted solution diagrams, arises the definition of works stations and of the intermediate phases necessary for a harmonious integration of the new system in the company.

7. References

An Lu, Wilfred Ng, 2009: Maintaining consistency of vague databases using data dependencies. Data & Knowledge Engineering, In Press, Corrected Proof, Available online 28 February 2009

Batini C., S. Ceri y S. B. Navathe, 1991, Database Design: An Entity-Relationship Approach, Prentice-Hall.

Ceri, S., Fraternali, P., 1997, Designing Database Applications with Objects and Rules: The IDEA Methodology Addison Wesley; 1st edition, ISBN: 0201403692.

Chen, P. S., 1976: The entity relationship model: to-ward a unified view of data, ACM Transactions on Data-base Systems, (1), 9-36.

Chu, f., Proth, J-M., Savi, V. M., 1993: Ordonnancement base sur les reseaux de Petri. Raport de recher-che No 1960 INRIA Francia.

Dey D., Storey V. C. and Barron T. M., 1999, Im-proving Database Design trough the Analysis of Relation-ship, ACM Transactions on Database Systems, 24 (4), 453-486.

Dullea J. and I. Y. Song, 1998, An Analysis of Struc-tural Validity of Ternary Relationships in Entity Relation-ship Modeling, Proceed. 7° Int. Conf. on Information and Knowledge Management, 331-339.

Eastman C, Stott Parker D. and Tay-Sheng Jeng 1997: Managing the integrity of design data generated by multiple applications: The principle of patching. Research in Engineering Design, Volume 9, Number 3 / septiembre de 1997

FAQ Merise et modelisation de donnees - Club d'entraides developpeurs francophones. http://uml.developpez.com/faq/merise/

González, J. A., Dankel, D., 1993: The Engineering of Knowledge-Based Systems. Prentice Hall.

Guoqi Feng, Dongliang Cui, Chengen Wang, Jiapeng Yu 2009: Integrated data management in complex product collaborative design. Computers in Industry, Volume 60, Issue 1, January 2009, Pages 48-63

He, X., Chu, W., Yang, H., 2003: A New Approach to Verify Rule-Based Systems Using Petri Nets. Information and Software Technology 45(10).

Larman Craig, 2001: Applying UML and Patterns: An Introduction to Object-Oriented. Analysis and Design and the Unified Process Prentice Hall PTR; 2d edition July 13, ISBN: 0130925691.

Melton J, Simon A R, 2002 Constraints, Assertions, and Referential Integrity SQL: 1999, 2002, Pages 355-394

MERISE - Introduction à la conception de systèmes d'ınformation. http://www.commentcamarche.net/merise/concintro.php3

Mounyol, R. MERISE étendue: Cas professionnels de synthèse. ISBN: 2729895574. Rojer Mounyol ed. Elipses

Post G., Kagan A., 2001: Database Management systems: design considerations and attribute facilities. Journal of Systems and Software, Volume 56, Issue 2, 1 March 2001, Pages 183-193

Song, I. Y., Evans, M. and Park, E. K., 1995: A comparative Análisis of Entity-Relationship Diagrams, Journal of Computer and Software Engineering, 3 (4), 427-459.

Tardieu, H., Rochfeld, A., Colletti, R., 1985 La Méthode MERISE. Tome 1. ISBN: 2-7081-1106-X. Ed. Les Edition d'organization.

Tardieu, H., Rochfeld, A., Colletti, R., Panet, G., Va-hée, G., 1987 La Méthode MERISE. Tome 2. ISBN: 2-7081-0703-8. Ed. Les Edition d'organization.

Ullman J. D. and J. Windom, 1997, A FirstCourse in Database Systems, Prentice-Hall.

Ullman Jeffrey D. & Freeman W. H., 1988, Principles of Database and Knowledge-Base Systems. Vol. 1, 1a edition, ISBN: 0716781581.

Wu, Q., Zhou, C., Wu, J., Wang, C., 2005: Study on Knowledge Base Verification Based on Petri Nets. Inter-national Conference on Control and Automation (ICCA 2005) Budapest, Hungry, June 27-29.

Yourdon, Inc., 1993: Yourdon Method, Prentice-Hall.

Zelasco J. F, Alvano, C. E., Diorio, G., Berrueta, N., O'Neill, P., Gonzalez, C., 1998: Criterios Metódicos Básicos para Concepción de Bases de Datos Orientadas a Objetos. Info-Net, III Congreso Internacional y Exposición de Informática e Internet. Proceding en CD. Mendoza, Argentina.

Zelasco, J. F., Donayo, J., Merayo, G., 2007, Complementary Utilities for UML and UP in Information Systems, EATIS 2007. (ACM DL). Faro, Portugal. ISBN:978-1-59593-598-4

Zelasco, J. F., Donayo, J., 2010, Database integrity in Integrated Systems INSTICC PRESS 2009,. Milán-Italia. May 2009. ISBN 978-989-8111-90-6

Zelasco, J. F., Donayo, J., 2011, Organizational Chart for Engineering of Requirements. IASTED SE 2011 Soft-ware Engineering, Innsbruck, Austria; 15-17 February 2011

Zhang, D., Nguyen, D., 1994: PREPARE: A Tool for Knowledge Base Verification. IEEE Trans. on Knowledge and Data Engineering (6).

2

An Architecture-Centric Approach for Information System Architecture Modeling, Enactement and Evolution

Hervé Verjus, Sorana Cîmpan and Ilham Alloui
University of Savoie – LISTIC Lab
France

1. Introduction

Information Systems are more and more complex and distributed. As market is continuously changing, information systems have also to change in order to support new business opportunities, customers' satisfaction, partners' interoperability as well as new exchanges, technological mutations and organisational transformations. Enterprise agility and adaptability leads to a new challenge: flexibility and adaptability of its information system. Most information systems are nowadays software-intensive systems: they integrate heterogeneous, distributed software components, large-scale software applications, legacy systems and COTS. In this context, designing, building, maintaining evolvable and adaptable information systems is an important issue for which few rigorous approaches exist. In particular information system architecture (Zachman, 1997) is an important topic as it considers information system as interacting components, assembled for reaching enterprise business goals according to defined strategies and rules. Thus, information system architecture supports business processes, collaboration among actors and among organizational units, promotes inter-enterprise interoperability (Vernadat, 2006) and has to evolve as business and enterprise strategy evolve too (Kardasis & Loucopoulos, 1998; Nurcan & Schmidt, 2009).

During the past twenty years, several works around system architecture have been proposed: they mainly focus on software system architecture (Bass *et al.*, 2003), enterprise and business architecture (Barrios & Nurcan, 2004; Touzi *et al.*, 2009; Nurcan & Schmidt, 2009). All of them mainly propose abstractions and models to describe system architecture. Research on software architecture (Perry & Wolf, 1992; Bass *et al.*, 2003) proposes engineering methods, formalisms and tools focusing on software architecture description, analysis and enactment. In that perspective, Architecture Description Languages (ADLs) are means for describing software architecture (Medvidovic & Taylor, 2000) and may also be used to describe software-intensive information system architecture. Such ADLs cope with software system static aspects at a high level of abstraction. Some of them deal with behavioral features and properties (Medvidovic & Taylor, 2000). Very few of the proposed approaches are satisfactory enough to deal with software-intensive system architecture dynamic evolution; *i.e.*, a software-intensive system architecture being able to evolve during enactment.

As an illustrative example of such a dynamically evolving software-intensive information system, consider the following supply chain information system that entails a manufacturing enterprise, its customers and suppliers. The supply chain information system is a software-intensive system comprising several software components. It is governed by an EAI (Enterprise Application Integration) software solution that itself comprises an ERP system. The ERP system includes components dedicated to handling respectively stocks, invoices, orders and quotations. These software elements form the information system architecture. In a classical scenario, a customer may ask for a quotation and then make an order. The order may or may not be satisfied depending on the stock of the ordered product. We may imagine several alternatives. The first one assumes that the information system is rigid (*i.e.*, it cannot dynamically evolve or adapt): if the current product stock is not big enough to satisfy the client's order, a restocking procedure consists in contacting a supplier in order to satisfy the order. We assume that the supplier is always able to satisfy a restocking demand. Let us now imagine that the restocking phase is quite undefined (has not been defined in advance – *i.e.*, at design time) and that it can be dynamically adapted according to business considerations, market prices, suppliers' availability and business relationships. Then, the supporting supply chain information system architecture would have to be dynamically and on-the-fly adapted according to the dynamic business context. Such dynamicity during system enactment is an important issue for which an architecture-centric development approach is suitable.

This represents an important step forward in software-intensive information system engineering domain, as software intensive information systems often lack support for dynamic evolution. When existing, such support doesn't ensure the consistency between design decisions and the running system. Thus, generally first the system model is evolved, and then the implementation, without necessarily mantaining the consistency between the two system representations. This leads to undesired situations where the actual system is not the one intended, or thought by the decision makers.

This chapter presents an architecture-centric development approach that addresses the above mentioned issues, namely dynamic evolution while preserving the consistency between the system design and implementation. Our approach entails architectural description formalisms and corresponding engineering tools to describe, analyze and enact dynamically evolvable software-intensive information systems.

It presents the overall development approach, briefly introducing the different models and meta-models involved as well as the different processes that can be derived from the approach (see section 2). Although the approach supports the entire development cycle, the chapter focuses on the way dynamic evolution is handled. More precisely it shows how information systems, described using suitable architecture-related languages (see section 3), can be architectured so that their dynamic evolution can be handled. Thus section 5 and 6 present the proposed mechanismes for handling respectively dynamic planned and unplanned evolutions of the information system architecture. These mechanisms are presented using evolution scenarios related to a case study which is briefly introduced in section 4. Section 7 presents related work. We end the chapter with concluding remarks in section 8.

2. On architecture-centric development

Considerable efforts have been made in the software architecture field (Medvidovic & Taylor, 2000; Bass *et al.*, 2003) (mainly software architecture modeling, architectural property expression and checking) that place the architecture in the heart of a software intensive system life cycle. "Software architecture is being viewed as a key concept in realizing an organization's technical and business goals" (Carrière *et al.*, 1999). Software architectures shift the focus of developers from implementation to coarser-grained architectural elements and their overall interconnection structure (Medvidovic & Taylor, 2000). *In architecture-centric development approaches, the architecture of the system under construction is considered at different abstraction levels. Starting with a rather coarse grain representation of the system, the process stepwise refines this representation producing more detailed representations. At each phase, architectural properties can be defined and analyzed.* Architecture Description Languages (ADLs) have been proposed as well as architecture-centric development environments, toolkits (graphical modelers, compilers, analysis/verification tools, *etc.*) (Schmerl *et al.*, 2004; ArchStudio) which support software architects' and engineers' activities.

We consider the architecture-centric information system development as a model-driven engineering process (Favre *et al.*, 2006). Every process is centered on design models of systems to develop. Models are used for several purposes: to understand specific aspects of a system, to predict the qualities of a system, to reason on the impact of change on a system and to communicate with different system stakeholders (developers, commercials, clients, end-users, *etc.*). Among the objectives of such approaches is their ability to provide (at least partially) enough details to generate an implementation of the information system software components and their interconnections. Thus, the generated code is, itself, the expression of a model. In architecture-centric development approaches (Kyaruzi & van Katwijk, 2000) models represent mainly software architectures, but can also represent some expected properties or transformations that can be made on such architectures.

The architecture may be defined at several levels of abstraction. The transition from one level to another is done through a refinement process along which further details are added to the architecture description until reaching a desired concrete (implementation) level. The resulting concrete architecture can either be directly executed if the employed ADL has its own virtual machine or it can be used to generate an executable description for another target execution environment (*e.g.*, Java, C++, *etc.*).

As the system software architecture captures early design decisions that have a significant impact on the quality of the resulting system, it is important if not essential to check those decisions as early as possible. Software architecture analysis is an ineluctable activity within the development process. It focuses on structural and/or behavioral properties one can expect from both system functional and non-functional behaviors (*e.g.* are architectural elements always connected? Is the system behavior robust? *etc.*). Moreover, evolving a system must be accompanied by checking whether its correctness is still ensured or not after the changes. In software engineering processes, checking the correctness of a system relies on analyzing expected properties at either/both design time or/and runtime. This requires the availability of software tools/support for both checking if the desired properties are satisfied and detecting those that have been violated with the possibility of reconciling them. Ideally an approach that aims at considering the evolution along the whole lifecycle should provide mechanisms for analysis, detection of property violation and its reparation.

The introduction of architecture-centric approaches had as prior intent an improvement of the software development process, allowing people to gain intellectual control over systems ever more complex and thus providing solutions for a major software engineering concern. Software-intensive system evolution is another major concern in software engineering (Andrade & Fiadeiro, 2003, Mens *et al.*, 2003), as human-centric activities are more and more supported by software applications that have to evolve according to changing requirements, technologies, business, *etc.* Software-intensive systems should be able to adapt according to those changes (Belady & Lehman, 1985). As changes may impact the information system architecture, the way of evolving the architecture is part of the information system evolution problem. Moreover, the problem of handling the evolution of a software-intensive information system taking into account its architecture is closely related to the problem of keeping the consistency between two layers: the software system *concrete* (source code, implementation) architecture, and, the information system *conceptual* (abstract, design) architecture as well as continuous switching between these layers (Perry & Wolf, 1992).

We distinguish four types of evolution (Cîmpan & Verjus, 2005) according to two criteria: (i) the architecture evolution is carried out *statically* (*i.e.*, while some of the information system executing software components are stopped) or *dynamically* (*i.e.*, while the system is being continuously executing), (ii) has the evolution been planned (*i.e.*, at design time) or not (*i.e.*, unplanned, may occur at any time during the information system enactment). A static evolution, be it planned or not, is de facto supported by all architecture-centric approaches. It is more or less supported by analysis tools to check the system correctness after the change implementation. A dynamic evolution is more difficult to handle, in particular if it has not been planned at the design time. Indeed this requires: (i) mechanisms to provide change specifications without stopping information system executing software components, (ii) performing the changes while preserving the information system correctness and (iii) preserving the consistency between the system implementation and its conceptual architecture.

As depicted by Figure 1, our architecture-centric approach supports information system development processes based on software architecture models. Different models and meta-models are proposed, as well as relations among them. Part of them are platform independent (PIM, represented in the upper part of the figure), while others are platform specific (PSM, represented in the lower part of the figure). The approach is suitable to description languages which have a layered construction. They entail a core, generic (and in our case enactable) description language as well as extension mechanisms enabling the description of domain specific languages. The figure gives a complete view of the different models and meta-models, yet not all of them are mandatorily used. Thus, different processes can be drawn from this picture. A very simple one would for instance consist in representing architecture in the core language, and use the associated virtual machine to enact it. A possible enhancement of this process would consist in defining properties the architecture should obey and check if it indeed does. This implies the additional use of an architecture analysis language to define such properties as well as the use of associated tools to verify whether the properties hold for the given architecture. If the enterprise environment imposes the use of particular platform, it is also possible that rather then using the virtual machine (VM), code is generated in a target language, using specific transformation rules. In this chapter, we do not address exhaustively how such processes are defined and carried out. Rather we focus on how evolution is supported at system enactment time.

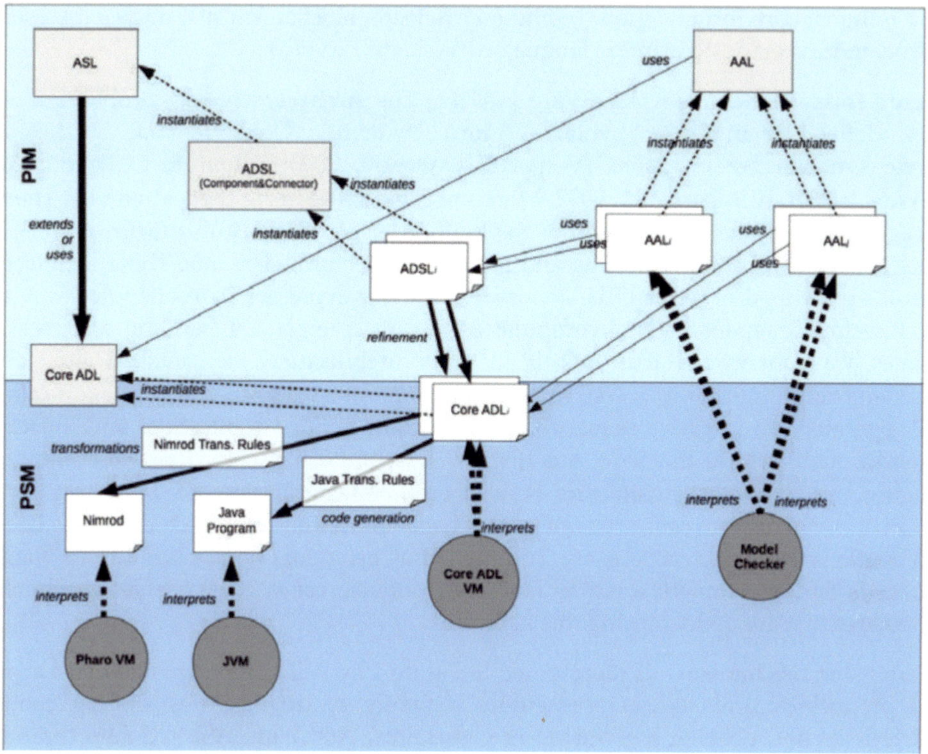

Fig. 1. Architecture centric development approach and processes

To illustrate how our architecture-centric information system development approach supports dynamic evolution of software-intensive information system architecture, we use as modeling language, an ADL allowing us to cope with unpredictable situations and dynamic changes: ArchWare ADL (Oquendo *et al.*, 2002; Oquendo 2004). This language is part of the ArchWare (ArchWare 2001) language family and can be used either as a specification language only or both as a specification and implementation language. In the first case, a target source code can be generated from specifications using mappings and adding implementation details related to the target environment. In the second case, an implementation is a specification, detailed enough, to be interpreted by the ArchWare ADL virtual machine. In both cases, user-defined expected architectural properties can be analyzed both at design time and runtime.

3. ArchWare architecture description languages, foundations and design

The ArchWare project (ArchWare, 2001) proposes an architecture-centric software engineering environment for the development of evolving systems (Oquendo *et al.*, 2004). The environment provides languages and tools to describe architectures and their properties, refine them as well as enact them using a virtual machine.

This section introduces part of the ArchWare language family – related to the description of architectures and their properties. The ArchWare language familly perfectly fits the above presented approach (cf. Figure 1). The description language family has a layered structure, with a minimal core formal language and an extension mechanism that allows the users to construct more specific description languages.

The core formal language - ArchWare π-ADL. The ArchWare project proposes a meta-model, defined by an abstract syntax and formal semantic (Oquendo *et al.*, 2002). Several concrete syntaxes are proposed (Verjus & Oquendo, 2003; Alloui & Oquendo, 2003), ArchWare π-ADL (Cîmpan *et al.*, 2002; Morrison *et al.*, 2004) being the textual one. The core language is a well-formed extension of the high-order typed π-calculus (Milner, 1999) that defines a calculus of communicating and mobile architectural elements. These architectural elements are defined in terms of behaviors. A behavior expresses in a scheduled way both an architectural element internal computation and its interactions (sending and receiving messages via connections that link it to other architectural elements). These actions (concerning communication as well as internal computing) are scheduled using π-calculus based operators to express sequence, choice, composition, replication and matching. Composite architectural elements are defined by composing behaviors, communicating through connections. An architecture is itself an architectural element. Moreover, π-ADL provides a mechanism to reuse parameterised behavior definitions which can be embedded in abstractions. Such abstractions are instantiated as behaviors by application. As the core language is Turing complete, a virtual machine (Morissson *et al.* 2004) enables enactment of architectures that are defined using this language.

The extension mechanism - is represented in Figure 1 by ASL. The extension mechanism is based on architectural styles, representing a family of architectures sharing common characteristics and obeying a given set of constraints. ArchWare ASL (Architectural Sytle Language) is a meta-model allowing the definition of styles, and hence of domain specific languages (Leymonerie, 2004). More precisely, architectural element types can be introduced by a style, forming the style vocabulary. When a style is defined using ASL, it is possible to associate a new syntax; thus the style provides a domain-specific architecture description language. Architectural styles and associated languages can then be constructed using a meta-level tower. If using the nth layer of the language family a style is defined, its associated syntax constitutes a $n+1$ layer. By construction, an architecture defined using the nth layer of the language family, has its corresponding description in the $n-1$ layer.

The component-connector layer - corresponds to a particular domain language, dedicated to the definition of component-connector models of software architectures. In Figure 1, ADSL is the generic term for such domain specific language. Using the extension mechanism (ASL) a level *1* language has been constructed starting from the core language (level *0*). This language, named ArchWare C&C-ADL is associated to an architectural style in which architectural elements are either components or connectors (Cîmpan *et al.*, 2005; Leymonerie, 2004). Components and connectors are first class citizens and can be atomic or composed by other components and connectors. An architectural element interface, represented by its connections, is structured in ports. Each port is thus composed by a set of connections, and has an associated protocol (corresponding to a behavior projection of the element to which it pertains). Atomic as well as composite architectural elements may entail attributes used in their parameterisation. A composite element behavior results from the parallel composition of its composing element behaviors. The composite element has its own ports, which ports of composing elements are attached to.

The architecture analysis language - corresponds to AAL in Figure 1. Architectural properties can be expressed in the ArchWare framework by using a dedicated language: ArchWare Architecture Analysis Language (AAL) (Alloui *et al.*, 2003; Mateescu & Oquendo, 2006). AAL is a formal language based on first order predicate logic and μ-calculus (Bradfield and Stirling, 2001). Predicate logic allows users to express structural aspects while μ-calculus provides the expressive power needed for the representation of dynamic aspects of an evolving system. A property is expressed in AAL using a predicate formula (concerns the architecture structure, *e.g.*, the existence of a connection among two elements), an action formula (concerns the architectural element behavior, *e.g.*, a component must have a recursive behavior), a regular formula (regular expression over actions, *e.g.*, after a certain number of actions of a given type, an architectural element will perform a given action; the goal of such regular expressions is not to increase the language expressive power, but rather to enhance the property readability) or a state formula (state pattern, *e.g.*, a given behavior leads to an expected state, such as true or false). AAL toolset entails theorem provers (Azaiez & Oquendo, 2005) and model checkers (Bergamini *et al.*, 2004). User-defined properties are linked to the description of architectural elements they are about. Their evaluation/analysis may be carried out at both design time and runtime.

The architecture execution languages - correspond to some concrete runtime architecture-centric languages. Specific defined transformation rules are applied to architectural models to generate more concrete and/or detailed architectural models. In the proposed approach (see Figure 1) either Core ArchWare detailed architectural models are generated for being executed by the ArchWare Virtual Machine (Morrison *et al.*, 2004), or Java code is produced to be executed by a Java Virtual Machine (Alloui *et al.*, 2003b), or a Nimrod architectural model (Verjus 2007) is produced to be interpreted by Nimrod (implemented in Pharo, www.pharo-project.org).

4. Case study introduction and evolution scenarios

Given the four identified kinds of evolution (cf. section 2) in this chapter we focus on the dynamic evolution, be it planned or not. To illustrate the mechanisms allowing such evolutions, we consider a supply chain architecture that entails a manufacturing enterprise, its customers (clients) and suppliers. The supply chain architecture is governed by an EAI (Enterprise Application Integration) software solution that itself includes an ERP system. The ERP system includes components dedicated to handling respectively stocks, invoices, orders and quotations.

Static evolutions are not considered in this chapter. Such evolutions require the running system to be stopped before any modification. Then, it is up to the architect to modifiy statically the system architecture and to launch the system again. Research approaches dealing with static evolution are manifold and the reader may look closer at works presented in section 7.

Initial scenario. Whenever a client places an order to the EAI, s/he first asks for a quotation. In order to simplify the scenario, the decision about order commitment by evaluating the quotation is not covered here. The ordering system (one may frequently meet the term *component* in most ADLs) takes the order and updates the stock according to the demanded product and quantity). The restocking system may ask for restocking if the current product stock is not big enough to satisfy the client's order. A restocking procedure consists in contacting a supplier in order to satisfy the order. We first assume that the supplier is always able to satisfy a restocking demand.

Dynamic planned evolution. The architecture that supports planned dynamic evolution is a self-contained architecture that is able to evolve in response to external and anticipated events. The architecture is able to dynamically and automatically evolve (*i.e.*, its structure and behavior may evolve - for example in our scenario by adding clients or modifying the invoicing system) without stopping the system and with no user's interaction. This kind of evolution requires anticipation: the evolution strategy is defined and embedded in the architecture description, before its execution. In our scenarios, the architecture evolves dynamically in order to support new clients or to change the ERP invoicing system (see section 5).

Dynamic unplanned evolution. In some situations (most real life systems), the evolution cannot be anticipated and the architecture is not able to self-adapt. We emphasize scenarios (section 6) for which the architecture has to evolve dynamically (*i.e.*, on-the-fly evolution), without stopping the system execution to support unpredictable situations. We show how the architect improves the restocking system by adding dynamically new suppliers and modifying the restocking process. This evolution scenario shows thus how our proposition addresses challenging topics such the dynamic and unplanned modification of the architecture structure (introducing new suppliers) and the dynamic and unplanned modification of the architecture behavior (changing the restocking process).

These evolution scenarios help to demonstrate how our approach supports controlled and consistent aware architecture dynamic evolution. For both planned and unplanned situations, the architecture consistency is ensured using architectural formal property verification.

5. Dynamic planned evolution: mechanisms and illustration using the supply chain architecture

The layer ArchWare C&C allows to handle dynamic planned evolution. As already mentioned, the language allows the definition of software architectures in terms of compositions of interacting components and connectors. The language (Cîmpan *et al.*, 2005) improves previous propositions, such as Dynamic Wright (Allen *et al.*, 1998), Piccola (Nierstrasz & Achermann, 2000) and π-Space (Chaudet *et al.*, 2000).

Being based on a process algebra, the language enables a system behavior representation. To represent architectural dynamic changes the C&C language introduces specific actions, such as a dynamic element creation and reconfiguration. Moreover, every architectural entity is potentially dynamic, its definition is used at the dynamic creation of several instances. Thus such a definition corresponds to a meta entity, a matrix containing an entity definition as well as information allowing the creation, suppression (dynamic or not) and management of several occurrences.

Components can be either atomic, either composite, *i.e.*, a composition of components and connectors. Independently of their atomic or composite nature, architectural elements can dynamically evolve. Their evolution has nevertheless particularities.

The evolution of atomic (cf. section 5.1) and composite elements (cf. section 5.2) is illustrated using the supply chain case study, for which the architecture has been defined in terms of components and connectors using the C&C language.

The Supply Chain architecture is presented in Figure 2. Defined as a composite component, the supply chain architecture entails two atomic components, a supplier and a client, and a composite component representing an ERP. The connector between the client and the ERP is equally represented, the other ones are basic connectors, and not represented in the figure. The ERP composite component entails four components, to handle respectively quotations, orders, stock availability and invoices. The quotation system and the order system are directly connected to one of the composite ports, allowing direct interaction with components from outside the composite. The stock control and the invoice system are intern to the composite, and are connected to the order system.

One of the supply chain architecture ports is dedicated to its evolution. Clients communicate with the ERP essentially for exchanging information related to quotes (quote demands and propositions) and orders (orders and invoices). Ports are dedicated to this purpose on both communicating parts.

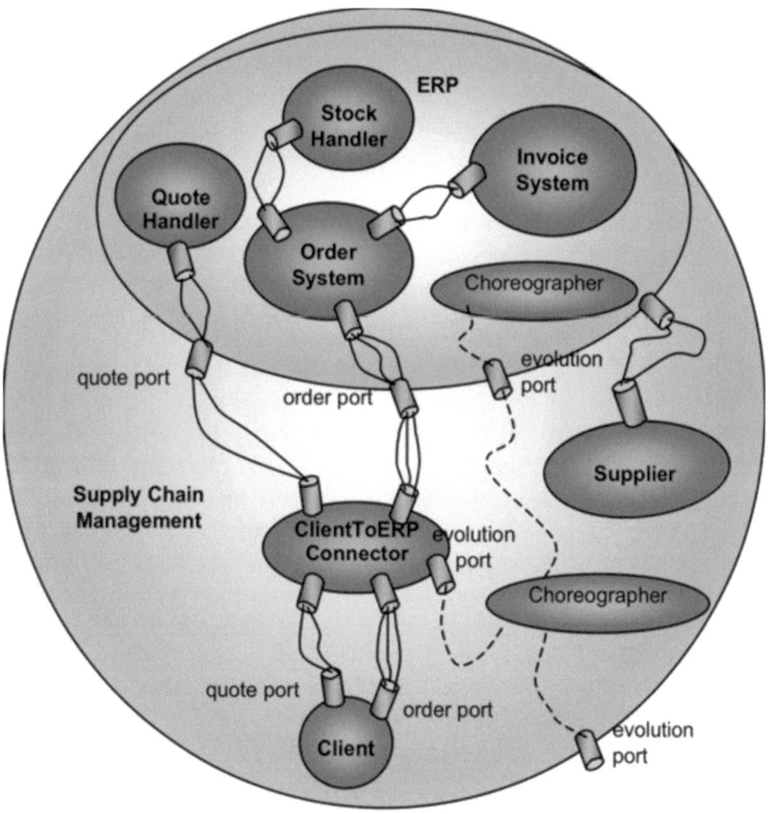

Fig. 2. The supply chain global architecture

The composite initialization and evolution are handled by its *choreographer*, as explained in section 5.2.

5.1 Evolution of atomic components and connectors

Atomic component and connectors definitions are structured in three parts, one for declaring attributes and meta ports, one to define the initial configuration (where instances of meta ports are created) and one representing the behavior. Component's behavior is named *computing*, while for connectors we use the term *routing*. The evolution of atomic components and connectors implies mainly changes in their interface, *i.e.*, addition or suppresion of ports. This has two implications on the behavior, who's representation does not change. The first implication is that part of it will be dedicated to handling the evolution while the rest of it, which we call nominal behavior, represents the main purpose of the element. The second implication is that the nominal behavior is generic, so that it can cope with the dynamic set of ports.

We will illustrate how dynamically evolving atomic architectural elements can be modeled by the example of the `ClientToERP` connector. The later has ports dedicated to the communication with clients and the ERP as well as an evolution port. As with all architectural elements described using ArchWare C&C-ADL, the declarations correspond to meta element declarations, meaning that several instances of the same meta element may co-exist at runtime. Thus, `clientQuotationP`, `erpQuotationP`, `clientOrderP`, `erpOrderP` as well as `newClientP` are meta ports. An instance of each is created in the configuration part. Additional instances may be created at runtime, as we will see. Meta elements provide an additional management level between types and instances, allowing to handle the dynamic evolution of architectures. In the initial configuration, an instance of each meta port is created (cf. Figure 3). Recursively, the connector has 3 choices: to transmit a demand/response for a product quotation, transmit a command, or handle an evolution request. The first two choices represent the nominal behavior. In the case of an evolution request, the connector creates two new instances of the `clientOrderP` and `clientQuotationP` ports, so that a new client can be connected to the ERP.

The nominal part of the behavior, which handles the quotation and the command transmissions, is generic, as it takes into account the fact that the number of clients, and hence the number of instances for `clientOrderP` and `clientQuotationP`, is unknown. Each meta entity (be it connection, port, component or connector) has a list containing its instances. The ith instance of the meta entity is accessed using its name follwed by **`#i`**, while a random instance is accessed using the name followed by **`#any`**. Thus, in the connector behavior, `clientQuotationP`**`#any=i`**`~quotationReq` is a reference towards the connection `quotationReq` of a random instance of the meta port `clientQuotationP`, while keeping the reference in the `i` variable. Saving the reference towards the connection concerned by the request allows the connector to identify the request demander, and thus to return the response to the correct client.

This represention allows the connector between the clients and the ERP to evolve dynamically to enable the connection of new clients. In the next section we will show how composite dynamically evolving architectural elements can be described.

5.2 Evolution of composite architectural elements

In this section we have a look at how the arrival of new clients is represented at the supply chain architectural level. The supply chain is represented as a composite component. Each composite element evolution is handled by a dedicated sub-component - the *choreographer*. The latter can change the topology whenever needed by: changing the attachments between architectural elements, dynamically creating new instances of architectural elements, excluding elements from the architecture, including elements which arrive into the architecture (coupling them with the rest of the architecture).

```
ClientToErpConnector is connector with {
   ports {  clientOrderP is OrderPort;
        clientQuotationP is QuotationPort;
        erpOrderP is OrderDemandPort;
        erpQuotationP is QuotationDemandPort;
        newClientP is port with {
             connections {
                  createI is connection(Any),
                  createO is connection(Any) }
             configuration { new createI; new createO }
             protocol {
                  via createI receive;
                  via createO send ;
                  recurse
             }
        }}
   configuration {   new clientOrderP; new clientQuotationP ;
        new erpOrderP; new erpQuotationP ; new newClientP}
   routing {
    choose{
        via clientQuotationP#any=i~quotationReq
             receive product:String, quantity:Integer;          quotation
        via erpQuotationP~quotationReq send product, quantity;  communication
        via erpQuotationP~quotationRep receive price:Float;
        via clientQuotationP#i~quotationRep send price; }
   or   {
        via clientOrderP#any=i~orderReq
             receive product:String, quantity:Integer;
        via erpOrderP~orderReq send product, quantity;
        via erpOrderP~orderRep receive ack:String;              command
        via clientOrderP#i~orderRep send ack;                   communication
        if (ack=="OK") then {
             via erpOrderP~invoice receive  invoice: String;
             via clientOrderP#i~invoice send invoice;} }
   or {
        via newClientP~createI receive ;                        evolution
        new clientOrderP; new clientQuotationP;                 management
        via newClient~createO send }
    then recurse }
}
```

Fig. 3. Connector between clients and the ERP

The `SupplyChain` choreographer (cf. Figure 4) handles the two evolution scenarios: the arrival of a new client and the reception of a new invoice system, which is transmitted to the `ERP` system. In the first case, the client is inserted into the `Client` meta component and an evolution message is sent to the `ClientToERP` connector, triggering the connector's evolution (cf. section 5.1). The `SupplyChain` choreographer attaches then the connector last created ports to the last client instance, *i.e.*, to the client that dynamically joined the supply chain.

```
SupplyChain is component with{
   ports {
       erpEvolveP is ERPEvolutionPort;
       newClientP is ClientPort;}
   constituents {
    clientComponent is Client;
    erpComponent is ERP;
    clientToErp is ClientToErpConnector;}
   configuration {
    new clientComponent; new erpComponent; new clientToErp;
    attach clientComponent~orderP to clientToErp~clientOrderP;
    attach clientToErp~erpOrderP to erpComponent~erpOrderP;
    attach clientComponent~quotationP
        to clientToErp~clientQuotationP;
    attach clientToErp~erpquotationP
        to erpComponent~erpQuotationP;}
   choreographer {
       choose {
           via erpEvolveP~newInvoice
               receive newInvoiceComponent:InvoiceSystem;
           via erpComponent~erpEvolveP~newInvoice
               send newInvoiceComponent;
           via erpComponent~erpEvolveP~ack receive ack:String;}
       or
       {   via newClientP~createOut receive c : Client;
           insert component c in Client ;
           via clientToErp~newClientP~createIn send ;
           via clientToErp~newClient~createOut receive ;
           attach clientComponent#last~orderP
               to clientToErp~clientOrderP#last;
           attach clientComponent#last~quotationP
               to clientToErp~clientQuotationP#last;}
     then recurse
   } }
```

Invoice system evolution

New client:

Demand the connector to evolve

Attach the new client to the connector

Fig. 4. The SupplyChain composite component

The ERP invoice system is replaced dynamically by a new one, and integrated in the ERP architecture. It is thus possible to change dynamically a system component. This is due, on the one hand, to the language formal foundations, the higher order π-calculus, which allows architectural elements to transit connections. On the other hand, the choreographer handles the connectivity among different architectural elements. It is thus possible to detach a component or to integrate a new one in a composite. The system topology changes in response to particular events.

New clients join the architecture dynamically; the connector evolves by creating communication ports for the new clients. This evolution scenario highlights the choreographer role in the evolution, its capacity to change dynamically the system topology. Other language mechanisms are used here, such as the management of meta elements' multiple instances and therefore the description of generic behaviors. The Client number of instances is unknown, and varies during execution. The Client meta entity handles the different instances, which can be on-the-fly created or come from outside the architecture. In this last case, typing constraints are imposed. The connector to which the Client component is attached has to evolve dynamically its interface (by adding new specific ports) and its behavior (the behavior definition does not change but is generic, so as to handle whatever number of clients).

The two evolution scenarios illustrate how ArchWare C&C-ADL allows the users to define the architecture of evolving systems. The evolutions presented contain some forms of mobility, as the new invoice system as well as new clients join the architecture at runtime. This is possible due to the use of the higher order π-calculus in the language foundations. Nevertheless we do not address other aspects related to mobility, only a rough management of the architecture state is made.

5.3 Property checking during evolution

Different kinds of properties are checked during the evolution. Some of them concern the typing and are intrinsically related to the language, and others are specified explicitly in order to represent domain-related properties to be checked. Concerning typing, for instance, the `newClient` connection of the `newClientP` port is typed so that only elements of type `Client` (or one of its sub-types) can transit via the connection. More precisely, in the previous example a component of type `Client` has to have two ports of type `QuotationDemandPort` and `OrderDemandPort`, *i.e.*, ports that have the same kind of connections and the same protocol. This ensures that a new component, to be integrated in the architecture as a client, is able to correctly interact with the rest of the system.

The explicit properties are more or less specific to the problem (in our case the supply chain). The main goal is to ensure the system integrity during the evolution, from structural as well as from behavioral points of view. An example of generic structural property is the *connectivity*: each element is connected to at least another element. While the system evolves the architectural elements have to remain correctly connected. Concerning the behavior, one can impose that each response to a command corresponds to an order made by a client. Properties can also combine both *structural* and *behavioral* aspects.

The following properties (structural and/or behavioral) are expressed using the ArchWare AAL analysis language (Alloui *et al.*, 2003a). Let us remind the reader that this language allows the users to define properties and comes with tools for property checking.

The property `connectivityOfERPArchitecture` expresses that each component has to be connected to at least another component. In our case study the architect has to verify that once the invoice system is changed, each component is connected to another component in the `ERP` composite component.

```
connectivityOfERPArchitecture is property {
-- each component is attached to at least another component
on self.components.ports apply
            forall { port1 | on self.components.ports apply
                 exists { port2 | attached(port1, port2) }}
}
```

The property `requestBeforeReplyOfOrderSystem` expresses the fact that the order system can send a response only after receiving a request. This property has to be verified also after the system evolution, *i.e.* when the invoice system is changed in the architecture.

```
requestBeforeReplyOfOrderSystem is property {
-- no reply without a request
  on OrderSystem.instances apply
   forall {os | (on os.actions apply isNotEmpty) implies
    (on os.orderP~orderReq.actionsIn apply
        exists {request | on os.orderP~orderRep.actionsOut apply
          forall {reply | every sequence {(not request)*. reply}
                          leads to state {false} }   } ) } }
```

This is expressed in AAL by a state formula that leads to `false` for all replies (belonging to `actionsOut`) sent before receiving a request (belonging to `actionsIn`).

The changes presented here were planned during the architecture design. The property checking takes place at design time too as the system evolves only in an anticipated way. That means each time that an architectural element is changed, related properties are checked on its new architecture description.

In the following section we will show how the unplanned architecture evolution can take place at runtime and how property checking is enabled before integrating the changes.

6. Dynamic unplanned evolution of the supply chain architecture

Let us go back to the original supply chain architecture. The case we are interested in is the one where no evolution was planned when the architecture was designed. So the architecture definition does not entail architectural changes to be triggered when given events occur (such as it was the case in the previous section) nor it is known what elements might evolve. Actually, the industrial reality shows that the maintenance and evolution of complex systems (client-server, distributed, *etc.*) is handled pragmatically, each case individually, without a methodical approach (Demeyer *et al.*, 2002).

The architecture proposed up to now (see section 4) responds to the problems the case study raises, without covering all possible evolution scenarios. What happens when the stocks for a product are not big enough to answer the demand, and the situation was not anticipated? What if the invoice system has to be outsourced, or if the supplier–client relation changes at runtime? The system initial architecture is unable to react to such unexpected events. So it has to evolve.

The scenario used for the unplanned dynamic evolution is different from the one presented in the previous section, although both are based on the initial scenario (section 3). More precisely a new restock system is to be added to the ERP.

6.1 Initial architecture: The supply chain system architecture before its evolution

We illustrate the dynamic unplanned evolution using an example described in the core language (rather than the C&C-ADL used for illustrating the dynamic planned evolution). Using the core language (also named π-ADL - see sections 2 and 3) enables to look at the evolution issue in its essence (independently from specific language layers) and to take advantage of the closeness with the virtual machine[1]. This induces a change in the architecture

[1] The virtual machine can only interpret the core ArchWare ADL language (Morisson *et al.*, 2004)

structure, as a description in the core language only uses the generic term of architectural abstraction (components and connectors used in the previous section are defined in terms of architectural abstractions (Cîmpan *et al.* 2005)). As the only terms are architectural abstractions, connected by connections (no ports, components nor connectors) we use a slightly different graphical notation as it is shown in Figure 5. There the architectural abstractions and their hierarchical composition for the initial architecture are presented.

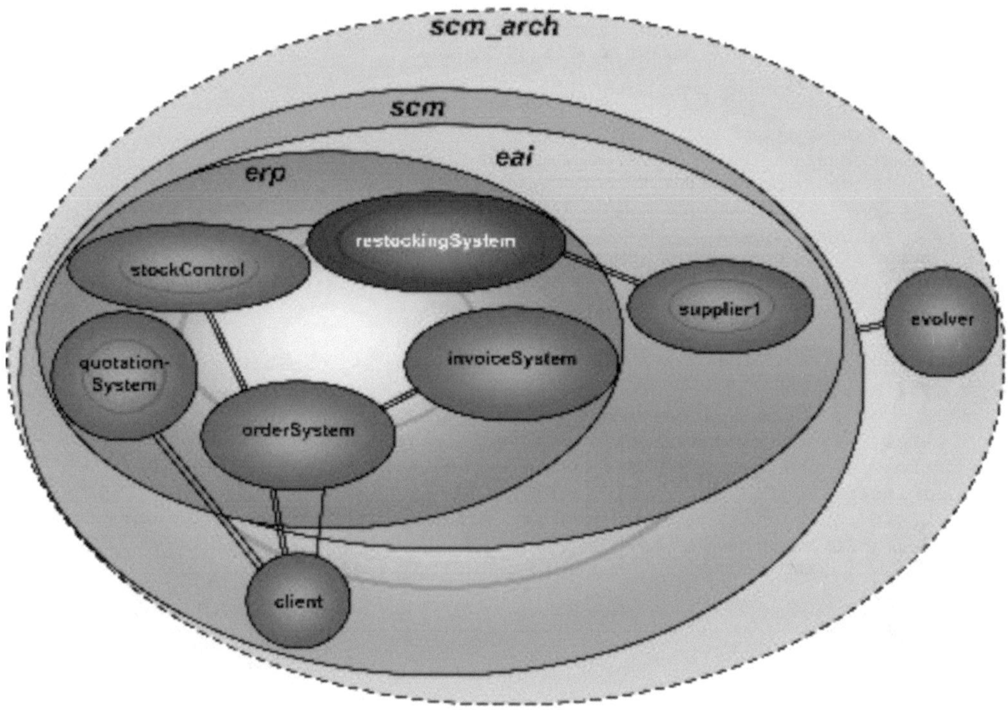

Fig. 5. The Supply Chain before its Evolution

The π-ADL descriptions for the client and supplier abstractions (cf. Figure 6) are rather simple. The client's behavior consists in sequencing the following actions: send a request for quotation, wait for the response; then, either make a request for quotation again (*i.e.*, when the previous one was not satisfactory), or place an order and wait for the invoice. The supplier receives a restocking request and satisfies it. In the initial scenario we chose a basic client-supplier relationship, in which any restock request is supposed to be satisfied (contractually this is of the suppliers' responsibility). The supplier acknowledges the request when it is ready to restock. We will see later how this relationship evolves.

```
value client is abstraction(String: quotationRequest, Integer: qty);{
   value quotationReq is free connection(String);
   value quotationRep is free connection(Float);
   value orderReq is free connection(String,Integer);
   value orderRep is free connection(String);
   value invoiceToClient is free connection(String);
   value quotationBeh is behaviour {
      via quotationReq send quotationRequest;
      via quotationRep receive amount:Float;
      unobservable; }
   quotationBeh();
   replicate {
        choose {
           quotationBeh();
         or
           behaviour {
              via orderReq send quotationRequest, qty;
              unobservable;
              via orderRep receive ack:String;
                if (ack == "OK) then {
                   via invoiceToClient receive invoice:String; } } } };
   done };
value supplier1 is abstraction(); {
   value restockingOrder1Req is free connection(String, Integer);
   value restockingOrder1Rep is free connection(String);
   replicate {
      via restockingOrder1Req receive wares:String, quantity:Integer;
      unobservable;
      via restockingOrder1Rep send "OK" };
   done };
```

Fig. 6. Descriptions for Client and Supplier

Building architectures in the core language is done by hierarchically composing abstractions. The ERP abstraction (cf. Figure 7) is composed by other abstractions. Let us remind the user that a behavior in the core language is closely related to a π-calculus process (Milner, 1999). Here the ERP abstraction is composed of abstractions representing systems for handling quotations, orders, invoices and restocks. The ERP abstraction is itself part of another abstraction, the EAI, itself part of another, and so on. The overall architecture (scm_arch) represents the supply chain management (cf. Figure 8) and its evolution capabilities. This abstraction composes the scm and evolver abstractions. In the π-calculus sense the two abstractions are autonomous processes, which are unified using their connection names and types (Oquendo *et al.*, 2002). Further in the chapter we will see the role played by each one of these abstractions.

```
value quotationSystem is abstraction(Float: price); {...}
value orderSystem is abstraction();{...}
value stockControl is abstraction(Integer: stock); {...}
value restockingSystem is abstraction();{...}
value invoiceSystem is abstraction();{...}
value erp is abstraction(Float: price, Integer: stock); {
        compose {       quotationSystem(price)
                and     orderSystem()
                and     invoiceSystem()
                and     stockControl(stock)
                and     restockingSystem() } };
value eai is abstraction(Float: price, Integer: stock); {
        compose {       supplier1(20)
                and
                        erp(price, stock) } } };
```

Fig. 7. The ERP abstraction

```
value scm_arch is abstraction(); {
        compose { scm()
                and
                evolver() } };
```

Fig. 8. The Supply Chain Abstraction (named scm_arch)

6.2 Language mechanisms for supporting dynamic unplanned evolution

The π-ADL evolution mechanisms are based on the π-calculus mobility (Milner, 1999). In π-ADL, an abstraction C (a behavior /process) can be sent from an abstraction A to another abstraction B. The latter can then dynamically apply it and may behave as the received abstraction C. As a consequence, the abstraction B has dynamically evolved, its current behavior might be radically different from the previous one (Verjus *et al.*, 2006). Such evolution is (1) dynamic because the new behavior (abstraction C) is dynamically received and (2) unplanned as the abstraction definition is unknown in advance. An architect can provide the abstraction definition at runtime, and thus represent the unplanned evolution (as opposed to the planned evolution illustrated in section 5).

To illustrate the evolution mechanisms let us consider a simple abstraction my_abst (cf. Figure 9). It receives a boolean (evolution) and an abstraction (evol_arch_part) on its connection evolRep. If the boolean value is true, my_abst behaves as the evol_arch_part abstraction definition received and applied. Otherwise (the boolean value is false), my_abst behaves in accordance to its initial description (// some code in Figure 9).

Thus, my_abst abstraction can be dynamically modified; such modification is unplanned as the evol_arch_part abstraction definition is unknown at design time and is provided at runtime by the evolver abstraction. The latter plays an important role in the evolution: it is always connected to the abstraction that is expected to evolve (the my_abst in this example).

```
value my_abst is abstraction(); {
   value evolReq is free connection();
   value evolRep is free connection(Boolean, abstraction() );
   . . . // some code
   via evolReq send;
   via evolRep receive evolution:Boolean,
                   evol_arch_part:abstraction(...);
   if (evolution) then {
      evol_arch_part(...) }
   else {
      . . .//some code } };
```

The new current abstraction's behaviour: the received abstraction is applied at runtime

Fig. 9. Abstraction Dynamic Evolution

```
value evolver is abstraction(); {
        value evolReq is free connection();
        value evolRep is free connection(Boolean, abstraction);
        value checkReq is free connection(abstraction);
        value checkRep is free connection(Boolean);
        evol_arch_part is ARCH-EVOLUTION;
        iterate{
        via evolReq receive;
        via checkReq send evol_arch_part;
        via checkRep receive propertyVerification : Boolean;
        if (propertyVerification)
                via evolRep send true, evol_arch_part ;
        }
};
```

Fig. 10. The Evolver Abstraction

The evolver abstraction is the communication means between the virtual machine and the external world *i.e.,* the architect who decides to evolve the architecture. As unplanned changes are to be implemented dynamically in the system, an important issue is the property preservation. Property verifications are made on the evol_arch_part abstraction, which represents (all) the evolved architecture (see section 6.4 for some insights on the evolved architecture according to the evolver abstractions' location(s)). This abstraction is sent using the mechanism we introduced to enable the on-the-fly exchange of abstractions: the use of a special abstraction type, ARCH-EVOLUTION. At design time, the evol_arch_part abstraction is declared of type ARCH-EVOLUTION (inside the evolver). This special type entails the evolution strategy, which can consist in using files, user's interfaces, *etc.* An example of such a strategy consists in using a file containing the new abstraction definition, at a place known by the virtual machine. The architect can place the evol_arch_part abstraction definition in this file. When the evolver sends the evol_arch_part abstraction, its definition is dynamically loaded by the virtual machine from the file.

However this is done only if property verification results are true, *i.e.,* the properties remain satisfied if changes contained in evol_arch_part are applied to the executing architecture. This verification is even more crucial than in the case of anticipated evolution since the content of evol_arch_part is not known in advance. The earlier property violations are detected, the lower the maintenance cost is. Thus the decision to evolve or not is taken in the evolver, depending on whether the properties are still verified after the evolution. Property verifications are made on the evol_arch_part abstraction, which represents the evolved architecture and which is sent by the evolver to the property checker, also represented by an abstraction. The checker verifies the properties attached to the abstraction to be evolved tacking into account the changes contained in the evol_arch_part abstraction. It sends then a boolean value (propertyVerification) to the evolver: true if the properties still hold, false otherwise. If the properties hold, then the evolver sends the evol_arch_part abstraction to the abstraction to be evolved. Other strategies can be implemented, such as prompting the architect with the analysis results. The architect's choice to proceed or not is then reflected on the boolean value. Finally the changes are implemented on the running system taking into account the architecture execution state (Balasubramaniam et al., 2004).

6.3 Illustration of the dynamic unplanned evolution

This evolution scenario is interesting: on the one hand it implies evolving the system architecture structure by adding a second and new supplier; on the other hand, it enforces to change dynamically the restocking process to take into account that a restocking request may not be satisfied; in this case, a new supplier is appearing and the initial restocking request has to be split (with some quantity computations) among the two suppliers. The system behavior has to be changed dynamically according to the new configuration and process (Figure 11 and Figure 12).

The new architecture description is presented in Figure 12.

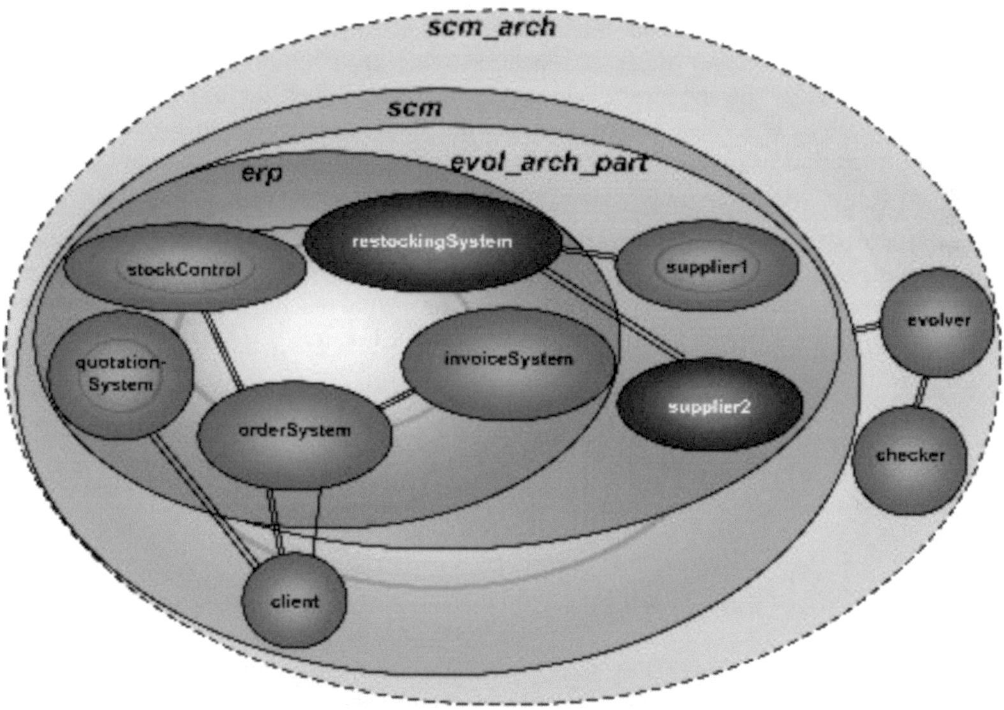

Fig. 11. The Evolved Architecture

```
value scm is abstraction(); {
   value evolReq is free connection();
   value evolRep is free connection(Boolean, abstraction()
);
   compose {
       behaviour {
         via evolReq send;
         via evolRep receive evolution:Boolean,
                   evol_arch_part:abstraction(Float,Integer);
         if (evolution) then {
                 evol_arch_part(100.00, 32) }
         else { eai(100.00, 32) }}
     and
        client("rollings", 12) } };

value scm_arch is abstraction(); {
   compose {   scm()
        and    evolver()
        and    cheker()}
 };
```

The received abstraction is dynamically applied

Fig. 12. The evolved architecture (scm abstraction description)

Changes between the initial architecture (before evolution - Figure 5) and the modified architecture (after evolution - Figure 11) take place in the scm abstraction. The scm abstraction definition contains π-ADL code that manages the evolution: the scm abstraction behavior includes and applies both the eai and client abstractions (before evolution), and both the evol_arch_part and client abstractions (when the evolution occurs). Thus, when the evolution occurs, the evol_arch_part abstraction substitutes the eai abstraction. The evolver abstraction is unified with the abstraction that is supposed to evolve (scm). As explained in section 6.2, the evol_arch_part abstraction is dynamically received and then applied after property verification by the property checker.

As in the case of planned evolution, architectural properties may hold on both the structure and behavior of the system. Note that in the present case, the properties are expressed in AAL using the core ADL concepts; this is because the virtual machine can only interpret the core language (Morisson *et al.*, 2004). Examples of properties are:

Structural:

- connectivity: all architecture elements must be connected (no isolated element) in scm_arch;
- cardinality: there must be at least one supplier in scm_arch;

Behavioral :

- no regression of services provided within the architecture: client's request must always be satisfied;
- no regression of behavior safety: a supplier must first receive a request before any other action.

These properties are formalised using ArchWare-AAL as follows.

Architecture connectivity

In scm_arch, each architectural element (abstraction) abst1 is connected to at least another architectural element abst2 (non empty intersection of their connection sets).

```
connectivityOfscm_arch is property {
-- each abstraction must be connected to at least another one
    on self.abstractions apply
        forall { abst1 | on self.abstractions apply
        exists { abst2 | (abst2 <> abst1) and ((abst2.connections
          apply intersection(abst1.connections)) apply isNotEmpty) }  } }
```

Supplier cardinality

In scm_arch, there must be at least one abstraction supp of type Supplier.

```
atLeastOneSupplierInscm_arch is property {
-- there must be at least one supplier within the system
       on self.abstractions apply
         exists { sup | (sup.type="Supplier") }  }
```

Client's request satisfaction

Every client's request must be satisfied (through receiving an OK reply on orderReq connection). This property is expressed using a state formula on client's actions: every request followed by zero or more non OK reply followed by an OK reply is the expected behavior (leads to state True).

```
clientRequestSatisfaction is property {
-- the client must always have his(her) request satisfied
  on Client.instances apply
   forall {c | (on c.orderReq.actionsOut apply
        forall {request | on c.orderRep.actionsIn apply
          exists {reply | (reply = "OK") AND
                (every sequence { request.(not reply)*.reply }
                           leads to state {true}) }   } ) } }
```

Supplier's safe behavior

Each supplier must receive a request before any other action. This is expressed by a state formula on supplier's actions: every sequence starting with zero or more actions that are not of the restocking order type (*i.e.*, couple (wares, quantity)) and ending by a reply, is not an expected behavior (leads to state false).

```
requestBeforeReplyForSupplier is property {
-- no reply action before receiving a request
  on Supplier.instances apply
   forall {s |
    (on s.restockingOrderReq.actionsIn apply
       exists {request | (request.type='(String, Integer)')
              AND (on s.restockingOrderRep.actionsOut apply
                  forall {reply |
                     every sequence {(not request)*. reply}
                           leads to state {false} } )  }) } }
```

Before implementing changes contained in ARCH-EVOLUTION, user-defined properties are analyzed taking into account those changes. In our scenario, the four properties remain satisfied when introducing a second supplier: (a) the connectivity is still ensured, (b) there is still at least one supplier, (c) the client's request can be satisfied by supplier1 and if needed with the help of supplier2, (d) the supplier1's behavior and now the supplier2's behavior must remain safe. Consequently evolving the scm_arch this way does not a priori threaten the stability of the system architecture as unexpected behaviors are detected during property analysis.

Once the property verification successfully performed by the property checker and the evol_arch_part abstraction applied, the scm abstraction adopts a new behavior, defined dynamically by the architect, according to the adopted evolution strategy. This behavior adds a new supplier (supplier2) and the restocking process in the ERP is changed taking into account this new supplier. The Figure 13 does not show non-modified abstractions (for conciseness and clarity purposes). One can note that the new supplier (supplier2) does not behave as the existing supplier (supplier1) (*i.e.*, both suppliers are different): the evolution we introduced (see section 4) requires two different suppliers; we assume that a restocking request to the new supplier (supplier2) will only be satisfied if the requested quantity is less or equal to the supplier2's stock quantity (for a given product). The restocking process takes now into account the existence of a new supplier, and the initial demand may be split (according to the quantity requested) and handled respectively by the two suppliers.

We have shown in this section that: (i) the system is able to dynamically evolve with architectural elements that are dynamically and on-the-fly provided (not known in advance), (ii) required changes are transmitted to the executing architecture through a particular abstraction (evolver), (iii) the architect can check the architecture before and/or after the evolution using user-defined properties that are expressed in a dedicated architecture property definition language, (iv) changes are applied according to the results of the property verification.

```
value supplier2 is abstraction(Integer capacity); {
  value restockingOrder2Req is free connection(String, Integer);
  value restockingOrder2Rep is free connection(String, Integer);
  via restockingOrder2Req receive wares:String, quantity:Integer;
  unobservable;
  if (quantity > capacity) then {
       via restockingOrder2Rep send "NOK",capacity; }
  else { via restockingOrder2Rep send "OK",capacity;       }
  done };
value restockingSystem is abstraction(); {
  value restockingReq is free connection(String, Integer);
  value restockingOrder2Req is free connection(String, Integer);
  value restockingOrder2Rep is free connection(String, Integer);
  value restockingOrder1Req is free connection(String, Integer);
  value restockingOrder1Rep is free connection(String);
  via restockingReq receive wares:String, quantity:Integer;
  via restockingOrder2Req send wares, quantity;
  via restockingOrder2Rep receive ack:String, qtyReceived:Integer;
  if (ack == "NOK") then {
       via restockingOrder1Req send wares, (quantity-qtyReceived);
       unobservable;
       via restockingOrder1Rep receives ack2:String; }
  unobservable;
  done };
value erp is abstraction(Float: price, Integer: stock); {
       compose {    quotationSystem(price)
            and     orderSystem()
            and     invoiceSystem()
            and     stockControl(stock)
            and     restockingSystem() } };
value ARCH-EVOLUTION is abstraction(Float:price, Integer: stock); {
       compose { erp(price, stock)
            and     supplier1()
            and     supplier2(20)  } };
```

The abstraction that will be sent to the scm abstraction and applied by this latter

Fig. 13. Definition of the ARCH-EVOLUTION abstraction

6.4 Discussion

Let us now focus on evolution mechanisms illustrated in this section. When unpredictable situations occur, the architect has to dynamically (at runtime) provide an abstraction definition entailing the desired architectural changes. This abstraction, typed ARCH-EVOLUTION is (1) checked against architectural properties, (2) sent to the abstraction that is supposed to evolve and (3) dynamically applied by this latter (see section 6.2). The scope of an architectural modification is related to the dedicated abstraction (evolver) that manages such modification. More precisely it is related to the exact place the evolver takes in the architecture, *i.e.*, which abstraction it is bound to. A given modification that is defined within an ARCH-EVOLUTION abstraction may only impact the abstraction (and sub-abstractions) that receives this ARCH-EVOLUTION abstraction from the evolver. As a consequence, the evolvers (abstractions) are architectural evolution elements. They may be considered as non-functional architectural elements. Thus, it is up to the architect to decide, at design time, where to place evolvers. The architect has to decide which abstractions may evolve without knowing how these abstractions will evolve. The architect adopts a strategy that can vary from using a unique evolver attached to the abstraction that composes the entire system to using as many evolvers as abstractions in the architecture. Both strategies have advantages and drawbacks. The first alternative forces the architect to dynamically provide the code that corresponds to the new (modified) entire architecture even if only a small change is occurring; it implies that that property checking is also performed on the entire architecture. The second alternative is quite heavy as it imposes that an evolver should be unified with every existing architectural abstraction (but when a change is occurring, only the code that corresponds to the evolved abstraction is redefined). This decision is related to the number of architectural abstractions and the underlying complexity of the full specification code (expressed in ArchWare ADL): it is an architectural design issue that can be solved.

Furthermore as the ADL proposes abstraction composition and evolution-dedicated abstractions, a given architecture may considerably evolve with cascading evolution situations. An open issue is, then, when and how an architecture is deviating so far from its initial configuration that we may consider it as another architecture (not as an evolved one).

During planned evolution or unplanned evolution, user-defined properties are evaluated taking into account the new architecture. It is worth noting in the scenarios of section 6.3, that while some property expressions like `connectivityOfScm_arch` are not affected by the change, other properties like `requestBeforeReplyForSupplier` should evolve to express `supplier2's` expected safe behavior as well.

7. Related work

This section presents the work related to the dynamic evolution of software-intensive information systems using a software architecture-centric approach.

(Bradbury *et al.*, 2004) presents a survey of self-management in dynamic software architecture specifications. The authors compare well known architecture description languages and approaches in a self management perspective; dynamic architectural changes have four steps : (1) initiation of change, (2) selection of architectural transformation, (3) implementation of reconfiguration and (4) assessment of architecture after reconfiguration. This chapter focuses on the three first steps. In the Bradbury *et al.* survey, most of the studied ADLs support all of the basic change operations (adding or removing components and connectors) but other more complex operations are not fully satisfied. Particularly, dynamically modifying internal component behavior remains an issue that is successfully addressed only by few ADLs.

The representation of evolvable software-intensive information system architectures is related to architecture description languages and their capabilities, *i.e.*, ADLs that allow the architect to express dynamic evolvable architectures, including adaptive architectures. Few ADLs support dynamic architecture representation: Darwin (Magee *et al.*, 1995), Dynamic Wright (Allen *et al.*, 1998), π-Space (Chaudet & Oquendo, 2000), C2SADEL (Medvidovic *et al.*, 1999; Egyed & Medvidovic, 2001; Egyed *et al.*, 2001), Piccola (Nierstrasz & Achermann, 2000), Pilar (Cuesta *et al.*, 2005), ArchWare π-ADL (Oquendo *et al.*, 2002; Oquendo 2004), ArchWare C&C-ADL (Cîmpan *et al.*, 2005). Most of them are not suitable to support unplanned dynamic architecture evolution as they consider different representations for the concrete and abstract levels, and use reflection mechanisms to switch among these representations: a dynamic architecture is first defined at abstract level and is then reflected (1) into a dynamic evolvable concrete software-intensive system (Cazzola *et al.*, 1999; Tisato *et al.*, 2000) or (2) into another, evolved abstract representation (Cuesta *et al.*, 2001; Cuesta *et al.*, 2005). The link between the abstract level and the concrete one is not maintained, leading to a situation in which only anticipated modifications can be supported dynamically. ArchWare π-ADL uses a unique representation for both levels (Verjus *et al.*, 2006).

Thus, handling the software evolution is closely related to the problem of keeping the consistency between the abstract and the implementation levels and continuously switching between these levels. This issue is particularly important in the case of runtime evolution. The consistency among the abstract and the concrete levels can be seen in two directions: top-down from the abstract level to the concrete one (such as considered in model-driven and architecture refinement approaches) and bottom-up from the concrete level to the abstract one (such as considered by architecture extraction approaches). Our approach adresses the top-down consistency.

Going from abstract architectural representations to more concrete ones is inherent in architecture-centric development, and to the model-driven development in general. The architecture-centric development highly depends on maintaining the consistency among levels. Traditionally, when changes on the abstract architecture occur, it is up to the developer to modify the code accordingly (sometimes assisted by semi-automated code generation tools). Some architecture-based development approaches maintain mappings between single versions of the architecture and their corresponding implementations (Carriere *et al.*, 1999; Medvidovi *et al.*, 1999; Erdogmus, 1998; Egyed 2000; Van der Hoeck *et al.*, 2001; Egyed *et al.*, 2001; Dashofy *et al.*, 2002; Aldrich *et al.*, 2002).

(Egyed & Medvidovic, 2001) approach introduces an intermediate "design" level between architectural (abstract) level and implementation (concrete) level. The consistency between these levels is managed using mapping rules between UML diagrams with OCL constraints (at design level) and C2 concepts (at architectural level). The transformation-based consistency checking is ensured by IVita (Egyed & Medvidovic, 2001). This approach assumes that changes are applied off-line.

ArchEvol (Nistor *et al.*, 2005) proposes to accurately determine which versions of the component implementations belong to the initial version of the architecture and which belong to the branched version of the architecture. ArchEvol defines mappings between architectural descriptions and component implementations using a versioning infrastructure (by using conjointly Subversion, Eclipse and ArchStudio) and addresses the evolution of the relationship between versions of the architecture and versions of the implementation. ArchJava (Aldrich *et al.*, 2002) is an extension to Java that unifies the software architecture with implementation, ensuring that the implementation conforms to the architectural constraints. The latter mainly concern the communication integrity, *i.e.*, implementation components only communicate directly with the components they are connected to in the architecture. The limitations of ArchJava are inherent to Java systems, that are difficult to dynamically evolve without stopping the executing system. In (Garlan *et al.*, 2004), the code is monitored, changes are made on abstract architectures using a change script language and then mapped into the code. Each change operator has its transformation into lower level changes. If the change script execution fails at the code level, the change is aborted. As this work is made in the context of self-adaptation, issues such as how the change is triggered are taken into account. The evolution takes place at runtime, and concerns both the design and the code.

(Huang *et al.*, 2006) focus on dynamic software architecture extraction and evolution by catching the executing component-based system state and system behavior: an architectural representation is deduced and can be modified at runtime. The approach can be seen as a unifying one. However, the deduced architectural representation is incomplete and the approach is limited to existing component-based systems.

Thus, the issue of dynamic unplanned changes is not satisfactory addressed. Aside ArchWare, none of the existing proposals unifies the abstract level and the implementation level in a complete and consistent manner. This is related to the fact that these proposals consider software-intensive information system architecture at abstract levels only. Most of the ADLs provide high level architectural means by focusing on abstract architectures. As we can see, there is an unbalance between the two identified issues, namely the description of dynamic architectures and the handling of unexpected changes. The former is rather well addressed by existing proposals, but the latter is practically uncovered. For an ADL, to consider both issues is important, the ADL should not only be a design language but also an implementation one, *i.e.*, architectures become executable representations. We have investigated in this chapter dynamic evolvable software-intensive information system architectures in a model-based development perspective. Model-based development is centered around abstract, domain-specific models and transformations of abstract models into more specific underlying platforms. Our approach addresses both abstract and concrete architectural models in a model-based development framework and is quite related to the Monarch approach (Bagheri & Sullivan, 2010). Nevertheless Monarch does not deal with dynamic architecture evolution support.

8. Conclusion

In this chapter we have presented an architecture model-based development approach guiding the development of dynamic evolvable software-intensive information system architectures. Our approach supports dynamic evolvable architecture development process covering modeling, analysis and execution. As the evolution is an important facet of a software-intensive system (Lehman, 1996), our proposal aims at integrating evolution modeling and evolution mechanisms into an executable and formal ADLs that can serve at both abstract and concrete levels (bridging the gap between both levels). In this chapter, we use ArchWare languages and technologies. Our proposal deals with the dynamic evolution of architecture using specific architectural elements and ADL built-in mechanisms. We claim that software-intensive system architectures have to incorporate, at the design time, evolution mechanisms making those architectures evolution-aware at runtime.

Architectural changes can occur at different levels of abstraction and may concern architecture structure and behavior, internal architectural elements' structure and behavior as well as their related properties. The dynamic support elements and mechanisms we have introduced and formally defined serve not only at classical architectural (abstract) level but also as implementation means. In other words, the software architecture, if completely detailed and defined, can be the entire executing system itself. In our proposal, even in the case of information systems incorporating heterogeneous and existing components or legacy systems, information system components' "glue" is described as behavior that can be modified at runtime. Then, components can be dynamically removed, modified or added and the way they interoperate can also be dynamically modified.

This issue positively impacts software-intensive information system maintenance activities and underlying costs, budgets, efforts and skills.

As for proposed mechanisms for unplanned evolution, through the concept of evolver and the ADL virtual machine, we consider them as a significant research advance as at the best of our knowledge. Moreover as the framework relies on core ADL concepts of abstraction composition and evolution-dedicated abstractions, a given architecture may considerably evolve with cascading evolution situations. We did not discuss when and how an architecture is deviating so far from its initial configuration so that we may consider it as another architecture/system (and not as an evolved one). This issue can be further addressed and related to architectural evolution patterns and paths introduced in (Garlan *et al.*, 2009). We also think that the ADL-based evolution support we propose is a good candidate for self-adaptation system design and analysis but further investigations and case studies are mandatory.

The scenarios used in this chapter, illustrate changes that are related to the composition of the system (by adding for example a supplier) as well as the behaviour of the system (in other words the business process) by modifying the restocking process. Other case studies have been realized using the ArchWare approach and technologies, *i.e.*, for a Manufacturing Execution System for a Grid-based application in a health-related project (Manset *et al.*, 2006). Other reserarch activities are directly inspired from these results (Pourraz *et al.*, 2006).

9. References

Abrial, J.R. (1996). *The B Book*, Assigning Programs to Meanings, Cambridge University Press, Cambridge, 1996.

Aldrich, J.; Chambers, C. & Notkin, D. (2002). ArchJava: Connecting Software Architecture to Implementation, *Proceedings of the 24th International Conference on Software Architecture (ICSE 2002)*, Orlando, Florida, May 2002.

Allen, R. ; Douence, R. & Garlan D. (1998). Specifying and Analyzing Dynamic Software Architectures, *Proceedings on Fundamental Approaches to Software Engineering*, Lisbon, Portugal, March 1998.

Alloui, I. & Oquendo, F. (2003). UML Arch-Ware/Style-based ADL, Deliverable D1.4b, ArchWare European RTD Project, IST-2001-32360, 2003.

Alloui, I. ; Garavel, H. ; Mateescu, R. & Oquendo F.(2003a). The ArchWare Architecture Analysis Language, Deliverable D3.1b, ArchWare European RTD Project, IST-2001-32360, 2003.

Alloui, I. ; Megzari, K. & Oquendo F. (2003b). Modelling and Generating Business-To-Business Applications Using an Architecture Description Language - Based

Approach, *Proceedings of International Conference on Enterprise Information Systems (ICEIS)*, Anger, France, April 2003.

ArchStudio http://www.isr.uci.edu/projects/archstudio.

Andrade, L.F. & Fiadeiro, J.L. (2003). Architecture Based Evolution of Software Systems, In *Formal Methods for Software Architectures*, M.Bernardo & P.Inverardi, pp. 148-181, LNCS 2804, 2003.

ArchWare Consortium (2001). *The EU funded ArchWare – Architecting Evolvable Software – project*, http://www.arch-ware.org, 2001.

Azaiez, S. & Oquendo, F. (2005). Final ArchWare Architecture Analysis Tool by Theorem-Proving: The ArchWare Analyser, Delivrable D3.5b, ArchWare European RTD Project IST-2001-32360, 2005.

Bagheri, H. & Sullivan, K. (2010). Monarch: Model-based Development of Software Architectures, *Proceedings of the 13th ACM/IEEE International Conference on Model Driven Engineering Languages and Systems (MoDELS)*, Oslo, Norway, October 2010.

Balasubramaniam, D.; Morrison, R.; Mickan, K.; Kirby, GNC.; Warboys, B.C.; Robertson, I.; Snowdon, B; Greenwood, R.M. & Seet, W. (2004). Support for Feedback and Change in Self-adaptive Systems, In *Proceedings of ACM SIGSOFT Workshop on Self-Managed Systems (WOSS'04)*, Newport Beach, CA, USA, ACM, October /November 2004.

Barrios, J. & Nurcan, S. (2004). Model Driven Architectures for Enterprise Information Systems, In *Proceedings of 16th Conference on Advanced Information Systems Engineering, (CAISE'04)*, Springer Verlag (pub), Riga, Latvia, June 2004.

Bass, L.; Clements, P. & Kazman, R.(2003). *Software architecture in practice*, Second Edition, Addison-Wesley, 2003.

Belady, L. & Lehman, M.(1995). *Program Evolution Processes of Software Change*, Academic Press, London, UK, 1995.

Bergamini, D.; Champelovier, D.; Descoubes, N.; Garavel, H.; Mateescu, R. & Serwe, W. (2004). Final ArchWare Architecture Analysis Tool by Model-Checking, *ArchWare European RTD Project IST-2001-32360*, Delivrable D3.6c, December 2004.

Bradbury, J.S.; Cordy, J.R.; Dingel, J.& Wermelinger, M.(2004). A survey of self-management in dynamic software architecture specifications. In *Proceedings of ACM SIGSOFT Workshop on Self-Managed Systems (WOSS '04)*. Newport Beach, CA, USA, ACM, October /November 2004.

Bradfield, J. C.& Stirling, C. (2001). Modal logics and mu-calculi: an introduction, In *Handbook of Process Algebra*, Elsevier, pp. 293–330, 2001.

Carriere, S.; Woods, S. & Kazman, R. (1999). Software Architectural Transformation, In *Proceedings of 6th Working Conference on Reverse Engineering*, IEEE Computer Society, Atlanta, Georgia, USA, October 1999.

Cazzola, W.; Savigni, A.; Sosio, A. & Tisato, F. (1999). Architectural Reflection : Concepts, Design and Evaluation, Technical Report RI-DSI 234-99, DSI, University degli Studi di Milano. Retrived from http://www.disi.unige.it/CazzolaW/references.html, 1999.

Chaudet, C. & Oquendo, F. (2000). π-SPACE: A Formal Architecture Description Language Based on Process Algebra for Evolving Software Systems, In *Proceedings of 15th*

IEEE International Conference on Automated Software Engineering, Grenoble, France, September 2000.

Cîmpan, S.; Oquendo, F.; Balasubramaniam, D.; Kirby, G. & Morrison, R. (2002). The ArchWare ADL: Definition of the Textual Concrete Syntax, *ArchWare European RTD Project IST-2001-32360*, Delivrable D1.2b, December 2002.

Cîmpan, S. & Verjus, H. (2005). Challenges in Architecture Centred Software Evolution, In *CHASE: Challenges in Software Evolution*, Bern, Switzerland, 2005.

Cîmpan, S.; Leymonerie, F. & Oquendo, F. (2005). Handeling Dynamic Behaviour in Software Architectures, In *Proceedings of European Workshop on Software Architectures*, Pisa, Italy, 2005.

Cuesta, C.; de la Fuente, P.& Barrio-Solorzano, M. (2001). Dynamic Coordination Architecture through the use of Reflection, In *Proceedings of the 2001 ACM symposium on Applied Computing*, Las Vegas, Nevada, United States, pp. 134 - 140, March 2001.

Cuesta, C.; de la Fuente, P.; Barrio-Solorzano, M. & Beato, M.E. (2005). An abstract process approach to algebraic dynamic architecture description, In *Journal of Logic and Algebraic Programming*, Elsevier, Vol. 63, pp. 177-214, ISSN 1567-8326, 2005.

Dashofy, E. M.; van der Hoek, A. & Taylor, R. N. (2002). Towards architecture-based self-healing systems, In *Proceedings of the First Workshop on Self-Healing Systems (WOSS '02)*,. D. Garlan, J. Kramer, and A. Wolf, Eds., Charleston, South Carolina, November 2002.

Egyed, A. & Medvidovic, N. (2001). Consistent Architectural Refinement and Evolution using the Unified Modeling Language, In *Proceedings of the 1st Workshop on Describing Software Architecture with UML*, co-located with ICSE 2001, Toronto, Canada, pp. 83-87, May 2001.

Egyed, A.; Grünbacher, P. & Medvidovic, N.(2001). Refinement and Evolution Issues in Bridging Requirements and Architectures, In *Proceedings of the 1st International Workshops From Requirements to Architecture (STRAW)*, co-located with ICSE, Toronto, Canada, pp. 42-47, May 2001.

Egyed, A. (2000). Validating Consistency between Architecture and Design Descriptions, In *Proceedings of 1st Workshop on Evaluating Software Architecture Solutions (WESAS)*, Irvine, CA, USA, May 2000.

Erdogmus H. (1998). Representing Architectural Evolution, In *Proceedings of the 1998 Conference of the Centre for Advanced Studies on Collaborative Research*, Toronto, Ontario, Canada, pp. 159-177, November 1998.

Favre, J.-M. ; Estublier, J. & Blay, M. (2006). *L'Ingénierie Dirigée par les Modèles : au-délà du MDA*, Edition Hermes-Lavoisier, 240 pages, ISBN 2-7462-1213-7, 2006.

Ghezzi, C.; Jazayeri, M. & Mandrioli D. (1991). *Fundamentals of Software Engineering*, Prentice Hall, 1991.

Garlan, D.; Cheng, S.-W.; Huang, A.-C.; Schmerl, B. & Steenkiste, P. (2004). Rainbow: Architecture-Based Self Adaptation with Reusable Infrastructure, *IEEE Computer*, Vol. 37, No. 10, October 2004.

Garlan, D.; Barnes, J.M.; Schmerl, B. & Celiku, O. (2009). Evolution styles: Foundations and tool support for software architecture evolution, In *Proceedings of the 7th Working*

IEEE/IFIP Conference on Software Architecture (WICSA'09), pp. 131–140, Cambridge, UK, September 2009.

Huang, G.; Mei, H. & Yang, F.-Q. (2006). Runtime recovery and manipulation of software architecture of component-based systems, In *Journal of Automated Software Engineering.*, Vol. 13, No. 2, pp 257-281, 2006.

Kardasis, P. & Loucopoulos, P. (1998). Aligning Legacy Information Systems to Business Processes , In *Proceedings of International Conference on Advanced Information Systems Engineering (CAISE'98)*, Pisa, Italy, June 1998.

Kyaruzi, J. J. & van Katwijk, J. (2000). Concerns On Architecture-Centered Software Development: A Survey, In *Journal of Integrated Design and Process Science*, Volume 4, No. 3, pp. 13-35, August 2000.

Lehman M. M. (1996). Laws of Software Evolution Revisited, In *Proceedings of European Workshop on Software Process Technology (EWSPT 1996)*, p. 108-124, Nancy, France, October 1996.

Leymonerie F. (2004). ASL language and tools for architectural styles. Contribution to dynamic architectures description, *PhD thesis, University of Savoie*, December 2004.

Magee, J.; Dulay, N.; Eisenbach, S. & Kramer J. (1995). Specifying Distributed Software Architectures, In *Proceedings of 5th European Software Engineering Conference (ESEC '95)*, LNCS 989, pp. 137-153, Sitges, September 1995.

Manset, D.; Verjus, H.; McClatchey, R. & Oquendo, F. (2006). A Formal Architecture-Centric Model-Driven Approach For The Automatic Generation Of Grid Applications. In *8th International Conference on Enterprise Information Systems (ICEIS'06)*, Paphos, Chyprus, 2006.

Mateescu, R. & Oquendo, F. (2006). π-AAL: an architecture analysis language for formally specifying and verifying structural and behavioural properties of software architectures, In *ACM SIGSOFT Software Engineering Notes*, Vol. 31, No. 2, pp. 1-19, 2006.

Medvidovic, N. & Taylor, R.N. (2000). A Classification and Comparison Framework for Software Architecture Description Languages, In *IEEE Transactions on Software Engineering*, Vol. 26, No. 1, pp. 70-93, 2000.

Medvidovic, N.; Egyed, A. & Rosenblum, D. (1999). Round-Trip Software Engineering Using UML: From Architecture to Design and Back, In *Proceedings of the 2nd Workshop on Object-Oriented Reengineering*, pp. 1-8, Toulouse, France, September 1999.

Mens, T.; Buckley, J.; Rashid, A. & Zenger, M. (2003). Towards a taxonomy of software evolution, In *Workshop on Unanticipated Software Evolution*, (in conjunction with ETAPS 2003) Varsaw, Poland, April 2003.

Milner, R. (1999). *Communicating and Mobile Systems: the π -calculus*, Cambridge University Press, 1999.

Morrison, R.; Kirby, GNC.; Balasubramaniam, D.; Mickan, K.; Oquendo, F.; Cîmpan, S.; Warboys, BC.; Snowdon, B. & Greenwood, RM. (2004). Support for Evolving Software Architectures in the ArchWare ADL, In *Proceedings of the 4th Working IEEE/IFIP Conference on Software Architecture (WICSA 4)*, Oslo, Norway 2004.

Nierstrasz, O. & Achermann, F. (2000). Supporting Compositional Styles for Software Evolution, In *Proceedings of International Symposium on Principles of Software Evolution*, IEEE, Kanazawa, Japan, pp. 11-19, November 2000.

Nistor, E.; Erenkrantz, J.; Hendrickson, S. & van der Hoek, A. (2005). ArchEvol: Versioning Architectural-Implementation Relationships, In *Proceedings of the 12th International Workshop on Software Configuration Management*, Lisbon, Portugal, September 2005.

Nurcan, S. & Schmidt, R. (2009). Service Oriented Enterprise-Architecture for enterprise engineering introduction, In *Proceedings of 13th IEEE International Enterprise Distributed Object Computing Conference*, pp. 247-253, Auckland, New Zeeland, September 2009.

Oquendo, F. (2004). π-ADL: an Architecture Description Language based on the higher-order typed π-calculus for specifying dynamic and mobile software architectures, In *ACM SIGSOFT Software Engineering Notes*, Volume 29, No. 3, pp. 1-14, 2004a.

Oquendo, F.; Alloui, I.; Cîmpan, S. & Verjus, H. (2002). The ArchWare ADL: Definition of the Abstract Syntax and Formal Semantic, *ArchWare European RTD Project IST-2001-32360*, Deliverable D1.1b, 2002.

Oquendo, F.; Warboys, B.; Morrison, R.; Dindeleux, R.; Gallo, F.; Garavel, H. & Occhipinti, C. (2004). ArchWare: Architecting Evolvable Software, In *Proceedings of the 1st European Workshop on Software Architecture (EWSA 2004)*, St Andrews, UK, pp. 257-271, 2004.

Perry, D.E. & Wolf, A.L. (1992). Foundations for the study of software architecture, In *ACM SIGSOFT Software Engineering Notes*, Vol. 17, No. 4, pp. 40-52, 1992.

Pourraz,, F. ; Verjus, H. & Oquendo, F. (2006). An Architecture-Centric Approach For Managing The Evolution Of EAI Service-Oriented Architecture, In *8th International Conference on Enterprise Information Systems (ICEIS'06)*, Paphos, Chyprus, 2006.

Tisato, F.; Savigni, A.; Cazzola, W. & Sosio, A. (2000). Architectural Reflection - Realising Software Architectures via Reflective Activities, In Proceedings of the 2nd Engineering Distributed Objects Workshop (EDO 2000), University of Callifornia, Davis, USA, November 2000.

Touzi, J.; Benaben, F.; Pingaud, H. & Lorre, J. (2009). A model-driven approach for collaborative service- oriented architecture design, In *International Journal of Production Economics*, Vol. 121, Issue 1, p. 5-20, 2009.

Van der Hoek, A.; Mikic-Rakic, M.; Roshandel, R. & Medvidovic, N. (2001). Taming architectural evolution, In *Proceedings of the 8th European Software Engineering Conference*, ACM Press, pp.1-10, Viena, Austria, September 2001.

Verjus, H. & Oquendo, F. (2003). Final XML ArchWare style-based ADL (ArchWare AXL), *ArchWare European RTD Project IST-2001-32360*, Deliverable D1.3b, June 2003.

Verjus, H. ; Cîmpan, S. ; Alloui, I. & Oquendo, F. (2006). Gestion des architectures évolutives dans ArchWare, In *Proceedings of the First Conférence francophone sur les Architectures Logicielles (CAL 2006)*, Nantes, France, September 2006, pp. 41-57.

Verjus, H. (2007). Nimrod: A Software Architecture-Centric Engineering Environment - Revision 2, *Nimrod Release 1.4.3, University of Savoie - LISTIC*, Number LISTIC No 07/03, June 2007.

Vernadat, F. (2006). Interoperable enterprise systems: architecture and methods, Plenary Lecture at *12th IFAC Symposium on Information Control Problems in Manufacturing*, Saint-Etienne, France, May 2006.

Zachman, J. (1997). Enterprise Architecture : The Issue of the Century, In *Database Programming and Design*, Vol. 10, p. 44-53, 1997.

3

Patterns for Agent-Based Information Systems: A Case Study in Transport

Vincent Couturier, Marc-Philippe Huget and David Telisson
LISTIC – Polytech Annecy-Chambéry, Université de Savoie
France

1. Introduction

Designing information systems is a complex task especially when these systems use agents to allow adaptability, cooperation and negotiation, and automatic behaviours. Difficulties arise due to the absence of understandable documentation associated with agent-based methodologies. These methodologies consider concepts defined implicitly and not explicitly requiring from engineers a good understanding of agent theory. This has as consequence an important learning curve for engineers trying to use agents for their information systems. This chapter proposes a collection of agent patterns to reduce time required to develop agent-based information systems.

We propose, in this chapter, to develop software patterns and to reuse them to design complex information systems such as the ones based on agents. According to Alexander (Alexander et al., 1977; Alexander, 1979), a pattern describes a problem, which occurs frequently in an environment as well as a solution that can be adapted for the specific situation. A software pattern (Beck & Cunningham, 1987) follows the same principle and offers a solution to developers when building software in a specific context.

Different categories of software patterns exist as mentioned in Section 2 and here, we present in this chapter, examples of agent patterns for analysis, design and implementation. They are illustrated on our case study in transport: enriched traveller information. These patterns are completed with reuse support patterns that help designing and building such agent-based information systems by guiding them among our collection of patterns.

The chapter is structured as follows. Section 2 presents the concept of pattern. Section 3 describes the categories of patterns dedicated to engineering Agent-based Information Systems (AIS) and the reuse process. Section 4 describes examples of such patterns. Section 5 illustrates these patterns on a transport information system example. Section 6 compares with previous works in literature. Finally, Section 7 concludes the chapter and draws perspectives.

2. The concept of pattern

Alexander introduced the concept of pattern in 1977 for the design and construction of homes and offices (Alexander et al., 1977; Alexander, 1979). This concept was adapted to software engineering and mainly to object-oriented programming by Beck and Cunningham in 1987 (Beck & Cunningham, 1987). These patterns are called *software patterns*.

In Alexander's proposition, a pattern describes a problem, which occurs over and over again in an environment as well as a solution that can be used differently several times. A *software pattern* follows the same principle and can be seen as abstractions used by design or code experts that provide solutions in different phases of software engineering. A pattern can also be considered as a mean to capitalize, preserve and reuse knowledge and know-how.

Patterns can be divided into five categories: **analysis patterns** (Coad, 1996; Fowler, 1997), **architectural patterns** (Buschmann et al., 1996), **design patterns** (Gamma et al., 1995), **idioms**--also known as **implementation patterns**--(Coplien, 1992), and **process patterns** (Ambler, 1998).

Analysis patterns are used to describe solutions related to problems that arise during both the requirement analysis and the conceptual data modeling phases. Among them, we can distinguish generic analysis patterns (Coad, 1992), which represent generic elements that can be reused whatever the application domain is. There exist as well analysis patterns for specific domains (Hay, 1996; Fowler, 1997) called *domain-specific patterns* or *domain patterns*. These patterns (Fowler, 1997) represent conceptual domain structures denoting the model of a business system domain rather than the design of computer programs. Fowler associates to domain patterns *support patterns* that show how domain patterns fit into information system architecture and how conceptual models turn into software. These patterns describe how to use domain patterns and to apply them to a concrete problem.

Architectural and design patterns are both related to the design process. Though, they differ in the level of abstraction where each one is applied. *Architectural patterns* express a fundamental structural organization schema for software systems and can be considered as templates for concrete software architectures (Buschmann et al., 1996). *Design patterns* (Gamma et al., 1995) provide scheme to refine the subsystems or components of a software system and thus are more abstract (and of smaller granularity) than architectural patterns.

Idioms are used at code level and deal with the implementation of particular design issues.

Finally, some patterns, called *process patterns* (Ambler, 1998) describe a collection of general techniques, actions, and/or tasks for developing object-oriented software. Actions or tasks can themselves be software patterns.

We present in next section categories of patterns dedicated to develop Agent-based Information Systems and their reuse process.

3. Categories of patterns dedicated to agent-based information system engineering

3.1 Pattern categories

The first patterns applied for engineering Agent-based Information Systems are *Agent Analysis Patterns*. They define agent structure and design multiagent systems at a high level of abstraction. They can be applied to design agents with or without decision behaviours. Thus, the designer will be able to reuse these patterns to design agents for his/her IS at a high level of abstraction.

Patterns dedicated to architectural representation and design of AIS are *Agent Architectural Patterns* and *Agent Design Patterns.*

The former has to be applied at the beginning of the design process and help defining the IS structural organization. They represent the different architectural styles for agent-based information systems which are means of capturing families of architectures and can be seen as a set of design rules that guide and constrain the development of IS architecture (levels, internal elements, collaborations between elements, etc.). Architectural styles depend on which architecture we choose: Market-based one, Subcontract-based one or Peer-to-Peer-based one.

Agent Design Patterns describe technical elements required to develop agent-based Information Systems. Analysis and conceptual models obtained by applying Agent Analysis Patterns are refined with behaviour, collaboration and software entities. Thus, the IS design model is obtained by adapting software elements specified in the design patterns solutions.

Finally, we have specified two kinds of support patterns: *Model Transformation Patterns* and *Reuse Support Patterns.*

Model Transformation Patterns help developers to build applications from design patterns and can be applied at the end of the design phase. They specify transformation rules to map design models to models specific to agent development frameworks such as JADE (Bellifemine et al., 2007) or Madkit (Gutknecht & Ferber, 2000).

Reuse Support Patterns (RSP) are process patterns, which help developers navigating into a collection of patterns and reusing them. They describe, by using activity diagrams, a sequence of patterns to apply to resolve a problem. There exists RSP for every category of patterns (analysis, architectural, design and model transformation).

The different patterns described here regarding the development cycle of an agent-based information system are shown on Figure 1.

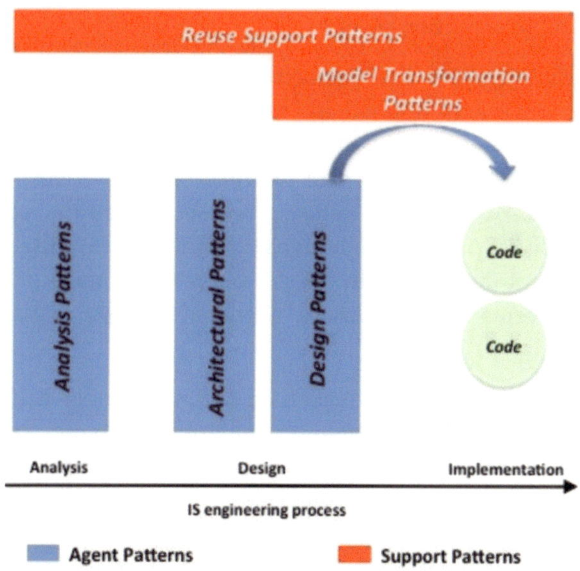

Fig. 1. The use of the different proposed patterns in the development cycle of an agent-based IS.

The description of our software patterns is composed of four parts:

- The *Interface* part contains the following fields: *Name* and *Classification* (used to categorize the pattern: Analysis pattern, Design pattern, etc.), *Context* (defines the conditions under which the pattern could be applied), *Rationale* (gives which problems this pattern addresses) and *Applicability* (gives the scope of this pattern: Information Systems in our case).
- The *Solution* part when proposed as a model-based solution is composed of the following fields: *Model* (an agent pattern presents a solution as a UML class diagram and/or a UML sequence diagram), *Participants* (explanation of the different elements defined on the diagram) and *Consequences* (advantages and drawbacks of this pattern to help developers deciding whether this pattern is the correct one). When the *Solution* part is proposed as a process-based solution (for instance for Reuse Support patterns), the *Solution* part is composed of a unique field entitled *Process* defined as a UML activity diagram.
- The *Example* part describes one or more illustrations on how to use this pattern.
- The *Relationship* part is composed of the following fields: *Uses* (describes the relationship: "the pattern X is using the pattern Y in its solution"), *Requires* ("the pattern X requires the pattern Y to be applied before"), *Refines* ("the pattern X refines the pattern Y if and only if the pattern Y solves the same issues than the pattern X") and *Looks like* ("the pattern X is a variant of the pattern Y").

Note: The different patterns presented here are reduced versions. We only describe the most important parts and fields required to understand what a pattern means. As a consequence, we remove the Example part, which is presented in Section 5.

3.2 Pattern reuse

The reuse of patterns dedicated to develop Agent-based IS consists in applying them during analysis, design and implementation phases.

First, developers analyze context and problem and should have to answer questions to decide which patterns have to be applied and in which order. This activity can be favoured by using *Reuse Support Patterns* which represent sequences of patterns that can be applied to develop Agent-based IS (See Table 1 for an example of RSP suited for navigating in our Analysis Pattern collection). They help to navigate into the pattern collection and to reuse them. Thus, developers adapt analysis, architectural or design pattern solution elements (instantiation) to represent the system they want to develop. Finally, the third activity aims at using Model Transformation Patterns to generate skeleton application from pattern instances.

It is worth mentioning that, here, reuse is realised by adaptation. Designers do not directly reuse the patterns but adapt the different solutions (instantiation) to their specific applications by modifying the level of abstraction given by the patterns. Moreover, as briefly depicted in the "Service Integration" RSP below, designers should have to answer questions to decide which patterns have to be applied. Another example is given in Table 1 where the "Restrict access to resources" pattern is used if and only if some policies are in use on resources.

Interface
Name
Base Agent Design
Classification
Reuse Support Pattern
Rationale
This pattern presents Agent Analysis Patterns that can be applied to develop a base agent. Here, a base agent is an agent that plays roles within organisations, lives in an environment and reacts to events in the environment, and optionally acts on resources (perception and action) if it has the associated permission.
Applicability
Agent Analysis Pattern Collection ^ Base Agent
Solution
Process
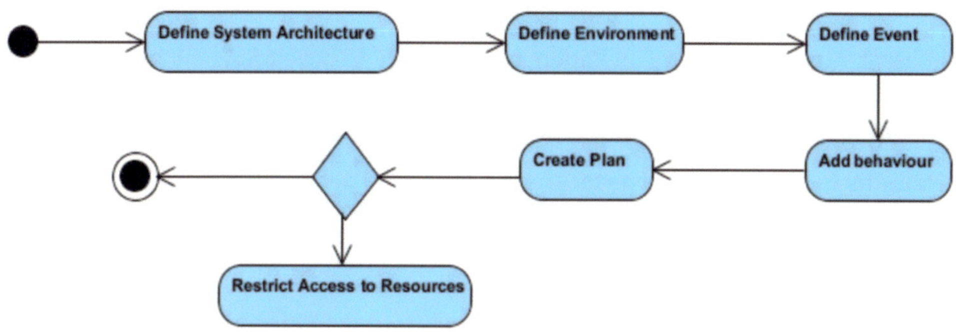 Designers first have to apply the pattern "Define system architecture", then the patterns "Define environment", "Define event", "Add behaviour" and "Create plan". After applying the "Create plan" pattern, it is possible either to terminate the process or to continue with the "Restrict access to resources" pattern depending on the necessity to have policies on resource access (a resource is for instance digital documents such as contracts, proposals, enterprise database, etc.). This decision is fuelled by considering the place of agents in the environment: do all agents access resources? Do some resources need to be kept private? Based on the answers, designers may decide to apply the "Restrict access to resources" pattern. *Note : only the "Define System Architecture" Analysis Pattern in this RSP is presented in Section 4.*
Relationships
Uses
"Define System Architecture", "Define Environment", "Define Event", "Add Behaviour", "Create Plan", "Restrict Access to Resources" Agent Analysis Patterns.

Table 1. Reuse Support Pattern "Base Agent Design"

Several other reuse support patterns (RSP) are proposed in our approach to address specific needs. Amongst them, we can quote the "Service Integration" RSP. The "Service Integration" RSP helps designers integrating the notion of services and service-oriented architectures within the information system. In this particular RSP, the process is not limited to a set of patterns to apply in a given order but obliges designers to think about the overall enterprise Information Systems:

- Do we need to agentify the services from the Information System?
- Do we consider agents as a wrapper of services?
- Do we need to present agent behaviours as services to Information Systems?
- Do we need to provide access to external Information Systems and partners then requiring interoperability and the definition of ontologies?

Based on designer's answers, a specific process will appear from the complete activity diagram in the "Service Integration" RSP.

Moreover, we have developed a toolkit, which is based on our software patterns. It takes as input a Reuse Support Pattern, guides the developer--by asking questions--through the different patterns to be used, and finally generates code skeleton. The process is then not fully automated due to interactions with developer. Thus, s/he can complete and refine the generated code and run his/her agents on a target platform.

We present, in next section, Agent Patterns we designed to develop Agent-based IS.

4. Patterns for engineering agent-based information systems

4.1 Patterns for the analysis phase

In following sections, we present patterns for the analysis phase of information systems engineering, which are *Agent Analysis Patterns.*

4.1.1 Agent analysis patterns

The analysis patterns described below are generic ones used for building agent-based information systems at a high level of abstraction. Due to space restriction, we only present two among twelve analysis patterns for building agents used in Information Systems.

4.1.1.1 Agent analysis pattern "define system architecture"

Interface
Name
Define System Architecture
Classification
Agent Analysis Pattern
Rationale
The aim of this pattern is to define the organisation and sub-organisations, their relations, and the roles played by agents in these organisations.
Applicability
Designing agents ^ Information systems
Solution
Model

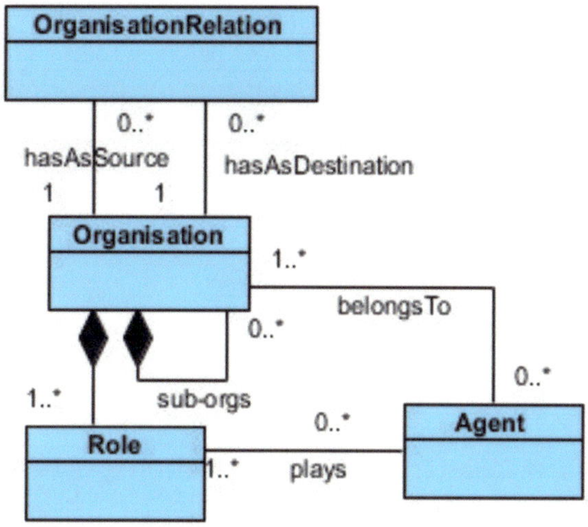

Participants
This pattern describes the overall structure of the multiagent system underlying the IS. A multiagent system is here an *Organisation* possibly composed of sub-organisations. Each (sub-) organisation is related to other (sub-) organisations by some *OrganisationRelation*. *Agent*s play *Role* in these organisations. The *Agent* concept corresponds to the notion of agent defined in the agent theory (Wooldridge, 2002). An agent is an autonomous and active entity, which asynchronously interacts with other agents and cooperates with others so as to solve a global problem. An agent is seen as an aggregation of *Role*. An agent is uniquely identified within the system. The *Role* concept describes a role that the agent will play. It defines a catalogue of behaviours played within the system. An association entitled *plays* links the *Agent* concept to the *Role* concept. This association has the following cardinalities: an *Agent* may have 1 or more roles, and a *Role* may be played by an agent. The *Organisation* concept defines the organisational structure used in the system. There could be a flat organisation or an organisation composed of sub-organisations.

Table 2. Agent Analysis Pattern "Define System Architecture"

4.1.1.2 Agent analysis pattern "define protocol"

Interface
Name
Define Protocol
Classification
Agent Analysis Pattern
Context

This pattern requires applying the "Define Communication between Roles" pattern before.
Rationale
This pattern defines the protocol with the messages between roles.
Applicability
Designing agents ^ Information systems
Solution
Model
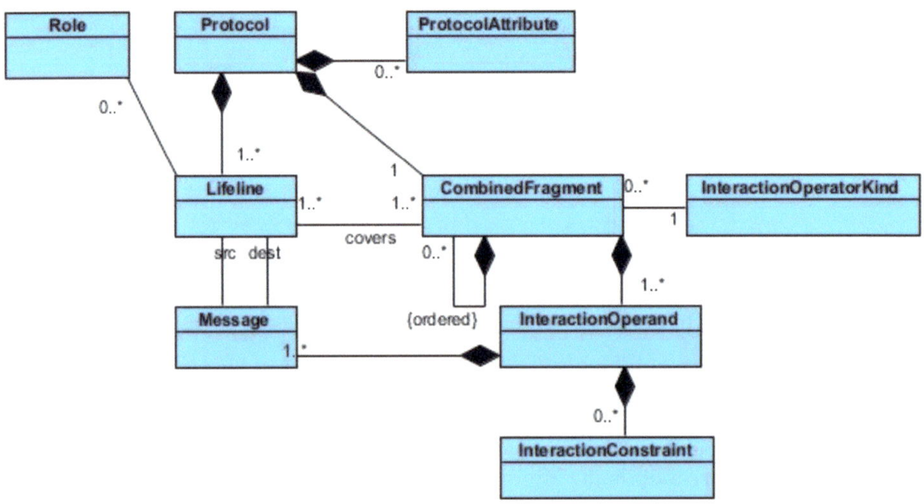
Participants
The different roles present in the *Protocol* are denoted by *Lifeline*. *Lifeline* specifies when a *Role* enters the conversation and when it leaves it. *Message* are exchanged between *Lifeline* and are gathered within *InteractionOperand*. These *InteractionOperand* correspond to sequence of messages. Some *InteractionConstraint* may alter how *InteractionOperand* can be used. Finally, *InteractionOperand* are gathered within *CombinedFragment* and the semantics of these fragments is given by *InteractionOperatorKind*. These *InteractionOperatorKind* are *alt* (one *InteractionOperand* is selected based on *InteractionConstraint), opt* (an *InteractionOperand* is applied if the corresponding *InteractionConstraint* are satisfied else nothing is done) and *loop* (a *CombinedFragment* is applied over and over again as long as the *InteractionConstraint* are satisfied). Some *ProtocolAttribute* may be defined for the *Protocol*, they correspond to parameters for the protocol.
Relationship
Requires
Agent Analysis Pattern "Define Communication between Roles".

Table 3. Agent analysis pattern "Define Protocol"

4.2 Patterns for the design phase

In this section, we present Agent Architectural and Design Patterns for the architectural and detailed design of AIS. These patterns have to be applied after analysis patterns described above.

4.2.1 Agent architectural patterns

We develop three architectural patterns related to the different architectures an AIS could have:

- Pattern "Market-based AIS": a marketplace is defined with this pattern. A marketplace is composed of several proposers and several task managers. Task managers try to find the best proposal for a service. Two approaches are possible to retrieve this best proposal: (1) A descending price auction or (2) A call for proposals.
- Pattern "Subcontract-based AIS": An AIS with subcontracts is a restricted version of the previous pattern "Market-based AIS". In this particular case, there is only one task manager and several proposers. The best proposal is found after a call for proposals.
- Pattern "Peer-to-Peer-based AIS": previous patterns impose to use a central server so as to store the address of the different task managers and proposers. This approach does not resist to the scalability problem and the bottleneck is located on querying the central server to retrieve the different task managers and proposers. In this pattern here, there is no central server and the different task managers and proposers know each other via social networks. This kind of architecture copes with the scalability problem.

Below, we only present the pattern "Subcontract-based Agent-based Information System".

Note: The different design and model transformation patterns described below are those required for building a Subcontract-based AIS.

Interface
Name
Subcontract-based Agent-based Information System
Classification
Agent Architectural Pattern
Rationale
This pattern gives the structure of a subcontract-based information system with a unique *Task Manager* and several *Proposers*.
Applicability
Designing agents ^ Information systems
Solution
Model

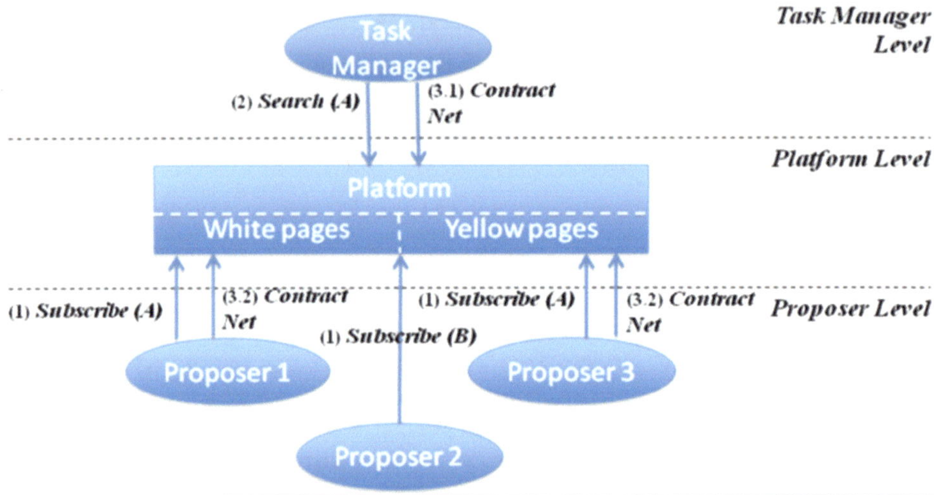

Participants

This kind of AIS architecture considers three layers: the *Task Manager* layer, the *Platform* layer and the *Proposer* layer.

The Task Manager layer contains one unique *Task Manager* playing the role of task manager in AIS. It is the one that requests services from Proposer.

The Proposer layer contains one or more *Proposer* playing the role of proposers who provide services.

The *Platform* layer contains two services proposed to the different task manager and proposers, that is the white pages and the yellow pages. White pages give the address of the different entities within the system and yellow pages return the service proposed by proposers.

Collaborations and communications within the architecture:

1. Proposers register their services within the yellow pages with the performative *subscribe*.
2. A task manager looks for proposers providing a specific service (here the service A) within the yellow pages with the performative *search*. It then retrieves their address within the white pages so as to contact them.
3. A Contract Net protocol (Davis & Smith, 1983) is then used between proposers and task manager so as to find the best proposal for a specific requested service (here the service A).

Table 4. Agent Architectural Pattern "Subcontract-based Agent-based Information System".

4.2.2 Agent design patterns

The following patterns describe the different concepts needed for designing an Agent-based IS. We only present here two examples of such patterns.

4.2.2.1 Agent design pattern "platform-based system architecture"

Interface
Name
Platform-based System Architecture
Classification
Agent Design Pattern
Rationale
This pattern describes the overall structure of the system taking count of the platform.
Applicability
Designing agents ^ Information systems
Solution
Model

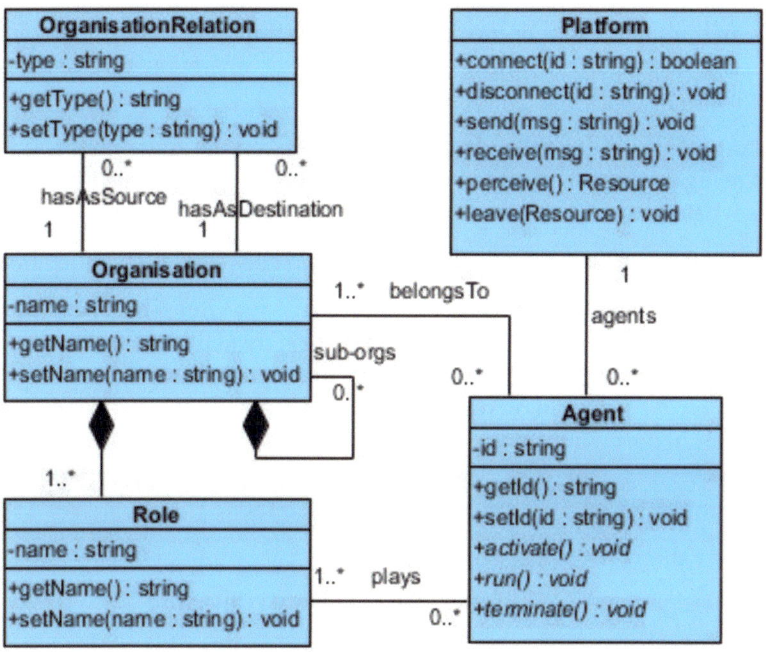

Participants

This pattern describes the overall structure of the multiagent system underlying the IS from the design point of view. A multiagent system is here an *Organisation* possibly composed of *sub-organisations*. Each (sub-) organization is related to other (sub-) organizations by some *OrganisationRelation*. Agents play *Role* in these organizations.

The *Agent* concept corresponds to the notion of agent defined in the agent theory (Wooldridge, 2002). An agent is an autonomous and active entity, which asynchronously interacts with other agents and cooperates with others so as to solve a global problem. An agent is seen as an aggregation of *Role*. An *Agent* is defined as an abstract class from object

theory since three operations mentioned below are abstract. An agent is uniquely identified in the system via the attribute *id*. Getter and setter operations are defined for the attribute *id*. Three other operations are defined abstract and have to be instantiated in the instance of this *Agent*. *Activate()* contains behaviours for initialising the agent. *Run()* is executed every time it is the turn of the agent to be executed. Finally, *terminate()* describes behaviours executed when ending the agent execution. The *Role* concept describes a role that the agent will play. It defines a catalogue of behaviours played within the system. The *Role* concept defines an attribute *name* and its corresponding getter and setter operations. An association entitled *plays* links the *Agent* concept to the *Role* concept. This association has the following cardinalities: an *Agent* may have 1 or more roles, and a *Role* may be played by an agent. The *Organisation* concept defines the organizational structure used in the system. There could be a flat organization or an organization composed of sub-organisations. An attribute *name* and its corresponding getter and setter operations are associated to the *Organisation* concept. An association *belongsTo* links the *Organisation* concept to the *Agent* concept. It expresses the fact that an agent may belong to several organizations and an organization has zero or more agents whatever their roles are. The *OrganisationRelation* concept describes the relation between two organizations. Finally, the *Platform* concept defines the platform and the different services provided by this one. These services are present by the operations available on the Platform concept: connection to the platform, disconnection from the platform, send a message, receive a message saved on the platform, perceive for sensing traces in the environment, and leave for adding traces in the environment.
Relationships
Requires
Agent Analysis Pattern "Define System Architecture".

Table 5. Agent Design Pattern "Platform-based System Architecture"

4.2.2.2 Agent design pattern "FIPA-based interaction with protocol"

Interface
Name
FIPA-based Interaction with Protocol
Classification
Agent Design Pattern
Rationale
This design pattern describes the notion of cognitive interaction in terms of protocols within roles. This interaction is FIPA-compliant.
Applicability
Designing agents ^ Information systems

Solution

Model

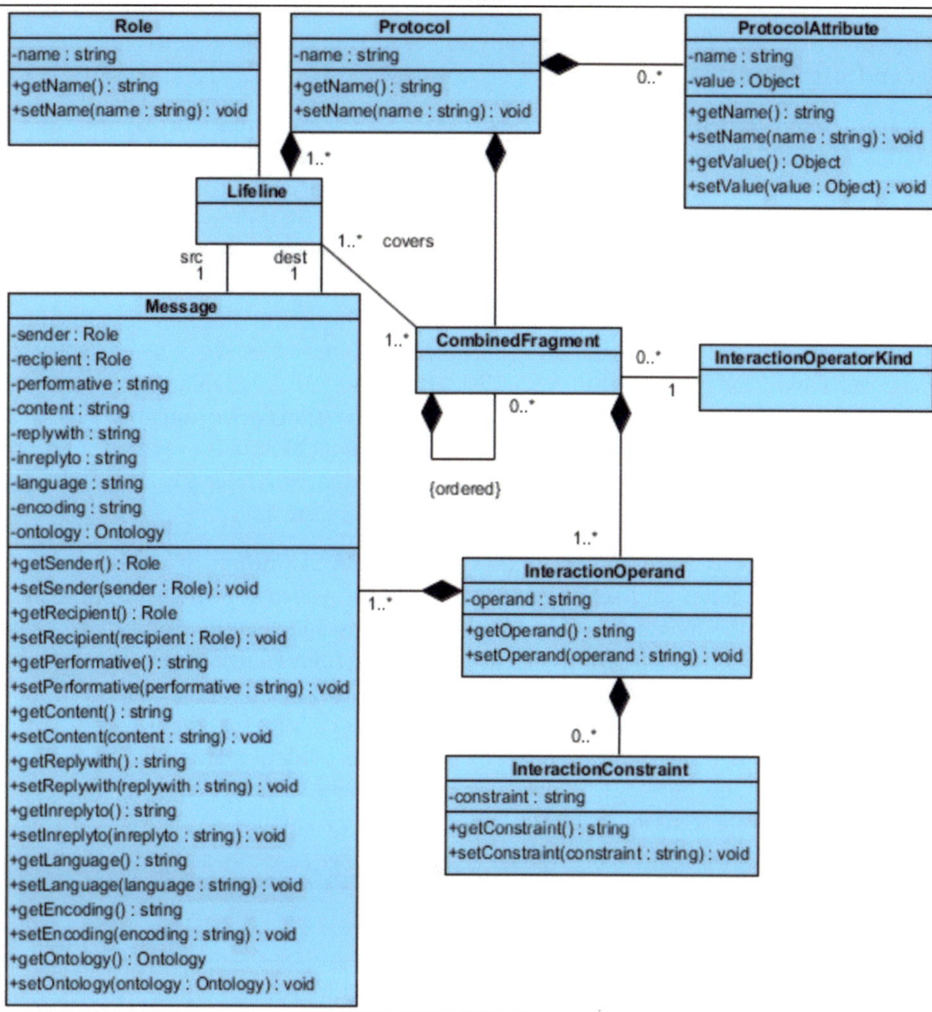

Participants

Interactions between roles are either based on pheromones left in the environment (we speak about reactive interactions) or based on communicative acts as humans do (we speak then about cognitive interactions). In this design pattern, we consider cognitive interactions through protocols. Protocols help directing the conversations between roles since only messages from the protocol are granted when agents interact with this protocol.

This design pattern is FIPA-compliant (FIPA, 2002) and is based on the UML 2.x sequence diagram specifications. We just remove some classes that are nonsense for agents.

The following concepts are present in this design pattern:

The *Role* concept describes a role that the agent will play. It defines a catalogue of behaviours played within the system. The *Role* concept defines an attribute *name* and its

corresponding getter and setter operations. The *Protocol* concept defines a protocol. It contains all the sequences of messages allowed for this protocol. The *Protocol* concept defines an attribute *name* and its corresponding getter and setter operations. A protocol may contain some *ProtocolAttribute.* These attributes correspond to local attributes required during the execution of the protocol. It could be for instance the set of recipients of a specific message. The *ProtocolAttribute* concept defines an attribute as a *name* and a *value*. The corresponding getter and setter operations are defined too. The different roles are denoted by the *Lifeline* concept in the protocol. Since this protocol definition is based on UML 2.x sequence diagram specification, a protocol is decomposed into *CombinedFragment*. Each *CombinedFragment* has an associated *InteractionOperatorKind* from the following list: *alt*, *opt* and *loop*. *Alt* denotes an alternative between several *InteractionOperand*. One and only one alternative will be chosen. *Opt* denotes an option on an *InteractionOperand*. This *InteractionOperand* is executed if and only if the conditions-represented by *InteractionConstraint*- are satisfied. Finally, *loop* denotes the execution of a set of messages as long as the conditions are satisfied. The *Message* concept is the concept following the FIPA definition. It contains a set of attributes and their getter and setter operations. *Sender, recipient, performative* and *content* denote from whom the message is sent to whom. A message is composed of two parts: a *performative* depicting the verb of the communicative act (*inform*, *request*, etc.) and a *content* on which this *performative* is applied. The other attributes are for administrative duties: *replywith* and *inreplyto* correspond to identifier respectively for the sender and the recipient. *Language* denotes the language in which the content parameter is expressed. *Ontology* defines which ontology is used for this message. Finally, *encoding* denotes the specific encoding of the content language expression.
Relationships
Requires
Agent Analysis Pattern "Define Protocol"

Table 6. Agent Design Pattern "FIPA-based Interaction with Protocol".

4.3 Patterns for the implementation phase: Model transformation patterns

We define several *Model Transformation Patterns* for developing AIS for different architectures (subcontract-based architectures, market-based ones and peer-to-peer-based ones) and for different execution platforms (JADE and Madkit). We only present here in Table 7, a short version---without method transformations---of a Model Transformation Pattern for Madkit implementation of a subcontract-based AIS.

Interface
Name
Madkit Implementation of a subcontract-based Agent-based Information System
Classification
Model Transformation Pattern

Rationale

This pattern performs the model transformation from a design model of a subcontract-based Agent-based Information System to the Madkit platform.

Applicability

Implementing agents ^ Subcontract-based Information Systems

Solution

Model

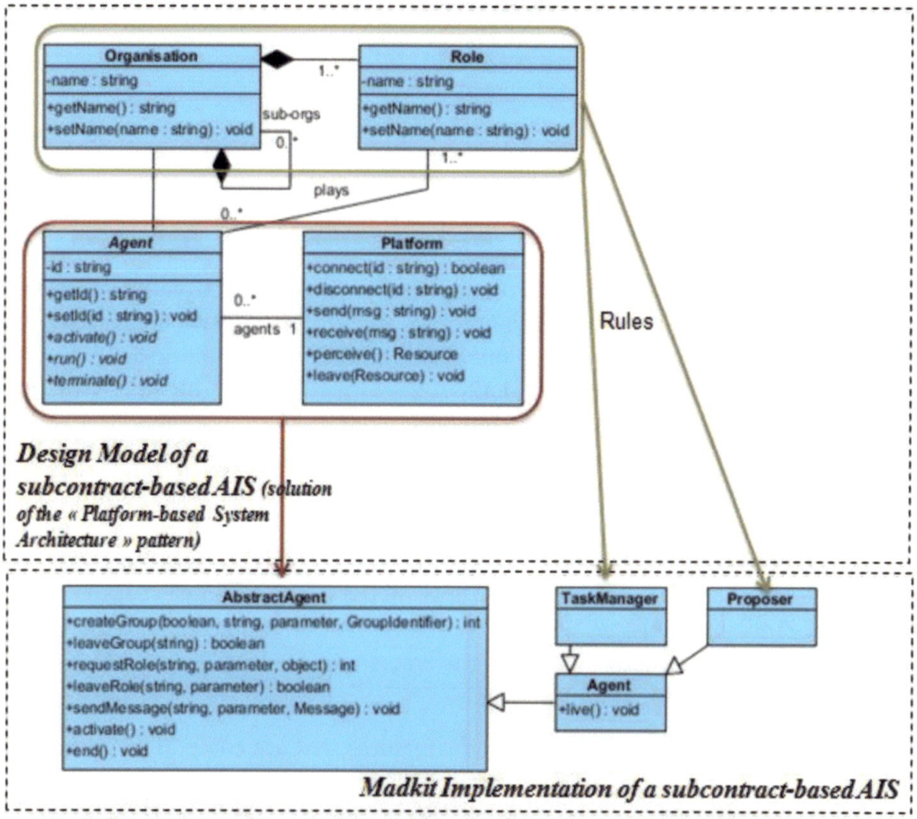

Rule 1: If the instance of Agent is linked to Organisation org1 then insert in activate() code of the instance the following line: *int g = createGroup(true, "community", "org1", null, null);*
Rule 2: If the instance of Agent is linked to Role role1 then insert in activate() code of the instance the following line: *int r = requestRole("community", "org1", "role1",null);*

Note: In this pattern and due to space restriction, we do not consider the OrganisationRelation concept since it is not mandatory for a subcontract-based AIS.

Participants

This pattern ensures the transformation from a design model of an AIS to a set of classes for the Madkit platform. Agents on the Madkit platform are defined as a specialization of the *AbstractAgent* class provided by the Madkit platform. The *AbstractAgent* class from the Madkit platform provides the different methods required for the Agent lifecycle (creation, invocation, execution and deletion). These methods correspond to the ones proposed in the *Agent* concept. The set of attributes and methods from the *Role* concept is added to the

Task manager and *Proposer* classes. The *Task manager* and *Proposer* are the two unique roles in a subcontract-based AIS according to the "Subcontract-based Agent-based Information System" architectural pattern (see Table 4). Two rules are added for model transformation. *Rule 1* expresses that organizations are created within agents in the *activate()* operation. Agents are responsible to create the organizations. *Rule 2* specifies that roles agents have, are taken within the *activate()* operation of the corresponding agent.
Relationships
Uses
Agent Design Pattern "Platform-based System Architecture".

Table 7. Model Transformation Pattern "Madkit Implementation of a Subcontract-based Agent-based Information System"

5. A case study

The objectives of our case study are to provide enriched traveller information. This enriched traveller information is in fact the collaboration of two different tools: (1) A route planner considering usual travel means such as buses and undergrounds but also taxis, personal vehicles, rent bicycles and walking, and (2) An adorned travel with points of interests related to traveller preferences (cultural interests, food preferences, etc.). The process of proposing a route to traveller is as followed. After entering origin and destination, the information system composed of all the different operators (bus, underground, taxi, and rent bicycle) cooperate to find the best route proposals based on the preferences (cost, duration, number of connections, etc.) and requirements (no stairs, disabled access, ease of use, etc.) of the traveller. Then, the system prunes all the proposed routes based on traveller requirements. Finally, points of interest providers adorn the routes with contextual information such as restaurants matching the traveller's food preferences if the route is during meal hours, shops or monuments, etc.

This information system exhibits some specific features that are compatible with an agent-based system. First of all, route planning is not realised according a client/server approach. Every operator is responsible of its data and is the only one to know how to deal with scheduled and/or unexpected events (delays, traffic jam, disruptions, etc.). As mentioned above, operators collaborate to find routes from origin to destination.

A second reason is the openness of the system. The list of operators (especially taxis) and points of interest providers is subject to evolve, especially during execution. The system should be able to take account of appearing and disappearing providers.

Finally, a third reason is the necessity for the information system to present some adaptability mechanisms. A route may change due to unexpected events or after traveller requests. The system should be able to modify the proposals during execution.

For all these reasons, an agent-based system is well-adapted since adaptability, openness, and context-aware are part of the intrinsic features of agents. We invite the reader to consult (Wooldridge, 2002) for details on agent-based systems and their characteristics.

We focus in this chapter on how designing and building the transport information system responsible to provide enriched traveller information.

Figures 2 and 3 give the instantiation for our case study of the two analysis patterns presented in Section 4.1.

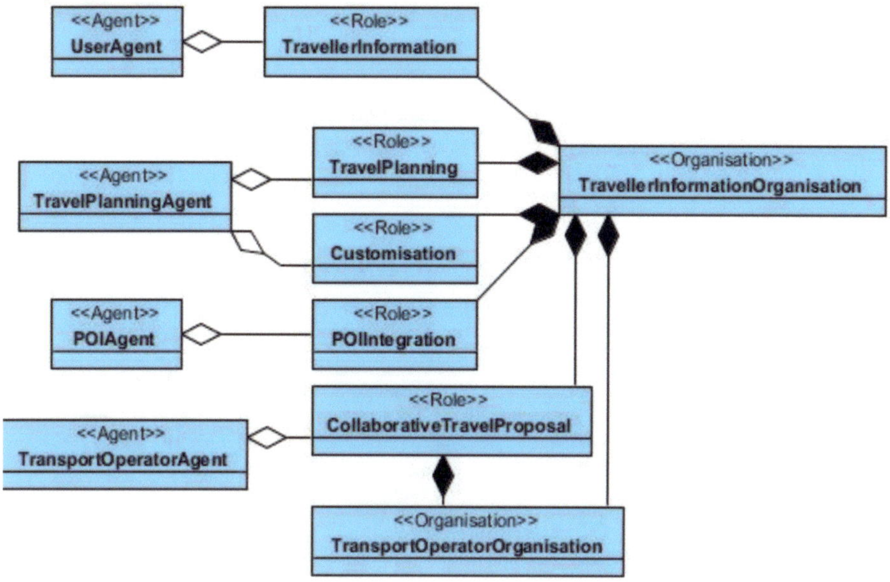

Fig. 2. Instantiation of the "Define System Architecture" Agent Analysis Pattern

Figure 2 describes the complete system architecture with one organisation *Traveller Information Organisation,* one sub-organisation *Transport Operator Organisation,* five roles *Traveller Information, Travel Planning, Customisation, POI Integration* and *Collaborative Travel Proposal,* and four agents *User Agent, Travel Planning Agent, POI Agent,* and *Transport Operator Agent.*

Each agent *Transport Operator Agent* represents a means to travel inside a city: underground if available, bus, taxi, rent bicycle, personal vehicle or by foot. These agents play the role *Collaborative Travel Proposal* since they try to collaborate so as to complete the travel from origin to destination. All these agents are part of the *Transport Operator Organisation.*

The *Transport Operator Organisation* is part of the *Traveller Information Organisation, which* carries information to travellers.

User Agent represents the traveller requesting the system. *Travel Planning Agent* is responsible to ask for a list of journeys to *Transport Operator Agent. Travel Planning Agent* has two roles: (1) *Travel Planning* to request journeys and (2) *Customisation* to prune the journeys based on user preferences and requirements. This role sends journeys back to the *User Agent.*

POI Agent represents point of interests within the city. These agents intervene when a journey is completed and add some points of interest based on user preferences. Points of interest might be restaurants, monuments, shops to name a few.

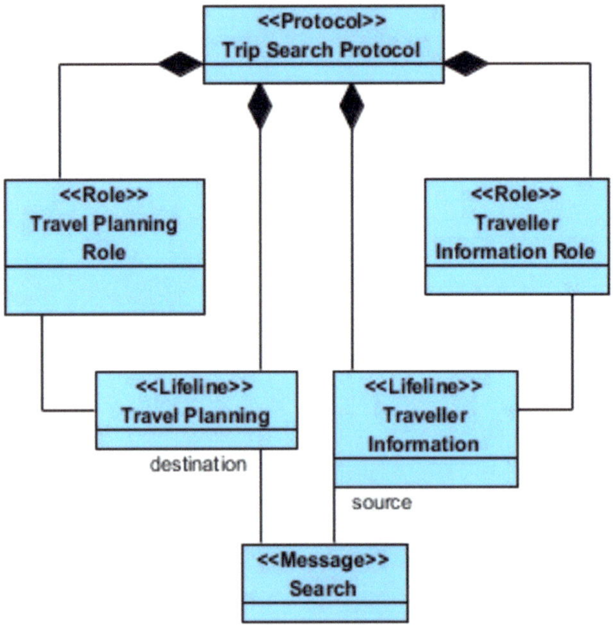

Fig. 3. Instantiation of the "Define Protocol" Agent Analysis Pattern

Figure 3 presents the protocol (instantiation of the "Define Protocol" analysis pattern) that initiates the search for a trip between the *Traveller Information* role acting for the user and the *Travel Planning*. The message sent is the *Search* message.

Figures 4 and 5 give the instantiation for our case study of the two design patterns presented in Section 4.2. The developer of a transport information system has to apply the agent analysis and architectural--not presented here--patterns before.

Figure 4 corresponds to Figure 2 after refining analysis model, i.e. inserting some attributes and operations. All the operations (except for the Platform concept) are getter and setter operations. We define below the different attributes for the concepts on this pattern:

UserAgent has attributes corresponding to the travel: there are an origin, a destination, a maximum amount s/he would like to pay and a maximum duration for the travel. *Preferences* and *Requirements* contain a *description* attribute describing the preferences or the requirements the user has.

TravelPlanningAgent has three attributes: *queries* containing the different user queries the enriched travel planning system has to satisfy, *plannedTravels* containing the raw travel planning answering user queries and finally *enrichedTravels* contain the list of enriched travels with points of interest to send to users.

POIAgent has a unique attribute *description* describing the point of interest (position, description, etc.) for inclusion in travel plans.

TransportOperatorAgent has an attribute *TransportOperatorDB* corresponding to the database of all the details about the journeys proposed by the operator. When the operator is a rent bicycle one, the database contains the different locations of rent and where bicycles are.

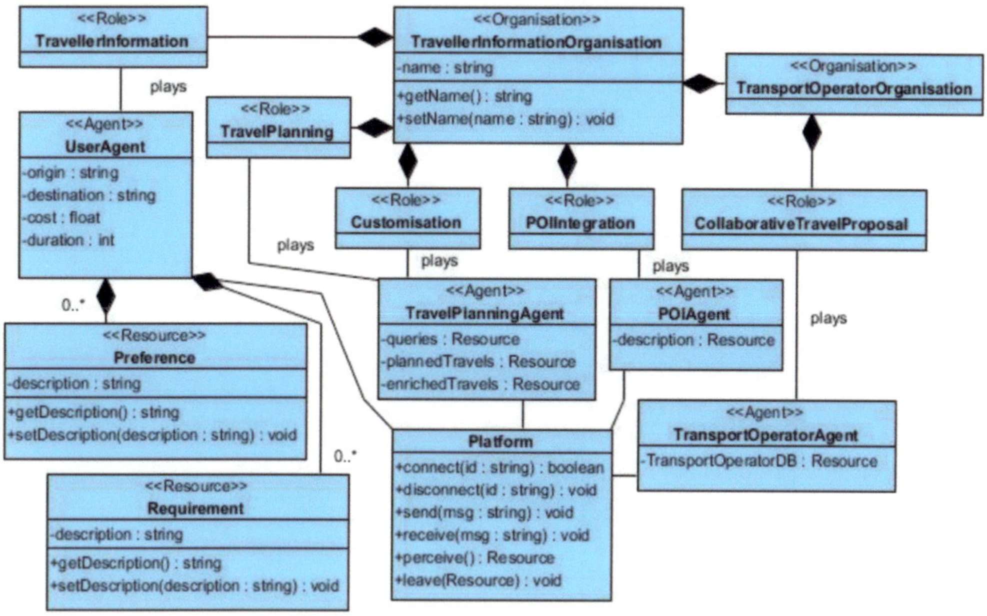

Fig. 4. Instantiation of the "Platform-based System Architecture" Agent Design Pattern

Figure 5 presents the sequence diagram corresponding to the situation where a user asks for a travel from an origin to a destination. This figure is the instantiation of the "FIPA-based Interaction with Protocol" Agent Design Pattern. His/her *UserAgent* leaves the query in the environment. This insertion generates an event, a *TravelPlanningAgent* can perceive. If this *UserAgent* is a newcomer in the system, the *TravelPlanningAgent* asks the *UserAgent* about its user's preferences and requirements.

TravelPlanningAgent then leaves in the environment a travel from origin to destination but without schedule. This empty travel is perceived by *TransportOperatorAgent* that tries to complete it. Every *TransportOperatorAgent* tries to update this travel or to propose an alternative. When this travel was considered by all *TransportOperatorAgent*, it turns into a planned travel. The *TravelPlanningAgent* perceives it and turns it into an enriched travel to let *POIAgent* to perceive it.

POIAgent tries to update it with points of interest and leaves the enriched travel plans in the environment. Finally, *Customisation* prunes the different proposals based on user's preferences and requirements and informs *UserAgent* of the best proposals.

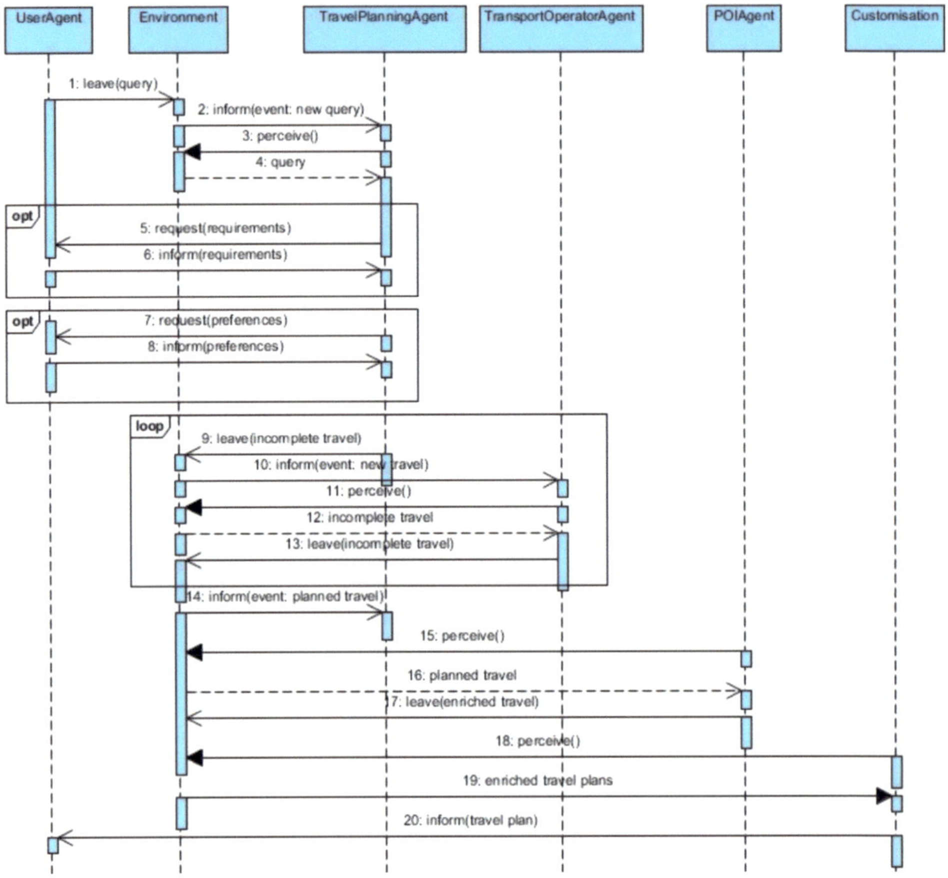

Fig. 5. Instantiation of the "FIPA-based Interaction with Protocol" Agent Design Pattern

6. Related work

We can find two kinds of patterns related to Information Systems and agent-based systems engineering in literature:

- Agent-based patterns
- Patterns for Information Systems engineering

Patterns for Information Systems engineering (for instance, patterns for cooperative IS (Couturier, 2004) (Saidane, 2005), e-bidding applications (Jureta et al., 2005; Couturier et al., 2010), distributed IS (Renzel & Keller, 1997), enterprise application architecture (Fowler, 2002), etc.) are generally domain-dependent and/or do not deal with advanced information systems requiring adaptability, cooperation or negotiation such as agent-based ones.

On the other hand, the concepts of agent technology, which include, among others, autonomy, proactivity, reactivity, social behaviours, adaptability and agents, differ from those of traditional software development paradigms. The various concepts and the relationships among them generate different agent-oriented software engineering problems for which agent-oriented patterns have been written.

According to Oluyomi et al. (Oluyomi et al., 2007), numerous efforts have been made by agent software practitioners to document agent-oriented software engineering experiences as patterns and they establish a listing of ninety-seven agent-oriented patterns gathered from literature.

Oluyomi et al. classify agent-oriented patterns based on the definition of the software tasks/concepts of agent technology and the stages of development.

According to this first point of view, numerous works such as (Kendall et al., 1998) (Aridor & Lange, 1998) feature agent-oriented concepts as object-oriented ones and adapt existing object-oriented patterns to their needs. This is not suited for agent-based system engineering due to the differences between agent technology concepts and object ones and their implementation languages.

According to the second point of view, existing agent patterns are not designed to capture all the different phases and processes of agent-oriented software engineering. Indeed, proposals ((Hung and Pasquale, 1999), (Tahara et al., 1999), (Sauvage, 2003), (Schelfthout et al., 2002) to name a few) focus either only on the implementation phase of development or only on some aspects of the design phase but scarcely to analysis. Other works are based on implementation of only a particular application of agent technology, for example, mobile agents (Aridor and Lange, 1998), or reactive or cognitive ones (Meira et al., 2001) for instance. It is worth mentioning that it is difficult to reuse these proposals to realise a complete agent-based information system: either the proposals only deal with a specific agent type, or the collection of patterns is partial and not homogeneous enough.

We add a third classification: proposals specifying patterns with or without providing tools or a methodology to help reusing these patterns. Some patterns underlie methodologies such as Tropos (Do et al., 2003) or PASSI (Cossentino et al., 2004). These methodologies aim at guiding developers when using patterns to develop agent-based systems. However, Tropos only proposes patterns for detailed design. These patterns focus on social and intentional aspects frequently present in agent-based systems. Patterns in PASSI methodology deal with detailed design and implementation. One hurdle in PASSI is this is not trivial selecting the appropriate patterns especially for new agent developers. Most of works do not propose a methodology or a guide to reuse patterns.

Thus, it becomes difficult for a developer to reuse these proposals to design and implement an agent-based information system:

- Proposed patterns are too generic and do not match with information systems issues.
- It is very difficult for non-agent software practitioners to easy understand the different aspects of agent based systems development.
- Users do not have adequate criteria to search for suitable patterns to solve their problems (lack of methodology).
- All stages of software development are not covered and combination of agent-oriented patterns written by different authors, into a well-defined pattern collection is nearly impracticable.

Our proposal, which covers all the phases of agent-based information systems engineering, is suitable for each kind of agent (agents with or without decision behaviours) and addresses information systems issues such as business rules, legacy systems, services and enterprise resources, for instance. We also propose a methodology based on our Reuse Support Patterns.

7. Conclusion

This chapter describes our work about specifying and reusing patterns so as to engineer Agent-based Information Systems. The different patterns presented here represent the building blocks which, after adaptation, can be used to develop analysis and design models for a new IS, define the architecture and ease implementation. The patterns cover all the phases of IS engineering and a methodology, based on our Reuse Support Patterns, is provided to favour their reuse. We have also developed a toolkit so as to ease engineering Information System applications and specifically, intelligent transport systems. This toolkit is based on our software patterns. It takes as input a Reuse Support Pattern, guides the developer through the different patterns to be used, and finally generates code skeleton.

Our approach and the different patterns are experimentally validated on a specific IS for transportation. Reusing the patterns help eliciting the business entities (analysis model), architecting the system (the architecture is a subcontract-based one since there is a unique task manager and several proposers), defining the design model and generating code skeleton for the Madkit platform.

Future work aims at reusing the different patterns presented here so as to develop other Enterprise Information Systems (schedule management for instance).

8. References

Alexander, C.; Shikawa, S.; Silverstein, M.; Jacobson, M.; Fiksdahl-King, I., & Angel, S. (1977). *A pattern language: towns, buildings, construction*, Oxford University Press, ISBN 0195019199, New York

Alexander, C. (1979). *The timeless way of building*, Oxford University Press, ISBN 0195022483, New York

Ambler S.W. (1998). *Process patterns: building large scale systems using object technology*, ISBN 0521645689, Cambridge University Press

Aridor, Y. & Lange, D.B. (1998). Agent Design Patterns: Elements of Agent Application Design, *Proceedings of the second international conference on autonomous agents*, ISBN 0897919831

Beck, K. & Cunningham, W. (1987). *Using pattern languages for object-oriented programs*, technical report CR-87-43, Computer Research Laboratory, Tektronix

Bellifemine, F.L.; Caire, G. & Greenwood, D. (2007). *Developing Multi-Agent Systems with JADE*, Wiley, ISBN 0470057475, New York

Buschmann, F.; Meunier, R.; Rohnert, H.; Sommerlad, P. & Stal, M. (1996). *Pattern-oriented software architecture: A system of patterns*, John Wiley & Son, ISBN 0471958697, Chichester, UK

Coad, P. (1992). Object-Oriented Patterns. *Communications of the ACM*, 35(9), 152-159.

Coad, P. (1996). *Object Models: Strategies, Patterns and Applications*, Prentice Hall, ISBN 0138401179

Coplien, J. O. (1992). *Advanced C++ Programming Styles and Idioms*, Addison-Wesley, ISBN 9780201548556

Cossentino, M.; Sabatucci, L. & Chella, A. (2004). Patterns Reuse in the PASSI Methodology. In *Engineering Societies in the Agents World*, Springer, LNCS, Vol. 3071/2004, 520, ISBN 978-3-540-22231-6

Couturier, V. (2004). *L'ingénierie des systèmes d'information coopératifs : une approche à base de patterns*. Unpublished doctoral dissertation, Université Jean-Moulin Lyon 3, France (in French).

Couturier, V.; Huget, M.-P. & Telisson, D. (2010). Engineering agent-based information systems: a case study of automatic contract net systems, *Proceedings of the 12th International Conference on Enterprise Information Systems* (ISAS - ICEIS 2010), Portugal, Volume 3, pp. 242-248

Davis, R. & Smith, R. G. (1983). Negotiation as a Metaphor for Distributed Problem Solving, *Artificial Intelligence*, 20(1), pp. 63-109.

Do, T.T.; Kolp, M.; Hang Hoang, T.T. & Pirotte, A. (2003). A Framework for Design Patterns for Tropos, *Proceedings of the 17th Brazilian Symposium on Software Engineering*, Brazil

FIPA (2002). FIPA ACL Message Structure Specification, 2002.

Fowler, M. (1997). *Analysis Patterns: Reusable Object Models*, Addison-Wesley, ISBN 0201895420

Fowler, M. (2002). *Patterns of enterprise application architecture*, Addison Wesley, ISBN 978-0321127426

Gamma, E.; Helm, R.; Johnson, R. & Vlissides, J. (1995). *Design patterns: Elements of reusable object-oriented software*, Addison Wesley, ISBN 0201633612

Gutknecht, O. & Ferber, J. (2000). The MADKIT agent platform architecture. In T. Wagner (Ed.), LNCS : vol. 1887. *International Workshop on Infrastructure for Multi-Agent Systems*, London, Springer-Verlag, pp. 48-55

Hay, D. C. (1996). *Data Model Patterns: Conventions of Thought*, Dorset House, ISBN 0932633293, New York

Hung, E. & Pasquale, J. (1999). *Agent Usage Patterns: Bridging the Gap Between Agent-Based Application and Middleware*, technical report CS1999-0638, Department of Computer Science and Engineering, University of California

Jureta, I.; Kolp, M.; Faulkner, S. & Do, T.T. (2005). Patterns for agent oriented e-bidding practices, *Knowledge-Based Intelligent Information and Engineering Systems (KES'05)*, Lecture Notes in Computer Sciences 3682, Springer, pp. 814 - 820

Kendall, E. A.; Murali Krishna, P.V.; Pathak, C.V. & Suresh, C.V. (1998). Patterns of intelligent and mobile agents. In Proceedings of the *Second International Conference on Autonomous Agents*, Minneapolis, Minnesota, USA, pp. 92–99

Meira, N. ; Silva, I.C. & Silva, A. (2001). An Agent Pattern for a More Expressive Approach, *Proceedings of the EuroPLOP'2000*, Germany

Oluyomi, A.; Karunasekera, S. & Sterling, L. (2007). A comprehensive view of agent-oriented patterns, *Autonomous Agents And Multi-agent Systems*, Volume 15, Number 3, pp. 337-377, DOI: 10.1007/s10458-007-9014-9

Renzel, K. & Keller W. (1997). Client/Server Architectures for Business Information Systems - A Pattern Language, *Pattern Languages of Program (PLOP'97)*, September 3-5, Monticello, Illinois, USA

Risi, W.A. & Rossi, G. (2004). An architectural pattern catalogue for mobile web information systems, *International journal of mobile communications*, vol. 2, no3, pp. 235-247, ISSN 1470-949X

Saidane, M. (2005). *Formalisation de Familles d'Architectures Logicielles Coopératives : Démarches, Modèles et Outils.* Unpublished doctoral dissertation, Université Joseph-Fourier - Grenoble I, France (in French).

Sauvage, S. (2003). *Conception de systèmes multi-agents: un thésaurus de motifs orientés agent.* Unpublished doctoral dissertation, Université de Caen, France (in French).

Schelfthout, K.; Coninx, T.; Helleboogh, A.; Steegmans, E. & Weyns, D. (2002). Agent Implementation Patterns. *Proceedings of workshop on Agent-Oriented Methodologies, 17th Annual ACM Conference on Object-Oriented Programming, Systems, Languages, and Applications*

Tahara, Y.; Ohsuga, A. & Honiden, S. (1999). Agent system development method based on agent patterns. In Proceedings of the *Fourth International Symposium on Autonomous Decentralized Systems.*

Wooldridge, M. (2002). *An introduction to Multi-Agent Systems*, John Wiley & Sons, ISBN 0470519460

4

Health Care Information Systems: Architectural Models and Governance

Paolo Locatelli, Nicola Restifo, Luca Gastaldi and Mariano Corso
Politecnico di Milano, Fondazione Politecnico di Milano and IHCO
Italy

1. Introduction

Health care is an information intensive industry (Rodrigues, 2010), in which reliable and timely information is a critical resource for the planning and monitoring of service provision at all levels of analysis: (i) organizational (Nemeth & Cook, 2007), (ii) regional (Harno, 2010; Pascot et al., 2011), (iii) national (Heeks, 2002; Brown, 2005) and international (Rada, 2008).

As a consequence, *Information and Communication Technologies* (ICTs) have become "indispensables" in the health care sector. The general perception that the use of ICT in health care is ten years behind that of other industrial sectors—such as banking, manufacturing, and the airline industry—is rapidly changing (Raghupathi, 2003).

The adoption of ICT within health care has been characterized by a series of phases evolving since the 1960s (Khoumbati et al., 2009). Health informatics adoption started mainly from financial systems, providing support to the organization's billing, payroll, accounting and reporting systems. Clinical departments launched a major initiative during the 1970s that supported such internal activities as radiology, laboratory and pharmacy (Wickramasinghe & Geisler, 2008), where machinery could support high-volume operations with the implementation of standardized procedures. Financial systems once again became prominent in the 1980s, with major investments in cost accounting and materials management systems (Grimson, 2001). During the 1990s, attention turned towards enterprise-wide clinical systems, including clinical data repositories and visions of a fully computerized *Electronic Medical Record* (EMR) (Bates, 2005).

Systematic reviews (e.g. Wickramasinghe and Geisler, 2008) show that, in most cases, all these ICT-based solutions tended to be uncritically adopted by health care organizations under the pressure of technologically-pushing forces (Burke et al., 2002)—with limited analysis of the organizational consequences during ICT adoption, and limited focus on both the support of the core care processes as well as the improvement of effectiveness (Uphoff and Krane, 1998; Martin et al., 2003; Greenberg et al., 2005). These factors can be linked to an historically low level of emphasis on ICT governance, and determined by an inhomogeneous development of *Health Care Information Systems* (HCISs) (IHCO, 2009e).

In recent years, however, health care providers—faced with an unprecedented era of competition and pressures to improve care quality and effectiveness—are changing this behaviour (Corso and Gastaldi, 2009), and exploring comprehensive perspectives that allow ICT to improve the quality of health care and of managerial processes, while simultaneously reducing their cost (Anderson, 2009; Christensen et al., 2009; Corso & Gastaldi, 2010b; 2011; Finchman et al., 2011).

This new perspective considers the HCISs made up of different systems as a whole, to be integrated and orchestrated so as to support care in a patient-centric view of organizations and processes. From this viewpoint, HCISs have much to offer to support health care cost management and to improve the quality of care (Kolodner et al., 2008). As a matter of fact, in addition to the embedded role of ICT in clinical and diagnostic equipment (Corso & Gastaldi, 2011), HCISs are uniquely positioned to capture, store, process, and communicate timely information to decision makers for better coordination of health care at all the aforementioned levels of analysis (Finchman et al., 2011).

Over the past decade, the topic of HCIS has flourished, and has germinated an emergent body of theoretical frameworks, empirical research, and practitioner-based literature that has many peculiarities if compared to the traditional streams of research active on information systems (Tan, 2008).

This chapter aims to shed light on this developing research stream—summarizing the status of the research on the topic, pointing out the most interesting aspects that are currently under study, and defining theoretical and empirical gaps to be filled with further analyses.

Consistent with these main intents, the objectives of this chapter are the following:

- Define HCISs as well as the peculiarities that differentiate them from information systems developed and adopted in other industries (§2);
- Describe the architectural models that characterize the HCISs, with a specific emphasis—for their centrality in the creation of value within an health care systems—on Hospital Information Systems (§3);
- Analyse the main challenges that are faced in the governance of HCIS—both inside an health care entity (e.g. a hospital) as well as among the different entities active in the health care sector (§4);
- Outline the gaps that the research on HCISs has to fill in the near future (§5).

All the considerations presented in this chapter are not only rooted in the literature on HCISs but also based on the empirical evidence progressively collected through a permanent research initiative promoted since 2007 by the Politecnico di Milano School of Management, i.e. the *ICT in Health Care Observatory* (IHCO).

The IHCO focuses on the analysis of ICT-driven innovation in the health care industry, with a specific emphasis on HCISs; and the production of actionable knowledge (Mohrman & Lawler, 2011) utilizable by the academics and practitioners who want to implement them (Corso & Gastaldi, 2010a).

The IHCO has traditionally studied the Italian health care industry; however, since 2011, the study of Danish, Swedish and Norwegian health care systems through an annual set of cross-comparative surveys, extensive case studies, periodical and engaging focus groups, and clinical inquiry research projects has been launched. The complete methodology that describes their overall usage is described in Corso and Gastaldi (2011).

Here the main objective is to highlight two characteristics of the research process:

- *The adoption of a collaborative framework to conduct the research*: collaborative implies (Pasmore et al., 2008) research efforts that include the active involvement of practitioners and researchers in: (i) the framing of the research agenda, (ii) the selection and pursuit of the methods to be used, and (iii) the development of implications for action. Through its collaborative framework, the IHCO increases the possibilities of relating its insights to the problems of health care practitioners.
- *The adoption of a multi-company and longitudinal framework to conduct the research*: the idea behind this approach is to reconstruct past contexts, processes, and decisions in order to discover patterns, find underlying mechanisms and triggers, and combine inductive search with deductive reason (Pettigrew, 2003). Through its multi-company and longitudinal framework, the IHCO increase the possibilities of accumulating solid knowledge over time and of generalizing its findings.

2. Health care information systems: definition and peculiarities

Rodrigues (2010) defines HCISs as powerful ICT-based tools able to make health care delivery more effective and efficient. Coherently, Tan (2005) views HCISs as a synergy of three other disciplines—namely, health care management, organization management, and information management. Rada (2008) agrees with these views, and recognises that HCISs are only partly based on the application of management information system concepts to health care. According to his view, HCISs comprise several different applications that support the needs of health care organizations, clinicians, patients and policy makers in collecting and managing all the data related to both clinical and administrative processes.

These data can be used across a number of systems for many different purposes (Wickramasinghe & Geisler, 2008), have to be integrated with the data from other entities in order to be effective (Pascot et al., 2011), and—especially for patient data—must be subject to strict rules in terms of confidentiality and security safeguards (Lobenstein, 2005).

Despite its importance, the health care domain has been underrepresented in the debate on the development of information systems—from both an empirical (Callen et al., 2007) as well as theoretical (Fichman et al., 2011) viewpoint.

Only recently a progressive proliferation of health care information systems research has been pushed by (i) the growing amount of investments made in the sector (World Health Organization, 2009), (ii) the increasing pervasiveness of ICT-based solutions within the health care domain (Stegwee & Spil., 2001), and (iii) the recognized capability of ICT to respond to the double challenge of rationalizing health care costs while, at the same time, increasing the quality of the health care processes (Stebbins et al., 2009).

Reasons behind this evidence have to be linked with the peculiarity that characterized and still characterizes health care industry itself (Anderson, 2009). At a general level, a striking feature of this industry is the level of diversity of (Fichman et al., 2011):

- Its final "customers" (the patients);
- The professional disciplines involved in the process to deliver the health care services (doctors, nurses, administrators, etc.); and

- The various stakeholders with interests in the sector (providers, regulators, etc.).

Fichman et al. (2011) have pointed out the effects of this diversity on the distinctiveness that characterizes the development of an HCIS in comparison to an information system in another industry. Generalizing their view, there are six elements that make HCISs so specific:

1. *The gravity associated with information mismatches*: health care quality is diligently pursued and vigilantly executed, and information systems can facilitate this pursuit by highlighting and monitoring errors at various stages along the continuum of care (Fichman et al., 2011). Even a small error in any one of the various pieces of information stored and used in the HCIS could have dramatic consequences that directly influence the quality of human lives (Aron et al., 2011).
2. *The personal nature of most of the information managed by health information systems*: most of the information transfer between the different health care actors involves risks—both actual and perceived—that the information could fall into the wrong hands. The perception of compromised privacy associated with each information exchange always makes the latter extremely complex in the health domain.
3. *The influence played by regulators and by providers' competition over information management*: health care is a sector highly subjected to regulatory policies on patients' data (World Health Organization, 2009). If one adds to this consideration the difficulties that the providers of ICT-based solutions experience during the exploitation of the advantages associated to their offers (IHCO, 2010; Ozdemir et al., 2011), it is easy to understand why ICT-driven innovation's realization within the health care industry is always so complex.
4. *The professional-driven and hierarchical nature of health care organizations*: one of the barriers to the full exploitation of all the potential associated with health information systems is that powerful actors in care delivery often resist technology (IHCO, 2011; Kane & Labianca, 2011). Given the hierarchical nature of health care (Fichman et al., 2011), aversion to technology by an influential physician is likely to irremediably affect other caregivers' behaviours (Venkatesh et al., 2011; IHCO, 2010).
5. *The multidisciplinarity of the actors who access HCISs*: despite the presence of multiple barriers to the use of ICT in health care, an overall unity in the use of HCISs can emerge because of the interdisciplinary nature of most of the health care services (Oborn et al., 2011). Moreover, the heterogeneity of the health care disciplines makes the pattern of ICT usage complex and entangled—forcing an approach that goes beyond the too simple classification usually performed in other industries between the adoption and the rejection of information systems.
6. *The implications for learning and adaptation associated to the implementation of an HCIS*: the health care delivery setting is characterized by a tension between the need for orderly routines and the need for sensitivity to variation in local conditions (Fichman et al., 2011). This tension magnifies the importance of effective learning and adaptation surrounding HCISs implementation (Goh et al., 2011), because the solutions that work in one specific context can not necessarily work in others .

3. Architectural models for health care information systems

3.1 Overview of health care information systems

From a functional viewpoint, an HCIS supports three main levels of a health care system:

- *Central government at national and regional level*: this comprises central planning capabilities, resources management, the definition of the rules and the procedures to be followed, general controls over financial performance, monitoring of quality and safety. This level is organized differently depending on the model of each national health care system, whose main paradigms can follow the mutual-private model typical in the United States, or the Anglo-Saxon model.
- *Primary Care Health Services*: this level includes all the systems that support the services delivered to the citizens throughout the national or regional territory. It includes all the service providers like general practitioners, local practices, etc.
- *Secondary Care Health Services*: this level refers mainly to the systems that support health care processes among health care providers.

The three levels are usually interconnected only as regards administrative and accounting flows (Locatelli, 2010; Corso & Gastaldi, 2010b), but the potential data exchange among the different layers makes ICTs essential for both the exchange and the manipulation of large sets of clinical data. This evidence provides enormous potential for the future development of health care. As a matter of fact, the ICT-based solutions that are currently present in the health care industry have the ability to not only simplify the relationship between the citizens and the physicians—improving the overall performance of health care services—but also enable a better control of the whole health care system.

For example, in Italy the national health care system is completely public, and provides health care services to all the citizens as a constitutional right. The different Italian HCISs have been based on a set of pillars (Lo Scalzo et al., 2009):

- The digitalization of the information flows at a national and a regional level;
- The development of a national as well as regional social security card;
- The development of a regional infrastructure supporting online services to citizens;
- The development of a strong set of interconnections between health care providers (secondary care) and general practitioners (primary care);
- The creation of a regional *Electronic Health Record* (*EHR*) to be subsequently integrated at a national level;
- The digitalization of the service-delivery processes in secondary care.

As health care is a subject ruled by cooperation between the central government and regions, most of the efforts aim to organize regional activities and to control costs (Corso et al., 2010). On the regional level, central institutions develop plans and projects that address high-level objectives fixed at a national level, and define regional guidelines/policies to be respected by single health care organizations on the territory (e.g. as regards the EHR).

This kind of model is reflected as well by the organization of HCISs, which are powered by a central network dealing with administrative and financial information flows, but have a much more local connotation as regards support to care processes. Moreover, many Regional governments have spent the last ten years creating a pervasive networking infrastructure, digitalizing information flows on activities performed by public providers, developing social health care identification cards, developing at least basic online services (e.g. booking), and activating the key elements for a regional EHR (Lo Scalzo et al., 2009).

If these efforts have proved quite patchy among the different regions, informatisation of health care providers is even more fragmented.

Inside the Italian health care system, it is possible to identify the CRS-SISS, a forward looking project promoted by the regional government of Lombardy, which aims to promote innovation within public health care organizations for an intensive e-health strategy, through the increasing and pervasive usage of ICTs (Corso et al., 2010).

The central elements of the CRS-SISS project are (IHCO, 2011):

- The social security citizen identification card, a powerful tool for citizens to access every health care service in the Lombardy region;
- A pervasive network linking all the health care providers, general practitioners and regional entities;
- The regional EHR, a central database where qualified health care organizations publish digitally signed documents on each clinical episode (e.g. outpatient visit reports, clinical reports, prescriptions, etc.).

The case of Croatia, described in Box 1, is an interesting example of a pervasive initiative driven by ICT and able not only to improve but also to completely redesign the national health care system.

Croatia is a country of about 56,000 square kilometres in Eastern Europe, with a population of 4.5 million inhabitants, of which about 17% are over 65 years.

Among its main initiatives, the Ministry of Health wanted to reduce the administrative burden and bring more transparency into the Croatian health care system. According to this objective, the Ministry launched the Care4U project that not only digitalized the workflows within and among health care organizations, but also integrated on a national scale all the primary care providers.

The project started in 2004, with the involvement of the National Public Health Institute and most of the Croatian health insurance agencies. Since March 2007, the Croatian HCIS operates on a national scale, connects all the offices of the general physicians (about 2,300) spread on the territory, and manages over 4 million citizens. At the end of 2010, a major system upgrade integrated into the system more than 1,100 pharmacies, 100 biochemical analysis laboratories and 66 hospitals.

The features that the HCIS makes available to all these actors are (i) an integrated management of medical records, (ii) the management of the main information exchanges (with electronic prescribing solutions, reservation, drug management, ADT, laboratories management, radiology, etc.), and (iii) the reporting of information flows to the Ministry of Health as well as all the member insurance companies.

The system has led to the achievement of substantial economic benefits—which are mainly related to the reduction in costs of hospitalization—while, at the same time, an increase not only in the effectiveness of the health care processes but also the quality perceived by patients, physicians and nurses. All these advantages have raised Croatia to the third-place ranking in the EuroHealth Consumer Index assessment performed in 2009 on 27 European countries.

Box 1. The National Health Care Information System in Croatia

3.2 Hospital information systems

The core level where ICTs can exploit their full potential both in terms of cost-efficiency as well as quality improvement is that of secondary care, i.e. the health care providers level.

A Hospital Information System (HIS) is a set of organizational structures, information flows and ICT-based solutions that support core and secondary processes of a hospital. HISs are responsible for supporting secondary care, and are the combination of a variety of interconnected systems that manage a huge amount of narrative, structured, coded and multimedia data (Corso and Gastaldi, 2010).

The HIS has not only to manage complex and widespread processes but also to store and make accessible all the information needed by the staff of the hospital.

The organization of the processes of a general health care provider can be described by a classic value-chain model (Caccia, 2008), with two main kinds of processes:

- *Primary (or core) processes*, related to direct patient care:
  - *Admission*: disease prevention, inpatient or outpatient event booking and hospitalization admission;
  - *Anamnesis*: definition of patient's clinical status from a medical and nursing standpoint;
  - *Diagnosis*: definition of patient's therapeutic and care plan;
  - *Care*: therapy, treatment, rehabilitation;
  - *Discharge and follow-up*: patient discharge and possible transfer to outpatient or home care for follow-up activities.
- Secondary (or support) processes:
  - *Strategic services*: strategy, planning and controlling, supervision of regulations;
  - *Administrative services*: administration and accounting, information systems, quality assurance, human resources;
  - *Technology services*: clinical machinery, biotechnologies, building automation, auxiliary systems;
  - *Sourcing and logistics.*

From a technological viewpoint, the concept of HIS includes the technological infrastructure, the organizational components (structures, policies, procedures) and the portfolio of the applications implementing them. Biomedical devices are not considered a part of the HIS, as they should be considered part of the clinical engineering area.

From a functional viewpoint, the main areas of an HIS are (Locatelli, 2010):

- The *administration and management area*, which supports strategic and administrative processes;
- The *front-office area*, which supports the admission of inpatients, outpatients, or emergency/first aid patients;
- The *clinical area*, which supports the core health care processes (the processes through which health care organizations provide treatment to patients).

Typically, these areas implement a number of different systems that have been progressively acquired over a period of years, to later be integrated with the aim of progressively bringing higher levels of process flexibility and organizational coordination.

In the rest of the paragraph the three functional areas will be described, emphasizing their main functional modules and their role in relation to providers' processes. Fig. 1 provides a comprehensive picture of how the different areas interact with each other thanks to a bunch of centralized services and a comprehensive integration layer called "middleware".

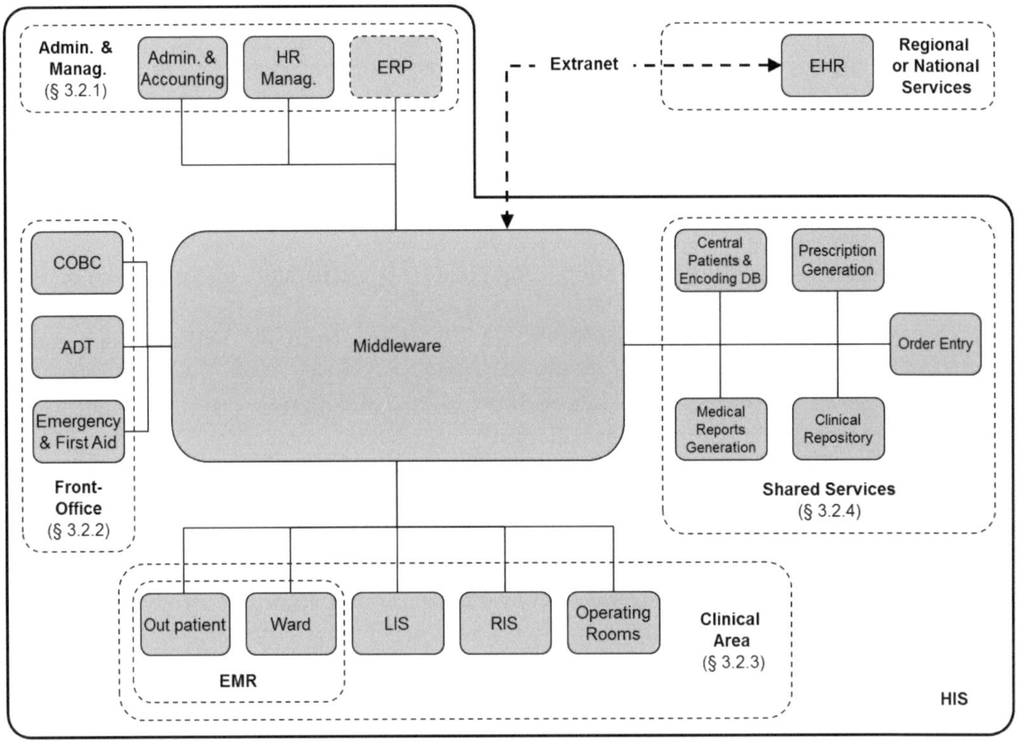

Fig. 1. Conceptual Architecture of a HIS

3.2.1 Administration and management area

The administration and management area supports processes like general administration and procurement, planning and management control, and resource (especially human resources) management (Locatelli, 2010). As administration processes are highly similar across almost all industries, the related systems are technically analogous to the ones used in other industries (Rodrigues, 2010; Tan, 2008; Greenhalgh et al., 2005; Raghupathi, 2003)—even if in health care they have to be slightly modified to better fit the peculiarities of the industry (e.g. its accounting rules).

The components related to this area have the responsibility to support the company in managing the activities of an administrative/accounting nature.

In particular, we typically identify two main components (IHCO, 2009d):

- *Administration and accounting suite*: for the management of accounting and business budget, procurement, storage of assets (general ledger, accounts payable, receivables, payments and bills for treasury management, tax professionals, management of requests for supplier bids, contract management, logistics management department, cost accounting, etc.).
- *Management of human resources*: for legal aspects, economic and security staff (allocation of personnel, analysis and reporting, etc.).

Each one of these components can have its own system that has been historically developed by each department following its own business requirements. Alternatively, the health care organization can implement the so-called *Enterprise Resource Planning* (ERP) suites similar to the ones being used in other industries since the 90s (Umble et al., 2003; Stegwee and Spil, 2001).

Application fragmentation in the administration and management area—added to a similar non-homogeneous configuration of clinical support systems—has led to problems like (i) misalignments and incompleteness of data sources, (ii) data inconsistency, (iii) difficulties in manipulation and aggregation of data, (iv) inconsistency among the results coming from different departments (IHCO, 2011).

For this reason, ERP projects are increasingly becoming frequent in health care—especially starting from the naturally more performance-oriented private providers. In fact, modern ERP platforms have a central data warehouse able to merge information flows from all hospital information sources, and, thus, enable advanced functions—e.g. decision support systems and balanced scorecard tools—that provide managers with up-to-date information on current activities, profit and loss accounts, and general performance indicators of the organization (IHCO, 2009a).

3.2.2 Front-office area

The front office area deals with patient reception, and typically distinguishes between inpatients, outpatients and patients in the emergency unit. These sub-areas are usually supported by enterprise-wide solutions that manage the workflows related to the waiting lists or the appointment management. Common solutions are the *Centralized Outpatient Booking Centre* (COBC) and the procedures related to *Acceptance-Discharge-Transfer* (ADT) (IHCO, 2010). Systems supporting the emergency and first aid wards typically also deal with clinical information (IHCO, 2011).

COBC supports the processes to manage outpatients:

1. The internal agendas for outpatient diagnostic service booking (RIS, LIS, AP), with potential connections to regional booking centres;
2. The communication of work lists to clinical services,
3. The collection and the verification of informed consents;
4. The billing for services and accounting.

The proper functioning of the COBC system is made possible by a front- and back-office service, responsible for programming functions and access management, as outlined below. Back-office cares for the maintenance and planning/preparation for the reservation of extraordinary activities. These activities are grouped into the main functions of management and planning the agenda reservation, supporting the booking and delivery point, and monitoring the management of waiting lists. The COBC is composed of several channels that allow access to the booking process, and handle different types of interaction.

ADT systems manage the processes related to hospitalized inpatients. In accordance with the hospital's organization (Lo Scalzo et al., 2009), ADT systems can provide the services in (i) centralized mode, (ii) distributed in the wards, or even (iii) in mixed mode (e.g. acceptance can be centralized while transfers and dismissals can be handled by wards).

Specifically, ADT systems support the following activities:

- The management of waiting lists, through integration with the cross-booking management service;
- The management of pre-admission;
- The registration of patient informed consent;
- The management of post-admission;
- The admission, the discharge and the transfers of patients within the hospital.

Emergency and first aid systems are made up by the process for both the organizational aspects of emergency events as well as the direct impact on citizens who request services considered essential for their health.

In this context, not only the impact of operational functions (use of informatics tool in an emergency context) but also the organization of the process (priority based on seriousness of the case) is highly important. These systems must also be able to support the doctor in requesting diagnostic support (e.g. analysis, consulting) as well as in making decisions as quickly and safely as possible (Corso et al., 2010; Locatelli et al., 2010).

The most important features are the following:

- The management of all the organizational aspects in the emergency and/or first aid department;
- The management of triage;
- The management of the EMR and the patient summary specialist folder (for the functions or the activities of both the physicians and the nurses);
- The management of the requests of consultations and examinations;
- The management of clinical and legal documents for both the patient as well as the authorities;
- The management of drug prescriptions;
- The transfer of data to the ADT system, in the case of a transfer to inpatient wards;
- The management of all the first aid discharge activities, including reporting.

3.2.3 Clinical area

The third key block of an HIS is the clinical area, which is the most complex and most delicate area due to its broad support to all the core processes of a hospital. It is also the most challenging area in terms of management, due on the one side to the involvement of critical patient data, and on the other side, to pre-existing systems implemented independently by each department or ward in different periods—usually without a consistent strategic direction by the *Chief Information Officers* (CIOs) (IHCO, 2011).

Clinical systems are mainly (i) departmental systems or (ii) *Electronic Medical Records* (EMRs). The former support both clinical and administrative tasks in diagnostic services (e.g. anatomical pathology), and are fed by the requests coming from wards or outpatient offices. The latter should be responsible for the digitally-integrated management of clinical information flows to support care, and—acting as a unique bedside working tool—for the role as the unique point of reference for clinical decisions (Locatelli et al., 2010).

Departmental systems receive requests from COBC or from the order management systems in the wards, they support the execution phases of tests, notify the application regarding the execution of the examination, and produce reports that are stored in the clinical repository.

The most common departmental systems are (IHCO, 2009d; Locatelli, 2010):

- The *Radiology Information Systems* (RIS), which manage the acquisition of radiological images, their analysis and the relative reporting. These systems are often linked to Picture Archiving and Communication Systems (PACSs), which acquire, store and distribute images and videos.
- The *Laboratory Information Systems* (LIS), which automatically manage the exam requests from the clinical units and the auto-analyser connected to the LIS, supporting sophisticated controls with validation of the results.
- The *applications for the operating room*, which are dedicated to the management of the interventions, to the logging of both the events and the data relevant to surgery and to the production of clinical surgery documentation.

The *Electronic Medical Record* (EMR) is the central element of the HIS. The fundamental function of an EMR is to collect information on the clinical history of patients during hospitalization—acting as a tool to support the multidisciplinary communication between professionals, operations management and decisions.

Literature (e.g. Handler & Hieb, 2007; IHCO, 2009d; Locatelli et al., 2010) allows the identification of five functional areas that characterize EMRs:

- The *ADT Area*: often integrated with the ADT system, this area manages patient admissions, discharges and transfers within the hospital, as well as vital statistics and administrative documentation (e.g. informed consent);
- The *Diagnostic Area*: the features in this area allow the requests of exams and the delivery of reports to/from wards;
- The *Clinical Dossier*: this area embraces the management of all medical and nursing sheets, including initial assessment, automated vital signs monitoring, anaesthesiology documents, OR reports, etc.;
- *Therapy management*: this area includes support to prescription and administration of drugs, transfusions, nutrition, etc.;
- *Out-patient management*: this area manages admission and medical reporting for out-patients, and feeds the patient's EMR with information like preliminary reports or follow-up examinations.

As depicted in Fig. 2, the most diffused functions of an EMR are inpatient ADT (80%), diagnostic procedure management (with electronic clinical exam requirements and reports available in 80% of cases) and outpatient management (67%). Even if clinical dossier and therapy management are the less diffused areas, at the same time, they are also the ones with the greatest expected growth for the future. Hindrances are mainly related to the difficulties in change management, in the migration of therapy procedures from paper to digital forms, in the needs of smart bedside support, and in legal constraints to digital data management.

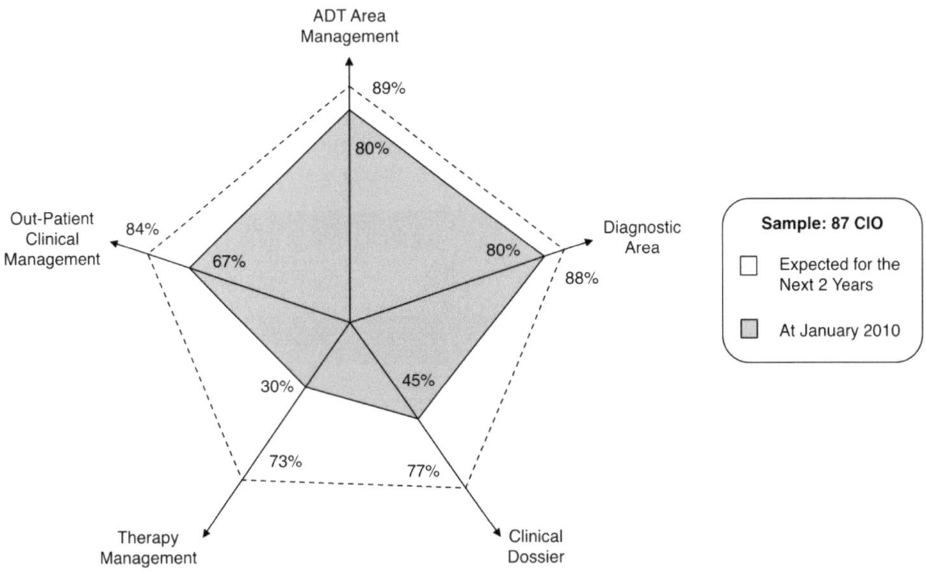

Fig. 2. *The Expected Diffusion* of Functional EMR Areas (ICHO, 2010)

Unfortunately these last areas not only have a key impact on clinical activities, but also are the ones that need higher levels of integration in order to allow the EMR to become a truly useful clinical tool. Case studies performed by the IHCO have confirmed that the lack of integration with the rest of the HIS and the absence of an enterprise-wide approach are the main limitations of current EMR projects. However, many efforts are made not only to standardize the EMR architecture, but also to drive its evolution towards a mature tool able to comprehensively support all the health care processes (IHCO, 2009d).

Another important opportunity coming from digitalization of clinical processes regards the opportunity to feed researchers with first-hand, complete and highly reliable datasets on clinical cases collected in the EMR during daily care and then filtered for clinical research purposes. The case of the Istituto Besta (see Box 2) briefly highlights how this can happen.

Fondazione IRCCS Istituto Neurologico "Carlo Besta" is a centre of excellence for care and scientific research on neurological diseases. Recently, a collaboration was started with the hospital A.O. Ospedale Niguarda "Ca'Granda" and Fondazione Politecnico di Milano, with the aim of transforming Niguarda's web EMR into a "clinical-scientific" portal to not only support patients' management during their entire care process, but also to feed scientific research with key information gathered during each clinical event.

Due to its open architecture, the portal was conceived as a unique access point to the HIS, based on a centralized patient reference registry. The first scientific features were provided in October 2008 supporting complete outpatient workflow and encoding pathological diagnoses according to international standards. Since 2009, most features of an EMR were also implemented to support inpatient management. This means that admission, anamnesis, diagnosis, clinical diaries, speciality neurology sheets have been standardized, reengineered and digitalized. Clinicians use RFId badges to access the clinical dossier on WiFi laptops fixed on mobile trays than can roll to bedside.

The most innovative feature of this system is however that the clinical portal's EMR is conceived to structure digital information both to support ward activities as well as to feed scientific research. Starting from the general EMR, specific design was done in order to satisfy the requirements of physicians and researchers working in the area of myasthenia gravis and peripheral neuropathy. A procedure was identified to enrich and structure usual clinical datasets, so that high quality data could be gathered by physicians during the clinical event and then it could also be used by the research area. Once the diffusion of the EMR reaches high coverage in wards, stored data are also made available to a clinical decision support system, through which users will directly access clinical and scientific indicators, improve the correctness of diagnosis and identify specific pathological patterns.

This approach at Istituto Besta is also applied to the Epilepsy Pathology Network of the Lombardy Region (EpiNetwork), introducing automatic feeds as a part of its clinical-scientific-epidemiological EMR. Here, the compliance of all organizations' HISs to syntactic and semantic standards is essential to feed the EpiNetwork, thereby increasing the amount and quality of available data.

Box 2. The EMR in Fondazione IRCCS Istituto Neurologico "Carlo Besta" (Milan, Italy)

Besides supporting clinical operations, over time the clinical information systems have assumed a growing role in risk management, e.g. as concerns the automated execution of critical tasks (e.g. laboratory examinations, drug dilution robotization), ensuring timely data gathering to clinical decision makers, automating patient monitoring and alerting upon inconsistencies, and so on (Chauldry, 2006).

Crosswise all systems and all applications, *Mobile & Wireless* (M&W) technologies emerge as a key element to close the bedside safety loop—filling the gap left by the traditional HIS. In fact, M&W technologies can on one hand deliver functionalities like decision-making support directly to the bedside, and on the other, they can strengthen the safe implementation of *Automatic Identification and Data Capture* systems (Bates, 2000). From this viewpoint, Box 3 describes an important example, as regards risk management as well.

The Fondazione IRCCS Istituto Nazionale dei Tumori in Milan (henceforth Istituto Tumori) is recognized as a top Scientific Research and Treatment Institution in Oncology.

Throughout the last decade the Istituto Tumori has implemented a state-of-the-art HIS based on a solid technical infrastructure and international standards (most of all HL7), effectively integrating information systems amongst each other. Regarding the five main functional EMR areas, in the Istituto Tumori ADT, Out-patient management and Diagnostics are the most historically consolidated.

As regards therapy management and bedside operations, the Istituto has recognized that lack of ICT support for bedside operations may be dangerous for patient safety. Therefore the Istituto is pervasively implementing M&W and Radio Frequency Identification (RFId) technologies in order to avoid errors and enhance patient safety and care quality of care at bedside.

An RFId enterprise platform, made of a set of process-tailored mobile applications and RFId devices integrated to the HIS applications, now enables traceability and process control (e.g. patient-to-treatment cross matches and workflow checks) as regards transfusions, radiotherapy treatments, radiology, surgical operation check and tissue samples. Traceability data are collected on mobile devices and gathered to the appropriate subsystem of the HIS, allowing specialists in departments (e.g. the Transfusion Service) to monitor ward activities.

An interesting project regards chemotherapy process reorganization, where the Istituto is leading the project "Towards a complete competence framework and an integrated solution for patient safety in chemotherapy" funded by the Italian Ministry of Health. Results and knowledge (in terms of risk analysis, process diagnosis evidences, workflow recommendations, and an ICT pilot system, ...) are now being applied with the design of an enterprise-wide therapy management system and a centralized lab to issue chemotherapy treatments for all wards. Here, RFId will be used to track all critical steps of preparation and administration at bedside, securing patient and drug identification and process monitoring.

Box 3. Therapy Management and Wireless Traceability at Fondazione IRCCS Istituto Nazionale dei Tumori (Milan, Italy)

In fact, to assess the potential impact and the convenience of digitalization in terms of risk management, many new methodologies have supported traditional *Business Process Reengineering* (BPR) theories (e.g. Davenport, 1993) and process-related risk management theories. The peculiarity of these approaches is that ICT is seen not only as a means to reduce process risk, but also as a potential source of new weaknesses in processes. The *Healthcare Failure Mode, Criticality and Effect Analysis* (HFMEA) is a recognized technique that has increasingly been adopted in practice (DeRosier, 2002).

3.2.4 Shared services of a hospital information system

Supporting the main aforementioned areas, there are other components that complement the HIS architecture. The best practices show that the architectural model of an HIS should be based on a common infrastructure, made of central services and a comprehensive integration middleware. More in detail, the shared services are (Locatelli, 2010):

- *Central Patients and Encoding Database:* this service has the responsibility to centrally manage patient identifiers (Master Patient Index, MPI) to make them available to other components of the HIS, and to manage clinical encodings shared among applications (e.g. encodings nomenclature or pharmaceutical handbook);
- *Prescriptions Generation:* this service allows the preparation, digital signature and issue of all prescriptions to be used outside the hospital;
- *Order Entry:* this service manages ward requests for internal exams and second opinion consultations;

- *Medical Reports Generation:* this module supports the issue of legally compliant medical reports for all hospital services;
- *Clinical Repository:* this is a central archive of (i) all kinds of digitally-signed medical reports, (ii) structured data, (iii) patient events (e.g. transfusions, surgery) and (iv) many others, from exam requests to therapy prescriptions. The clinical repository is a core component because it is the central collector of patient data, that all other systems can consult to retrieve official documents and data on past episodes. This component is also responsible for feeding the regional health record, via a dedicated network link (extranet)

Crosswise, the central middleware is responsible for linking all HIS components using standards, such as *Health Level Seven* (HL7). The importance of an infrastructural backbone can be fully understood with the example of St. Olav's Digital Hospital, described in Box 3. This is only one case amongst many (e.g. the Orbis Medisch Group hospitals, in Denmark, and the Julius-Maximilians University Hospital of Würzburg, in Germany) in which a pervasive infrastructure enables the implementation of an integrated technological platform aimed at digitalizing both management activities and clinical processes. A strong technological partner has proved essential in all cases.

4. Governance of health care information systems

HCISs are developed, maintained and innovated by a *complex ecology* of multiple agents that share knowledge (as well as other resources) in often previously unknown interaction paths (Simon, 1996; Anderson, 1999; IHCO, 2011). If, as a result of this complex process, HCISs emerge almost unpredictably over considerable time periods—as various agents in the ecology interact with and react to the actions of others—their governance is naturally characterized by a *shared and multilevel nature* (IHCO, 2010; 2011).

The challenge, in this case, concerns how to foster the necessary collaboration among many diverse organisations over long and uncertain time periods, while, at the same time, continuing to develop internal solutions able to respond to the specific necessities of the health care organisations' different lines of business (IHCO, 2010).

St. Olav 's of Trondheim (www.stolav.no) is the largest hospital in Norway, with 950 beds and 8,000 employees. The willingness to restructure the campus has given the opportunity for a pilot project whose goal is the realization of a completely digital hospital.

Three intervention pillars existed: (i) the review of information flows and clinical documentation for their complete dematerialization, (ii) the multichannel and continuous access to systems and information clinics, and (iii) the advanced infrastructure enabler.

The third pillar is the real basis of a digital hospital design, and it is made of a communication and integration infrastructure mainly based on IP and XML protocols. The main innovative element is on one side the infrastructure's pervasiveness, and on the other side the integration of the HIS—including clinical systems, remote control systems, telecommunications equipment support, building automation systems, asset management applications, automatic guided vehicles transports, and environment sensors.

The experience of St. Olav's is a case of excellence in terms of a state-of-the art infrastructure enabling a truly paperless organization. In fact, the communication infrastructure and the integration platform can support various application modules: the electronic medical record, the departmental systems, biomedical equipment, bedside entertainment, and so on.

As an example, pocket PCs are used to both replace cell phones, pagers, and terminals for patient entertainment as well as use EMR in mobility, also fed with vital sign data as well as by reports of departmental applications.

Box 4. St. Olav 's Digital Hospital (Trondheim, Norway)

As a matter of fact, the problem is that most of the theoretical and empirical research on information systems management is mainly focusing on firms and their performance (Hunter, 2009)—paying little attention to both the interaction among the different actors inside a specific sector as well as the development of shared solutions like the ones currently needed by the health care industry (Corso & Gastaldi, 2010b).

A comprehensive governance model must, thus, not only focus on what should be done inside each organization of the health care industry to make ICT-based solutions efficient and effective, but also (and especially) consider the decisions that each one of these organizations has to make during the interaction with the other actors in the sector. To simplify the discourse and make it a bit more effective, it is possible to talk about *the internal and external governance* of HCISs (IHCO, 2009e).

4.1 Internal governance

By the term *internal governance of HCISs* we mean the system of policies, processes, decisions and rules that set the way through which HCISs are run, managed and developed inside an health care organization (Corso and Gastaldi, 2009).

Empirical evidence (IHCO, 2008; 2009e; 2010; 2011) as well as literature (Corso et al., 2010; Venkatesh et al., 2011) emphasize that the low levels of formalization of the governance models of the HISs are greatly affecting the development of the HISs themselves. Low financial support—often pointed out as the main problem by health care CIOs —is mainly a reflection of the low commitment by the majority of the strategic board, which often neither has a clear idea about how ICT can have an impact that goes beyond mere efficiency, nor fosters the pursuit of a clear ICT strategy (Callen et al., 2007). The real reasons for a lack of effectiveness in the implementation of the HISs are multiple, and range from the lack of a technological perspective on the part of Chief Executive Officers (CEOs), Chief Financial Officers (CFOs) and Chief Medical Officers (CMOs), and the inability of CIOs to clearly propose all the advantages tied to ICT solutions, to the need to reach concrete organizational results for achieving higher investments in HISs.

As regards the ICT department, very few learning processes are launched to enhance the technical skills of employees, above all in the public sector. Leadership programs are practically inexistent. The turnover rate is very low, and many difficulties are found in attracting professionals from other sectors. CIOs tend to ascribe all these criticalities to exogenous causes, rather than internal inadequacy, and to blame operational workload instead of their own inability to face it. The CIO himself often has a narrow strategic view that hinders an open approach to innovation. This is due to: (i) a low level of managerial capabilities, (ii) a difficult alignment with corporate strategies, and (iii) an overuse of technical language in strategic board interactions.

ICT supplier involvement is almost always operational or consultancy-oriented, and in the few cases in which the relation is continuative, CIOs fail to sufficiently delegate—working along-side the ICT supplier, even in highly outsourced operations.

To solve this set of problems, CIOs need first to work on their capabilities, as already done in other sectors (Broadbent and Kitzis, 2005). The research conducted by IHCO (2008; 2009e, 2010) shows an operative role for 65% of health care CIOs. With these values it is impossible to manage the effective development of HISs, and, thus, their innovation. It is true that organizations could first work on the ICT department team, but getting out of the operative vicious circle without a true C-Level director is often a challenge (Smaltz et al., 2006).

Obviously, this simply is not enough: having CIOs with more capabilities does not necessarily simplify the development or the management of HISs. Real innovation will not be attained until the ICT department develops a deep knowledge of clinical processes, relational and change management capabilities, and the ability to exploit external knowledge, while working alongside medical offices (IHCO, 2008). Thus, internal governance models have to direct their attention to core health care businesses, redesigning the ICT unit's skills on three main pillars:

- *Demand management*: reconciling the needs expressed by clinical units (and often anticipating them) with the overall ICT strategy of the organization.
- *Project management*: applying process reengineering and change management methodologies to govern projects, face unexpected events, assure success.
- *Supply management*: implementing rigorous procedures for vendor selection and establishing long-term relationships with key vendors able to support innovation.

A possible solution that combines these aspects is the change from a vertical to a horizontal governance model of HISs. The former is completely focused on a hierarchical relationship with the strategic board—forced as ineffective, because of the CIO having historically an operative profile. The latter directs its attentions to the core of care, establishes the ICT department as the main interface between the supply and the demand of the health care organization, and more easily achieves the systemic innovations, the effectiveness, the confidence and the leadership necessary to play a strategic role in health care organizations.

In the most advanced situations studied by the IHCO (2008; 2009e; 2010), CIOs confirmed that good horizontal governance implied increased objectives-sharing and thus, not only more integration between departments, but also a more innovative HCIS.

Reasonably, the change in ICT governance style will expose the CIO and the ICT department to greater interaction with internal (as well as external) organizational actors. In order to not lose focus in these difficult tasks—which imply adapting to very different business needs—a project priority framework is needed (Corso and Gastaldi, 2009).

4.2 External governance

By *external governance of HCISs,* we mean the set of decisions that allow the development of the information system adopted in a health care organization to be coordinated with the other information systems used in the health care sector (IHCO, 2009e).

As opposed to other sectors, within health care, most of the value that an organization brings to its customers is highly dependent on the information localized in other organizations—e.g. those health care organizations in which the patients previously received treatments. From this viewpoint, the cooperation among the different organizations in the health care industry is core and, thus, there is an high emphasis in the development of external governance models able to align the different interests in the sector.

Working on Dougherty and Dunne (2011), and considering the empirical evidences collected by the IHCO (2011), is it possible to state that all the models that allow the achievement of good external governance of HCISs are characterized by three dynamics:

- The development of sufficient connections among health care agents;
- The development of sufficient deviation-amplifying activities that stretch the overall health care industry toward integrated solutions with a positive social impact;
- The development of coordinating mechanisms that recombine, reuse, and recreate existing solutions, slow down amplifications and keep the system under control.

The first dynamic regards the development of sufficient connections among health care agents (Anderson, 1999). The presence of these connections is the most basic condition necessary to allows the emergence as well as the progressive comparison of new patterns and new solutions in the governance of HCISs (IHCO, 2010; 2011).

The process through which these connection are constructed is initiated by a variety of fluctuations that occur outside the norm, so the various agents need to interact and react to feedback about the action of others (Lichtenstein & Plowman, 2009). More specifically, the research of the IHCO (2011) points out that each actor has to strive towards specific behaviours in order to create solid connections with the rest of the health care industry:

- *Involvement and listening of lower level actors*: e.g. a regional council has to continuously develop channels that allow it to be in contact with its hospitals;
- *Proactivity and availability toward higher level actors*: e.g. a physician has to be able to overcome his natural tendency toward localism, offering himself as an open interlocutor in the dialogues with his referring hospital;
- *Comparison and collaboration with the actors of the same level*: e.g. all the hospitals that share the same geographical area should maintain a continuous dialogue that would allow them to coordinate their tasks and learn from other experiences.

The second dynamic is composed of deviation-amplifying activities, such as positive feedback, that move the overall health care system toward a new kind of order (Dougherty & Dunne, 2011) that—being characterized by higher levels of integration among the different health information systems—is comprehensively better in terms of social impact (IHCO, 2011).

Floricel and Dougherty (2007) suggest that reciprocal value can be created and can persist if each actor enables the heterogeneity of the possible outputs to be explored and experimented through time. More specifically, the analysis performed with the Italian health care practitioners by the researchers of the IHCO (2011) points out that each stakeholder has to work locally in order to set and solve problems of orchestrating knowledge and capabilities across the health care ecology—fostering each potential form of strategizing across the whole health care industry in order to create shared IS applications.

The third dynamic enables new order to come into being and comprises coordinating mechanisms that recombine and recreate existing solutions, that slow down amplifications, and keep the new system persistent and under control (Lichtenstein & Plowman, 2009).

This dynamic relies mostly on the development of public policies and standardization choices that embrace the potential ambiguities that arise in the progressive development of shared HCISs. Even if currently research (Mahoney et al., 2009) tends to emphasize regulations as factors that constrain firms, rather than shaping collective action, public policies and standardization provide an overall direction to bundle knowledge and mitigate risks as well as provide the long-term continuity necessary to allow the new possibilities to emerge.

5. Future trends in health care information systems

According to the latest literature on HCISs (e.g. Fichman et al., 2011) as well as to the evidences collected by the IHCO (2010; 2011), there are three areas where major ICT-based advances are opening promising scenarios to further developments:

- Evidence Based Medicine;
- Health care analytics;
- Social Media in Health care.

Evidence-Based Medicine (EBM) is the conscientious, explicit, and judicious use of current best evidence in making decisions about the care of individual patients (Sackett et al., 1996). Recently, EBM has gained increasing attention as a tool to address the concerns about health care cost and quality—allowing earlier and more precise diagnoses, producing cheaper and more effective treatments, and minimizing the side effects associated to each treatment (Glaser et al., 2008; Christensen et al., 2009).

If the barriers to the widespread use of EBM are substantial, HCISs can play an important counteracting role. Generalising Fichman et al. (2011), there are four potential ways through which the research on HCISs can foster the adoption of EBM inside the health care industry:

- *Depth of knowledge about the efficacy of many common treatments*: the rise of digital storage of personal medical information gives researchers opportunities to discover precise knowledge about the links between treatments and outcomes;
- *Producing and sharing actionable knowledge*: health information systems researchers can study the antecedents and the consequences of sharing actionable knowledge through digital media in order to better influence practice;
- *Overcoming practitioner resistance*: health information systems can be used to promote education of all the health care stakeholders on the efficacy of diagnostic and treatment options so that they can hold caregivers more accountable;
- *Focusing on the implications that EBM brings in the field of HCISs:* both in terms of privacy as well as security.

Health care analytics is a rapidly evolving field of HCISs that makes extensive use of data, computer technologies, statistical and qualitative analyses, and explanatory and predictive modelling to solve problems that generally affect the entire health care sector.

The difference between analytics and EBM lies in the scale of the problems tackled by the two different solutions. If both of them focus on extracting knowledge from the amounts of digital data available in the health care industry, EBM maintains a focus on the individual while analytics impacts on a larger scale—analysing retrospective population datasets across multiple clinical conditions with models involving extensive computation. Common applications of analytics include the statistical analysis performed to understand historical patterns and, thus, predict and improve future treatments (Davenport, 2006).

According to the analyses conducted by the IHCO, there are three main behaviours that health care organizations have to adopt in order to increase the exploitation as well as the effectiveness of analytics in their industry:

- *Designing for consumability*: it will be progressively necessary to take into account the specific context, user, device and intended purpose of each quantitative analysis;
- *Exploiting natural variations in task performance as an "experimental test bed"*: as long as contextual variables are captured, variations in task performance across the enterprise will be progressively used as experiments to draw causal conclusions;
- *Building capacity and instrumentation to capture and use "external" data*: through the integration and the analysis of the data coming from (i) RFID tags on patients and providers, (ii) patient personal health record data, (iii) patient mobile device sensor data, (iv) data from other organizations, (v) social media data, etc.

Social media communities have been particularly active in the health care domain (Kane et al., 2009)—though with highly different rates across the different countries (IHCO, 2009c). The primary driver of value, in these communities, is a commons-based peer production of knowledge (Benkler, 2002) in which individuals, in a spontaneous way, collaborate on a large scale to produce work products without hierarchical control (firms) or market exchanges (price, contracts) to guide them (a famous example is *www.patientslikeme.com*).

Generalizing Fichman et al. (2011), it is possible to propose a set of the main interesting questions at the intersection between the new social media and the traditional information systems currently present in the health care sector:

- What conditions lead to the formation of health-oriented social media communities, and what is their impact on traditional health information systems?
- Which kinds of information are these communities going to share with the traditional health information systems?
- What are the most effective design rules for the platforms supporting these communities? How can they be seamlessly integrated with the traditional health information systems?
- What posture should large providers of ICT-based solutions be taking with regard to these natural developing platforms?

The conclusive case study presented in this chapter, in Box 4, is paradigmatic of the new horizons ICTs can nowadays open to health care organizations and public decision-makers.

Of course, a mixture of managerial skills, technological knowledge, commitment to innovate, and adequate resources is needed. However, the cases like the one of the University of Pittsburgh Medical Centre suggest that the continuous innovation of HISs and HCIS provides great results both in terms of efficiency and effectiveness in delivering care.

The University of Pittsburgh Medical Centre (UPMC) is a 9 billion USD health care organization affiliated with the University of Pittsburgh Schools of the Health Sciences. UPMC counts more than 54,000 employees, over 20 hospitals, and 400 doctors' offices.

UPMC is a top tier case as regards the integration of ICTs in health care processes. Since 2006 the company has invested 1,45 billion USD to: (i) review its infrastructural backbone, (ii) digitalize diagnostic services, (iii) implement a complete EMR, (iv) ensure widespread use of use of M&W devices (laptops, pagers, smartphones, etc.), and (vi) create a unified communications workspace for staff.

UPMC's current strategy for ICT is focused on three areas: (i) new telemedicine services, (ii) analytics development, and (iii) smart human-computer interfaces.

The first area regards the development of a set of telemedicine services. In this case technology allows the widespread application of new service models like telepathology, teleradiology, remote second opinion, remote monitoring for chronic patients. An interesting example, in this case, is the experimental pediatrics TeleICU project that the health care organizations is developing in partnership with the Mediterranean Institute for Transplantation and High Specialization Therapies (ISMETT). The project provides ISMETT surgeons with the virtual and real time support of Pittsburgh physicians.

The second frontier is analytics, seen as a tool for supporting both managerial governance (mainly in terms of financial control, outcome assessments, and process monitoring) and EBM. In the first case the HIS of UPMC generates key performance indicators that are provided to managers at different levels. In the second case interesting results have been achieved in profiling patients and in supporting clinicians with context-aware tools that display proper protocols, generate reference cases related to patient's condition, predict a treatment's expected outcome, and analyse in real time the history of similar cases stored in a centralized database.

The third area in which UPMC is working, in order to develop its HIS, is an innovative concept of a human-computer interface able to simplify and encourage the use of the HIS by the physicians. For example UPMC has created a new access to the Clinical Repository, where the whole patient history is graphically summarized, and key data from each clinical episode are characterized by graphical landmarks. This interface works as a launch point for all clinical applications, and allows semantic searches from multiple data sources.

Box 5. University of Pittsburgh Medical Centre (USA)

6. References

Anderson, J.G. (2009). Improving Patient Safety with Information Technology, In: *Handbook of Research on Advances in Health Informatics and Electronic Healthcare Application*, Khoumbati, K.; Dwivedi, Y.; Srivastava, A. & Lal, B. (Eds.), pp. 1-16, Medical Information Science Reference, ISBN 978-1-60566-030-1, Hershey (PA)

Anderson, P. (1999). Complexity Theory and Organizational Science. *Organizational Science*, Vol. 10, No. 3, pp. 216-232, ISSN 1047-7039

Arabnia, H.R.; Open Source Clinical Portals: a Model for Healthcare Information Systems to Support Care Processes and Feed Clinical Research. An Italian Case Study of Design, Development, Reuse, Exploitation. In: *Software Tools and Algorithms for Biological Systems*. Book series *Advances in Experimental Medicine and Biology - AEMB2*. Springer, New York, 2011

Aron, R.; Dutta, S.; Janakiraman, R. & Pathak, P.A. (2011). The Impact of Automation of Systems on Medical Errors: Evidence from Field Research. *Information Systems Research*, Vol. 22, No. 3, pp. 429-446, ISSN 1047-7047

Bates, D.W. (2000). Using information technology to reduce rates of medication errors in hospitals. *British Medical Journal (British Medical Association)*, 2000;320:788-791

Bates, D. W. (2005). Computerized Physician Order Entry and Medication Errors: Finding a Balance. *Journal of Biomedical Informatics*, Vol. 38, No. 4, pp. 259–261, ISSN 1532-0480

Broadbent, M.; Kitzis, E.S. (2005). *The new CIO Leader: Setting the Agenda and Delivering Results*, Harvard Business School Press, ISBN 978-1-59139-577-5, Boston (MA)

Brown, G.D. (2005). Introduction: The Role of Information Technology in Transforming Health Systems, In: *Strategic Management of Information Systems in Healthcare*, Brown, F.D.; Stone, T.T. & Patrick T.B. (Eds.), Health Administration Press, ISBN 978-1-56793-242-3, Chicago (IL)

Burke, D.E.; Wang, B.B.L.; Wan T.T.H. & Diana, M.L. (2002). Exploring Hospitals' Adoption of IT. *Journal of Medical Systems*, Vol. 26, No. 4, pp. 349–355, ISSN 0148-5598

Bracchi, G.; Francalanci, C. & Motta, G. (2009). *Organizational Information Systems*, McGraw-Hill, ISBN 9-788-83866-328-4, Milan (IT) (in Italian)

Caccia C. (2008). *Management of Health Care Information Systems*, McGraw-Hill, ISBN 9-788-83862-532-9, Milan (IT) (in Italian)

Callen, J.L.; Braithwaite, J. & Westbrook, J.I. (2007). Cultures in Hospitals and Their Influence on Attitudes to, and Satisfaction with, the Use of Clinical Information Systems. Social Science and Medicine, Vol. 65, No. 4, pp. 635-639, ISSN 0277-9536

Chauldry, B.; Wang, J.; Wu S.; et al.(2006). Systematic Review: Impact of Health Information Technology on Quality, Efficiency, and Costs of Medical Care. *Annals of Internal Medicine (American College of Physicians)*, Vol. 144, No. 10, pp. 742–752

Christensen, C.M.; Grossman, J.H. & Hwang, J. (2009). *The Innovator's Prescription: A Disruptive Solution for Health Care*, McGraw–Hill, ISBN 978-0-07-159209-3, New York

Corso, M. & Gastaldi, L. (2009). Managing ICT-Driven Innovation in the Health Care Industry: Evidence from an Empirical Study in Italy, *Proceedings of the 10th CINet Conference*, pp. 1-14, Brisbane, Australia, September 6-8, 2009

Corso, M. & Gastaldi, L. (2010a). A Multiple and Collaborative Research Methodology to Study CI Driven by ICT in the Italian Health Care Industry, *Proceedings of the 11th CINet Conference*, pp. 290-308, Zürich, Switzerland, September 5–7, 2010

Corso, M. & Gastaldi, L. (2010b). Managing ICT-Driven Innovation to Overcome the Exploitation-Exploration Trade-Off: A Multiple and Collaborative Research Methodology in the Italian Health Care Industry, *Proceedings of the 11th CINet Conference*, pp. 274-289, Zürich, Switzerland, September 5–7, 2010

Corso, M. & Gastaldi, L. (2011). Toward a Relevant, Reflective and Rigorous Methodology Able to Study CI at Affordable Resource-Consumption Levels, *Proceedings of the 12th CINet Conference*, pp. 230-254, Århus, Denmark, September 11–13, 2011

Corso, M.; Gastaldi, L. & Locatelli, P. (2010). Enhancing the Diffusion of Electronic Medical Record and Electronic Health Record: Evidence from an Empirical Study in Italy, *Proceedings of the 16th Congress of International Federation of Health Records Organizations "Better Information for Better Health"*, Milan, Italy, November 15–19, 2010

Davenport, T.H. (1993). *Process Innovation. Reengineering Work through Information Technology.* Harvard Business School Press, 1993

Davenport, T.H. (2006). Competing on Analytics. *Harvard Business Review*, Vol. 84, No. 1, pp. 1–12, ISSN 0017-8012

DeRosier, J.; Stalhandske, E.; Bagian, J.; Nudell, T. (2002). Using Health care Failure Mode and Effect Analysis (HFMEA). *Journal on Quality Improvement*, May 2002

Dolin, R.H.; Alschuler, L.; Boyer, S.; Beebe, C.; Behlen, F.M.; Biron, P.V. & Shabo, A. (2001). The HL7 Clinical Document Architecture, Release 2. *The Journal of American Medical Informatics Associations*, Vol. 13 No. 1, pp. 30-39, ISSN 1067-5027

Dougherty, D. & Dunne, D.D. (2011). Organizing Ecologies of Complex Innovation. Organization Science, Articles in Advance (published online ahead of print February 8, 2011), pp. 1-10, Doi 10.1287/orsc.1100.0605, ISSN 1047-7039

Finchman, R.G.; Kohli, R. & Krishnan, R. (2011) Editorial Overview—The role of IS in Healthcare. *Information Systems Research*, Vol. 22, No. 3, pp. 419-428, ISSN 1047-7047

Floricel, S & Dougherty D. (2007). Where Do Games of Innovation Come From? Explaining the Persistence of Dynamic Innovation Patterns. *International Journal of Innovation Management*, Vol. 11, No. 1, pp. 65-92, ISSN 1363-9196

Glaser, J; Henley, D.E.; Downing, G. & Brinner, K.M. (2008). Advancing Personalized Health Care Through Health Information Technology. *Journal of American Medical Association*, Vol. 15, No. 4, pp. 391-396, ISSN 0002-9955

Goh, J.M.; Gao, G. & Agarwal, R. (2011). Evolving Work Rountines: Adaptive Routinization of Information Technology in Healthcare. *Information Systems Research*, Vol. 22, No. 3, pp. 565-585, ISSN 1047-7047

Greenhalgh, T.; Robert, G.; Bate, P.; Macfarlane, F. & Kyriakidou, O. (2005). *Diffusion of Innovations in Health Service Organizations: A Systematic Literature Review*, Blackwell, ISBN 978-0-7279-1869-7, Oxford (UK)

Grimson, J. (2001). Delivering the Electronic Healthcare Record for the 21st Century. *International J. of Medical Informatics*, Vol. 64, No. 2–3, pp. 111–127, ISSN 1386-5056

Hamid A., Sarmad A. (2009). Towards an Evaluation Framework for E-Health Services, In: *Handbook of Research on Advances in Health Informatics and Electronic Healthcare Application*, Khoumbati, K.; Dwivedi, Y.; Srivastava, A. & Lal, B. (Eds.), pp. 1-16, Medical Information Science Reference, ISBN 978-1-60566-030-1, Hershey (PA)

Handler, T.J. & Hieb, B.R. (2009). CPR Generation Criteria Update: Clinical Documentation, In: *Gartner Research*, Available from www.gartner.com

Harno, K. (2010). Shared Healthcare in a Regional E-Health Network, In: *Health Information Systems: Concepts, Methodologies, Tools, and Applications*, Rodrigues J.J.P.C. (Ed.), pp. 554-568, Medical Information Science Reference, ISBN 978-1-60566-988-5, Hershey

Heeks, R. (2002). Information Systems and Developing Countries. *The Information Society*, Vol. 18, No. 1, pp. 101–112, ISSN 1087-6537

Hsiao, J.L. & Chang, I.C. (2005). An Empirical Study of Establishing Nursing Care Plan Systems. *Journal of Information Management*, Vol. 12, No. 2, pp. 27–43, ISSN 0268-4012

Hunter, M.G. (2009). *Strategic Information Systems: An Overview, In: Strategic Information Systems: Concepts, Methodologies, Tools and Applications*, Hunter, M.G. (Ed.), pp. xxxix-xiix, Information Science Reference, ISBN 978-1-60566-678-5, Hershey (PA)

IHCO (2009a). Clinical Governance Support Systems, *School of Management of Politecnico di Milano*, Available from www.osservatori.net (in Italian)

IHCO (2009b). Dematerialization in Health Care, *School of Management of Politecnico di Milano*, Available from www.osservatori.net (in Italian)

IHCO (2009c). Digital Services to Patients, *School of Management of Politecnico di Milano*, Available from www.osservatori.net (in Italian)

IHCO (2009d). Electronic Medical Record, *School of Management of Politecnico di Milano*, Available from www.osservatori.net (in Italian)

IHCO (2009e). ICT in Health Care: Innovation from Theory to Practice, *School of Management of Politecnico di Milano*, Available from www.osservatori.net (in Italian)

IHCO (2010). ICT in Health Care: Innovation is in the Network, *School of Management of Politecnico di Milano*, Available from www.osservatori.net (in Italian)

IHCO (2011). ICT in Health Care: Innovation in Search of an Author, *School of Management of Politecnico di Milano*, Available from www.osservatori.net (in Italian)

Kane, G.C.; Fichman, R.G.; Gallaugher, J. & Glaser, J. (2009). Community Relations 2.0. *Harvard Business Review*, Vol. 87, No. 3, pp. 45-50, ISSN 0017-8012

Kane, G.C. & Labianca, G. (2011). IS Avoidance in Health-Care Groups: A Multilevel Investigation. *Information Systems Research*, Vol. 22, No. 3, pp. 504-522, ISSN 1047-7047

Khoumbati, K.; Dwivedi, Y.; Srivastava, A. & Lal B. (2009). Foreword, In: *Handbook of Research on Advances in Health Informatics and Electronic Healthcare Application*, Khoumbati, K.; Dwivedi, Y.; Srivastava, A. & Lal, B. (Eds.), pp. xxvii, Medical Information Science Reference, ISBN 978-1-60566-030-1, Hershey (PA)

Kolodner, R.M.; Cohn, S.P. & Friedman, C.P. (2008). Health Information Technology: Strategic Initiatives, Real Progress. *Health Affairs*, Vol. 27, No. Special Issue, pp. w137-w139, ISSN 0278-2715

Liaw, S.S. (2002). Understanding User Perceptions of World-Wide Environments. *Journal of Computer Assisted Learning*, Vol. 18, No. 2, pp. 137–148, ISSN 1365-2729

Lichtenstein, B.B. & Plowman, D.A. (2009). The Leadership of Emergence: A Complex Systems Theory of Emergence at Successive Organizational Levels. *Leadership Quarterly*, Vol. 20, No. 4, pp. 617-630, ISSN 1048-9843

Lobenstein, K.W. (2005). Information Security and Ethics, In: *Strategic Management of Information Systems in Healthcare*, Brown, F.D.; Stone, T.T. & Patrick, T.B. (Eds.), pp. 237-255, Health Administration Press, ISBN 978-1-56793-242-3, Chicago (IL)

Locatelli, P. (2010). Health Information Systems, In: *Organizational Information Systems*, Bracchi, G.; Francalanci, C. & Motta, G. (Eds.), pp. 291-311, McGraw-Hill, ISBN 9-788-83866-328-4, Milan (IT) (in Italian)

Locatelli, P.; Restifo, N.; Gastaldi, L.; Sini, E. & Torresani, M. (2010). The Evolution of Hospital Information Systems and the Role of Electronic Patient Records: From the Italian Scenario to a Real Case, In: *MEDINFO 2010 – Proceedings of the 13th World Congress on Medical Informatics*, Safran C. Reti, S. & Marin, H.F. (Eds.), pp. 247-251, IOS Press, ISBN 978-1-60750-587-7, Amsterdam (NL)

Lo Scalzo, A.; Donatini, A.; Orzella, L.; Cicchetti, A. & Profili, S (2009). Italy: Health System Review. *Health Systems in Transition*, Vol. 11, No. 6, pp. 1–243, ISSN 1817-6127

Mahoney, J.T.; McGahan, J.G. & Pitelis, C.N. (2009) The Interdipendence of Private and Publix Interests. *Organizational Science*, Vol. 20, No. 6, pp. 1034-1052, ISSN 1047-7039

Martin, D.K.; Shulman, K.; Santigao-Sorrell, P. & Singer P.A. (2003). Priority Setting and Hospital Strategic Planning. *Journal of Health Services Research ad Policy*, Vol. 8, No. 4, pp. 197–201, ISSN 1355-8196

Mohrman, S.A. & Lawler, E.E. III (Eds.) (2011). *Useful Research: Advancing Theory and Practice*, Berret-Koehler, ISBN 978-1-60509-600-1, San Francisco (CA)

Nemeth, C. & Cook, R. (2007). Healthcare IT as a Force of Resilience. *Proceedings of the International Conference on Systems, Management and Cybernetics*, pp. 1-12, Montreal, Canada, November 15–19, 2007

Oborn, E; Barrett, M. & Davidson E. (2011) Unity and Diversity: EPR Use in Multidisciplinary Practice. *Information Systems Research*, Vol. 22, No. 3, pp. 547-564, ISSN 1047-7047

Ozdemir, Z.; Barron, J. & Bandyopadhyay, S. (2011). An Analysis of the Adoption of Digital Health Records Under Switching Costs. *Information Systems Research*, Vol. 22, No. 3, pp. 491-503, ISSN 1047-7047

Pascot, D.; Bouslama, F. & Mellouli, S. (2011). Architecturing Large Integrated Complex Information Systems: An Application to Healthcare. *Knowledge information Systems*, Vol. 27, No. 2, pp. 115–140, ISSN 0219-3116

Pasmore, W.A.; Stymne, B.; Shani, A.B. (Rami); Mohrman, S.A. & Adler, N. (2008). The Promise of Collaborative Management Research, In: *Handbook of Collaborative Management Research*, Shani, A.B. (Rami); Mohrman, S.A.; Pasmore, W.A.; Stymne, B. & Adler, N. (Eds.), pp. 7-31, Sage, ISBN 978-1-41292-624-9, Thousand Oaks (CA).

Pettigrew, A.M. (2003). Strategy as Process, Power, and Change, In: *Images of Strategy*, Cummings, S. & Wilson, D. (Eds.), pp. 301-330, Blakwell Publishing, ISBN 0-631-22610-9, Oxford (UK)

Rada, R. (2008). *Information Systems and Healthcare Enterprises*, IGI Publishing, ISBN 978-1-59904-651-8, Hershey (PA)

Raghupathi, W. (2003). Information Technology in Healthcare: A review of Key Applications, In: *Healthcare Information Systems (2nd Ed.)*, Beaver, K. (Ed.), pp. 9-27, Auerbach Publications, ISBN, Boca Raton (FL)

Rodrigues, J.J.P.C. (2010). Preface, In: *Health Information Systems: Concepts, Methodologies, Tools, and Applications*, Rodrigues J.J.P.C. (Ed.), pp. i-vi, Medical Information Science Reference, ISBN 978-1-60566-988-5, Hershey (PA)

Sackett, D.L.; Rosenberg, W.M.C.; Gray, J.A.M.; Haynes, R.B; Richardson W.S. (1996). Evidence Based Medicine: What It Is and What It Isn't. *British Management Journal*, Vol. 312, No. 7023, pp. 71-72, ISSN 1045-3172

Shaffer, V.; Runyon, B.; Edwards, J.; Handler, T.J.; Lovelock, J.-D.; Rishel, W. & Earley, A. (2010). The Top 9 Actions for the Healthcare Delivery Organization CIO, In: *Gartner Research*, Available from www.gartner.com

Simon, H. (1996). *The Sciences of the Artificial*. The MIT Press, ISBN 9-780-26219-374-0, London

Smaltz, D.; Sanbamurthy, V. and Agarwal, R. (2006). The Antecedents of CIO Role Effectiveness in Organizations: An Empirical Study in the Healthcare Sector. *IEEE Transactions on Engineering Management*, Vol. 53, No. 2, pp. 207–222, ISSN 0018-9391

Stebbins, M.W.; Valenzuela, J.L. & Coget, J.-F. (2009). Long-Term Insider Action Research: *Research in Organizational Change and Development*, Woodman, R.W.; Pasmore, W.A. & Shani, A.B. (Rami) (Eds.), pp. 37-75, Emerald, ISBN 978-1-84855-546-4, Bingley

Stegwee, R & Spil, T. (2001). *Strategies of Healthcare Information Systems*, IGI Global, ISBN 978-1-59904-889-5, Hershey (PA)

Tan, J. (2005). *E-health Care Information Systems: An Introduction for Students and Professionals*, Jossey-Bass, ISBN 978-0-78796-618-8, San Francisco (CA)

Tan, J. (2008). Preface, In: *Healthcare Information Systems and Informatics: Research and Practices*, Tan, J. (Ed.), pp. viii-xviii, Medical Information Science Reference, ISBN 978-1-59904-692-1, Hershey (PA)

Umble, E.J.; Haft, R.R. & Umble M.M. (2003). Enterprise Resource Planning: Implementation Procedures and Critical Success Factors. *European Journal of Operational Research*, Vol. 146, No. 2, pp. 241–257, ISSN 0377-2217

Uphoff, M.E. & Krane D. (1998). Hospital-Based Technology Assessment. *Public Productivity and Management Review*, Vol. 22, No. 1, pp. 60–70, ISSN 1044-8039

Venkatesh, V.; Zhang, X. & Sykes, T.A. (2011). "Doctors Do Too Little Technology": A Longitudinal Field Study of an Electronic Healthcare System Implementation. *Information Systems Research*, Vol. 22, No. 3, pp. 523-546, ISSN 1047-7047

Wickramasinghe, N. & Geisler, E. (Eds.) (2008). *Encyclopedia of Healthcare Information Systems*, Medical Information Science Reference, ISBN 978-1-59904-889-5, Hershey (PA)

World Health Organization (2008). The World Health Report 2008, Available from www.who.int/whr/2008/en/index.html

5

Globalization and Socio-Technical Aspects of Information Systems Development

Gislaine Camila L. Leal[1], Elisa H. M. Huzita[2] and Tania Fatima Calvi Tait[2]
[1]State University of Maringá, Department of Production Engineering
[2]State University of Maringá, Department of Computer Science
Brazil

1. Introduction

Globalization has reached the spheres including, economy and software development, making the approach known as Global Software Development (GSD) increasingly adopted. In that the physical, cultural and temporal distances are inherent. They can introduce advantages such as better use of resources in different places and thus stimulate cooperation for the software development. On the other hand, brings challenges related to communication, control and coordination of teams, which reflect in technical, social and cultural differences management.

According to Cukierman et al. (2007), is very common to deal social issues of software engineering as "non-technical"ones. So is assumed that most of the software engineering community believes thats is possible to divide the problems into "technical" and "non-technical". Laudon and Laudon (2011) suggest that project managers have to solve technical and non-technical problems by allocating people in the most effective way.

Currently, both the practice and research have shown, increasingly, that software engineering community must review projects considering both the technical as well as the social view point. So a more complete view of the context and impacts that these two points cause in the products generated are obtained. Further more, the GSD has features that making possible that the socio-technical aspects be considered in the overall development of information systems.

In the context of this chapter global development of information systems is the work that involves the collaboration of two or more organizations. These organizations may be in geographically dispersed locations, which can result in loading of cultural and techniques differences. So, find guidelines and best practices to support the management and also analyze the impact of socio-cultural and technical differences are crucial to achieving success in the global development of information systems.

This chapter is structured as following: Section 2 describes GSD emphasizing their advantages and challenges. The elements of sócio-technical view are presented in Section 3. Section 4 shows the socio-technical aspects involved in GSD. Section 5 brings an application example analysing the impact of the socio-technical factors considered in this chapter. Finally, Section 6 presents final considerations.

2. Global software development

In the last decade has been a great investment in the conversion of national markets into global ones, resulting new ways of competition and collaboration (Herbsleb *et al.*, 2000). In this context, in search of competitive advantage, many organizations have chosen to distribute the software development process adopting Global Software Development (GSD).

GSD can be defined as a strategy for software development. This strategy uses teams in several geographical locations with the involvement of people of different nationalities and different organizational cultures. It has been mainly characterized by collaboration and cooperation among departments and organizations by creating groups of developers working together, but located in different cities or countries, physically distant and time zone (PRIKLADNICKI and AUDY, 2008). According to Carmel (1999), the GSD projects consist of teams that working together to achieve common goals in the same project, however scattered geographically.

In this strategy the process is accelerated due to: reduced costs, access to human resources improvements in infrastructure (Internet and development and integration tools); advantage of new markets, the rapid composition of virtual teams, and improving time to market, with the use of development "around the sun" (BEGEL and NAGAPAN, 2008).

However, this dispersion has added new challenges to the development mainly related to communication, coordination and control, which may adversely affect productivity and therefore the software quality. These factors influence the way in which the software is designed, developed, tested and delivered to customers, thereby affecting the corresponding stages of the life cycle of the software.

This configuration of software development, the GSD, added new factors to the process, such as temporal distance, geographic dispersion, socio-cultural differences, which extended some of the challenges in of software engineering are and also added new demands that challenge the processes of communication, coordination and control of projects (LAYMAN *et al.*, 2006). According to ((Damian, 2002) (Herbsleb *et al.*, 2000) (Mockus and Herbsleb, 2001) (Sangwan *et al.*, 2007)) these challenges, can be related to technical factors (problems with network connectivity and differences between development and test environments) and non-technical (trust, communication, conflict and culture).

The main challenges found in GSD are related to cultural differences, geographic dispersion, coordination and control, communication and team spirit. Cultural differences often exacerbate problems of communication which can lead to frustration, displeasure and even disagreement between the teams. Holmstrom *et al.* (2006), report that culture has a determining effect on how people interpret certain situations, and how they react to these ones. Cultural differences involve the organizational and national cultures, language, politics, individual motivation and ethic of distributed teams (CARMEL, 1999).

In GSD, the large geographical distances adversely affect communication. Eckhard (2007) points out that solving the problems of communication is a challenge because of the complexity of projects GSD. Then complexity is caused by (i) heterogeneity as people, source code, hardware and software, difficulting the integration of tools, (ii) dependency among these elements, and (iii) and the constant changes in development environments. In addition, communication affects coordination and control (CLERC, LAGO and VLIET, 2007).

Coordination is the act of integrating each activity with each organizational unit. Integration usually requires intense and constant communication. Control is the process of adherence to the objectives, policies, standards and quality levels. For Mockus and Herbsleb (2001), coordination becomes a problem because the processes of each distributed team are different, that is, there is not a uniform process. Communication is the mediating factor that directly affects the coordination and control, and is considered the essential component of all practices of collaboration in software development. It represents the exchange of unambiguous and complete information, that is, the sender and receiver can reach a common understanding. According to Herbsleb *et al.* (2000), informal communication plays a key role in the success of distributed teams. The lack of efficient communication in GSD environments can result in a low level of trust among the teams and the loss of visibility into the work progress (DAMIAN, 2002).

3. Socio-technical view

The software development is not just a set of technical objects. It is designed, built and used by people. The socio-technical perspective provides a deeper analysis on the relationship between the methods, techniques, tools, development environment and organizational structure. Damasevieius (2007) also highlights that it is difficult to dissociate the social aspects of technological one, because they are mutually interdependent.

In the socio-technical view approach the organizational structure is composed by social or organizational aspects and technical aspects. However, the vision goes beyond the socio-technical division between technical and social aspects in seeking to put both at the same level, none is privileged over another. The integration between the social and the technical can to ensure the success and its absence can lead to failure of projects. Motta and Cukierman (2009) report the failure of a large Brazilian company in the pursuit of the implementation of CMMI model motivated by non-technical and cultural issues.

The socio-technical aspects involve the coordination of technology, organizations and persons who shall cooperate with each other and adjust to optimize the performance of the complete system. Thus, information systems can be considered a team effort, involving people with different technical, administrative and analytical skills (LAUDON and LAUDON, 2011).

Cukierman *et al.* (2007), consider that in the context of software engineering (SE), the social, cultural, and organizational policies are important. But, they do not receive addequated attention and recognition of their importance neither in literature and events of software engineering, and especially in practice. These are common questions referred to as "non-technical" by the SE community, which deals the division of problems into "technical" and "non-technical" ones.

Discussion on technical and non-technical elements in the development and management software are also covered by Fuggetta (2000) considering such elements as important to the success of projects. Cukierman et al. (2007) argue that to meet the growing challenges of software engineering is necessary break the barrier between "technical" and "non-technical" aspects. It is necessary deal they in a new design view, a new framework, a sócio-technical view, that consider both social and technical view concomitantly.

In seeking by physical and human resources shared,, the software development by distributed teams requires that the software project manager has new skills and concerns associated with those common in the management such as: plan, lead, coordinate and monitoring. The challenges stemming from the collaborative work also include the integration of teams with different cultures that need to share ideas and knowledge.

The sharing of ideas and knowledge is possible by communication among the teams that need store the information for decision making and better control of activities. Cultural differences increase the need for better communication and coordination.

4. Socio-technical aspects in GSD

The software development process is an extremely complex activity involving several technical and non-technical factors. For many managers, the technical aspects of the project or any matter related to the programming language used, databases, tools or technology, are absolutely paramount. Thus, often the non-technical problems are left aside.

According to Pilatti *et al.* (2007), the non-technical knowledge involves social, cultural, behavioral, linguistic and political aspects. In the case of distributed software development, sometimes the socio-cultural aspects are much more evident, since teams located in different countries with, language and habits totally different, are forced to work at the same project.

Managers see their software project that was developed in distributed way fail. Sometimes it is due to non adequate a combination of social, political, linguistic and cultural issues (KIEL, 2003). According to Carmel (1999), cultural diversity is among the five major challenges for the GSD project manager, along with inefficient communication, lack of coordination, geographic dispersion and loss of team spirit.

In GSD projects may exist groups with differences in behavior between people due to their different cultures. This can lead to complications in work planning, decision-making process, in the style of argument, in conversation, inconsistent work practices, among others (OLSON and OLSON, 2003). In countries with continental extensions, such as Brazil, Russia, China, United States, among others, cultural differences can occur even with people of same country due to local customers (ENAMI *et al.*, 2006).

Moreover global development, elements such as language (Cibotto *et al.*, 2009), religion (Kotabe and Helsen, 1998), customs, prejudices (Aquino, 1998), rivalry (Brenner, 1990; Vidal 2005), lack of education and professional qualification (Kotabe and Helsen, 1998) stand out in conjunction with infrastructure problems (Rigolon, 1998), economic and political aspects, organizational culture (Schein, 2004), among others. So besides allocate the best team for the development of a project, these other elements should be considered to facilitate the proper working of the team.

The division between technical and non-technical can lead to a classification that takes the as primary and that nontechnical as secondary. Among several tasks in the software project management area is one that deals with people whose actions collaborate to integrate socio-technical aspects (CUKIERMAN *et al.*, 2007). (Enami *et al.*, 2006), (Trindade *et al.*, 2008), among others, present elements that contribute to the socio-technical approach such as the integration of communication Tools that make possible people to perform activities in distributed development environment.

The development of a system is not a purely technical, but social since it contemplates the organizational structure and culture. Social structures influence and determine behavior at work and generation of artifacts making it important throughout the development (DAMASEVIÈIUS, 2007).

The present socio-technical challenges in GSD will be stratified by subdividing them into categories, so it is easier to characterize them. According to Soares (2011) can be identified three categories: people, business and infrastructure. These categories were extended including technical factors that we think should also be considered when they turn as socio-technical. We divided in four groups (Figure 1):

- **Group 1** - Factors caused by people involved in the project, ie, the adversities that arise from different cultures, habits, ways of thinking and working of each one.
- **Group 2** - Factors caused by the structure and working style of the company.
- **Group 3** - Factors caused by issues outside the company, ie, due to characteristics of the environment where they are inserted.
- **Group 4** - Factors caused by technical factors.

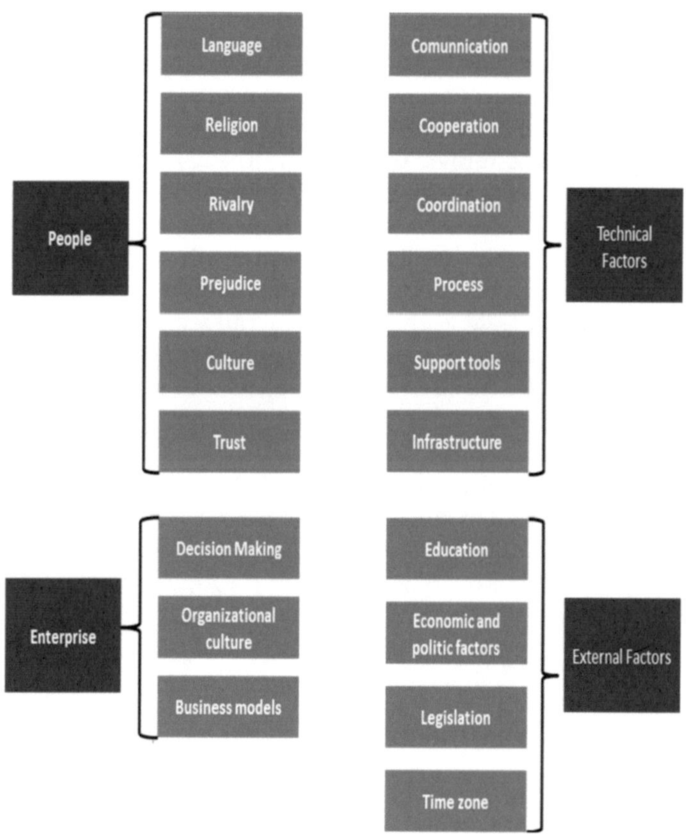

Fig. 1. Sociotechnical factors.

Next each item is discussed.

4.1 People

Language

The language is considered as the major cultural distinction. Even if the groups involved in the development have different customs and beliefs, but they use a common language among them, they can develop the project with less difficult. Otherwise, if these groups do not adopt a common language to communicate, probably they will have more difficult to develop the project. According to Mockus and Herbsleb (2001), Even with common language the lack of proficiency of some members and cultural differences that may influence the interpretation semantics during communication, create problems that can lead to mistrust or disagreements about the need for respect for hierarchy or even for punctuality. However, GSD often the spoken language may be different from one location to another. So, establish an effective communication with a language that is not his natural language, can be tricky if not well managed. Therefore establish a training programming in a common language that will be used to develop a project, followed by a face meeting, and also in loco visit on different places, are good practices that could be adopted.

Religion

An interesting comment refers about the importance of neutrality on religion. Religion has influenced the politics, economy and also the traditions of a people. In some countries there is a constant change by government agencies establishing laws and guidelines that influence the public and private life of the population. As an example, there are countries where some professional activities can be performed only by men. The women are prevented from acting in their respective professions. Moreover, they are forced to cover their face completely when they walk by streets. In business terms, these countries often do not see positively the presence of women in leadership positions or meetings. However, women in leadership positions become increasingly common in Western countries in both public and private organizations. Therefore, where the religion has great influence , it has been used to allocate teams politically and geographically dispersed. The religious situation must be observed by managers to ensure that neither the team nor the projects are in risk.

Rivalry

The rivalry can occur at several levels: countries that compete one each other; rivalries arising from sporting activities, territorial disputes, religious conflicts, among others. In the management of virtual teams, the rivalry issue becomes relevant because often leads to conflicts between the teams, ie, rivalry goes beyond the limits and starts to affect not only the development of daily tasks by team members but also their behaviour.

Sometimes the rivalry creates a team spirit among people who share the same opinions. It results the same type of behavior toward certain situations in which they have to decide or solve problems.

Prejudice

Another factor that has influenced the development of team activities in projects is the behavior prejudiced against the differences that there are among people. Prejudices such as racism, homophobia, anti-semitism, gender, among others, if not properly managed in the team result in conflicts among the people involved. A project manager who acts from the socio-technical perspective should certainly observe the characteristics of his/her team. Anyway it comes to patrolling the ideas expressed, but is important to be aware of the respect that should exist between people and the differences identified. Prejudice and discrimination lead to acts of violence both physically and psychologically, which configures in intolerance in relationship among people.

Some countries have different laws and opposing positions about criminal acts and prejudice as well as that related with to the tolerance and encouragement of these types of discriminatory acts. The project manager need much skills to deal with this kind of differences. He must always act without discriminate the people. The project manager that takes discriminatory positioning of any kind can put at risk the team's activities and, in the case of geographically dispersed teams this situation becomes quite complex as they are added elements from the religious faith and morals.

Trust

Teams are fragile social units, that can easily be broken. When problems such as distance, cultural differences and time zones appear, the synergistic effect that makes the team a cohesive unit, is often compromised. Trust is essential when people depend on each other to achieve common goals. Thus, according to Carmel (1999), trust is based on the individual to believe in the character, ability, strength and confidence of someone else. Therefore, a team without trust can not meet their commitments effectively.

Trust in an organizational environment is defined as "faith in each one of intentions and behaviors: trust builds trust, distrust leads to distrust." The importance of trust has become increasingly recognized as a critical element in the success of operations in organizations and, specifically, business, professional work and relationships. Trust is the basis of successful cooperation among individuals within and among organizations. It is essential to the functioning of an organization and the operating units within it. High level of trust within an organization improves performance, efficiency, productivity, creativity, and consequently the results obtained.

Trust is a recurring problem in GSD teams due to geographical, temporal, organizational, cultural and political differences. It is crucial to all business relationships since it enables a more open communication, increases performance to deliver better quality products, and greater satisfaction in the decision making process. Virtual teams with low cohesion require face to face interactions and synchronous ways to build trust and relationships and also to share views. An Indian experience has shown 'Customer references', 'Experience in outsourcing', 'Reputation', 'Client visits', 'Investment', 'Processes', 'Communication', 'Performance', 'Honesty', 'Commitment', 'Confidentiality', 'Cooperation', 'Understanding' 'Creditability', 'Capabilities', 'Pilot project performance', 'Personal visits', 'Investment' are important factors to establish the initial trust between customers and suppliers.

While developing offshore/nearshore can exist trust and good relationships. However it can be continued if the trust between the staff of involved organizations is broken. This can result in not a non-cooperative behavior in which e-mails are used to attack one each other. As a result, instead of working as a whole, begin to work discrediting the work of others, every opportunity being used to obstruct and denigrate colleagues. As a result the projects fail to meet specifications, over budget, late delivery occurs, and worse, resulting in delivery of low quality products.

Also, when starting a new project, the goals, objectives, definition of teams that will be involved and what will be done at each location must be communicated to all involved. Such information must be documented and provided and so obtain the commitments that everybody understood and so avoid misunderstandings from part of members (LINGS *et al.*, 2007). A leader to foster trust and commitment among members must be defined.

Culture

Culture can be defined as values and beliefs shared that are historically situated, and also emerging. They are constantly interpreted and negotiated in social relationships and interactions of a group of people within a particular socio-cultural context. The development of Information System is embedded in a socio-cultural and multi-level complex environment. It generate cultural diversity since the globally distributed team members have several cultural experiences: national, organizational and professional. Cultural difference can promote creativity and innovation that are important for knowledge intensive work. The other hand it can become a barrier to sharing and knowledge transfer.

Different cultural factors co-exist at different interaction levels and together produce different environments and group dynamics. The culturally diverse work groups are faced with difficulties in communication and interpersonal conflicts that may become less pronounced with synchronous and face to face interactions. The face to face interactions enhance the ability of team members to work with the spatial and cultural differences.

Culture has a deep impact on communication styles. Someone prefer direct communication while others prefer indirect communication. Thus, for example, German engineers have a communication style direct and assertive whereas the Indians have an indirect communication style and are reluctant to say "no". Often due to cultural differences the silence is established as a result of conversational style, that can generating misunderstanding. The knowledge acquired during the project development can support Information Technology professionals to develop strategies to achieve greater collaboration between people.

Another point to consider is that the 'compromise' is culturally different in India. When an Indian software developer says "yes" to a certain deadline, this usually means "yes I'll try that" instead of "yes I can do it." Punctuality is also taken very seriously by the Indians. If you have a meeting scheduled for 9:00 pm they usually get 5 minutes before and not 10 or even 20 minutes later as with the Americans.

Other cultural factors such as masculinity versus femininity, and individualism are covered by Evaristo (2004). The creation of a code of ethics to be practiced by all partners can help reduce the impact of these factors.

Cultural prejudices about punctuality, perfectionism, ethics, teamwork, quality and interaction can affect design decisions. Therefore, the effective management of cultural diversity is critical to success in the practices of global development.

4.2 Enterprise

Decision Making

Employees can often feel frustrated when they realize that organizational decisions, workflow, project and infrastructure among others are always centered and coming from a specific location. This occurs regardless if the teams are in the same group or organization working together on a project or performing some activities due the fact they are partners. To minimize this kind of feeling could be established a participatory process stimulating the motivation, cooperation and also promoting opportunities to release the creative potential of staff. In this way could leading to greater engagement and also sharing responsibility.

The determination of the authorities, responsibilities within the organization setting who does what within the project allows to establish the correct leadership, avoids omissions and prevent recriminations. It is also important to provide practitioners the opportunity to reflect and share their tacit knowledge acquired in practice.

Organizational culture

Organizational culture has apparent and adjacent features. According to Moscovici (1993) the apparent features are characterized by formality and documentation standard established by the organization. The issues surrounding these aspects are considered informal or hidden, but can influence the project development and team performance. For example, consider an organization that has clear rules for use of information technology, which indicate the shape and levels of access to equipment, the proper use of the Internet and computers. This organization need perfectly disseminate these rules and so they reflect the behavior of people in the organization.

However, sometimes people have friends outside the organizational structure. These include, the team of football, members who profess the same religious faith, among others, that although are in locations outside of the work environment, there they also can discuss problems related with the organization. This indicates that they may take similar stances on the problems or to support in performing the activities. Thus, it is sometimes given another format for the rules. In this context change simple rules as maintain confidentiality about individual password to access equipment becomes commonplace, since some people share their passwords with other when they help one each other in case of some faults or problems.

This simple example clearly shows the categorization of organizational culture in terms of formal and informal. While the rules are clear when is considered the formal aspects, when is considered informal aspects, sometimes the password that should be keep confidential, because it was informed in confidence, is not. It can generate problems with involved people.

In addition to these formal and informal aspects there is another view of the organizational culture that determines the behavior and ways to develop activities in the organization. Some companies have rules and customs that no there are overtime, appreciate people who participate in community activities, the use of company products, among other attitudes that become part of everyday life of organizational members.

The geographical dispersion understand that the organizational culture in each place becomes a challenge for project managers. While there is a specific local culture, there is also built-in organizational culture that reflects the behavior of individuals. Moreover the local culture is part of national culture, in the case of geographic dispersion of teams from different countries.

Managers would aware and trained to deal with cultural differences when they are to sent or brought from another country. According to Prikladnicki, Audy and Evaristo (2003), the definition of design patterns that can be adopted by the teams involved, help decrease arguments concerning the way of solving some problems. The use of standards, processes and certifications are also useful for the standardization of quality in different locations. When standardization is not possible, local conditions and concepts can make use of ontology to prevent confusion at the project level (LINGS *et al.*, 2007).

Business models

In a GSD environment the distribution can take some configurations, according to the distance between the teams and organizations involved in the project. Regarding the geographical distribution of the units involved in a project, when they are located in more than one country is called offshore distribution, if all they are in the same country has the distribution onshore. Considering the relationship established among the companies, there is the outsourcing scenario in which a company delegates the control of one or more activities to an external company which hired the service, and insourcing, when companies create their own software development centers. From these distribution these settings there are four business models, as are shown on Figure 2 and discussed as follow:

- *onshore insourcing*: in this business model there is a department within the company or a subsidiary in the same country (onshore), which provides software development service through internal projects (insourcing);
- *onshore outsourcing*: this business model indicates the hiring of a third company (outsourcing) for the development of certain software products or services to a company. The third company is located in the same country of the contracting company (onshore);
- *offshore outsourcing* or *offshoring*: this business model indicates hiring a third party (outsourcing) for the development of certain software products or services, and the third party is necessarily located in an other country than the contractor (offshore);
- *offshore insourcing* or internal *offshoring*: the latter business model indicates the creation of a subsidiary own company to provide software development services (insourcing). This subsidiary is necessarily located in a country different from the parent company, or contractor (offshore).

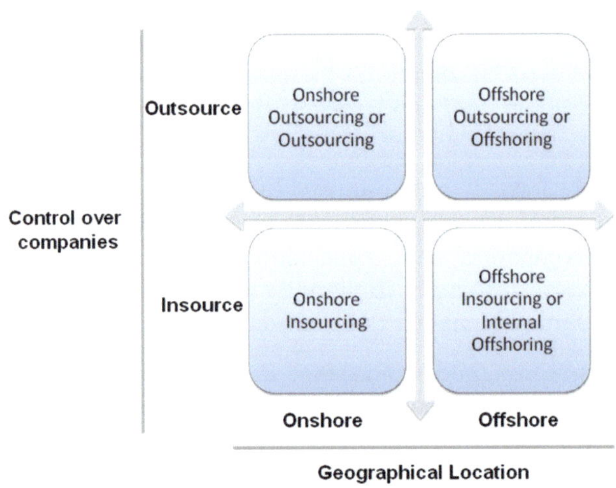

Fig. 2. Models of Distribution.

4.3 External factors

Education

The different business models allow participants from different places constituting the development teams. The geographical dispersion may, refer to two situations: in first one identify the professional expertise that will contribute greatly to generate a software product with higher quality. On the other hand one can identify professionals who are less expensive. Often these professionals cost less, can have a lot of willpower, but may not have availabity to participate as a team member or don't have the necessary skill or knowledge to perform project activities. In this case would be interesting that organizations offer the necessary training to these people whether at undergraduate, graduate or training.

Thus, companies located in places that do not have institutions that can offer the appropriate courses should encourage employees with opportunities for this qualification. One solution would be, for example, avail himself of the physical dispersion and look for other sites to establish an exchange in which a given employee could spend a certain period of time learning and after his return become the disseminator element. This person could offer training courses on site an thus offer for a large number of people in the company, the opportunity for a recycling.

Economic and politic factors

When considering the organization as an open system should be checked all the connections that exist among they and their surroundings. Figure 3 presents the various actors that are related to the organization, both directly and indirectly. Can be directly included suppliers, customers, employees. Can be cited as indirectly related the government and non-governmental organizations that do not determine the activities, but may influence the is which activities are carried out. Often, the need to reconcile the laws of different countries, especially when it comes to GSD, can impact the progress of a project. This may require adaptations for dealing with the human and material resources involved in the project.

Fig. 3. Organization in its environment. Adapted from Tait and Pacheco(2001).

The adjustments in software products can result from changes in legislation or changes in procedures to incorporate the new rules at the government level. To make the adjustments necessary to formalize the new procedure can result in higher costs and reallocation of staff.

In thinking about political and economic factors in a distributed environment, it is necessary to must identify factors in each site which can compromise the project. Countries with high economic instability and political instability are considered unsafe for the installation or maintenance of existing companies. The insistence into remain in unstable places can put at risk the security of project teams.

The political and economic factors are part of the organization's external environment and, in principle, should not have influence on internal activities. However, organizations depend on these factors to maintain their activities. Thus, it is more over challenge for software project managers to perform the planning and monitoring of projects developed by geographically dispersed teams.

Legislation

The legal aspect is one of the main problems between different locations. Groups may be subject to different laws, be they commercial, civil, labor, etc. This diversity affects the development of several ways. For example, in some countries it is forbidden to import hardware, while some others countries have reciprocal trade agreements and require that a company spends part of the revenue in the nation's economy where it is located. Other countries prohibit to transfer data to out of their national boundary or have government restrictions regarding access to the internet.

The laws of each country vary in many ways and in many cases, significantly. Each team must know the laws of the country in which it is installed. It should be noted that even in a single country, there may be substantial differences in taxes in different regions. In addition to general legislation, it is essential to know the labor laws under which the team is governed. Detailed knowledge of the laws allows each group, when necessary, take action in accordance with the regulations that surround them, avoiding legal problems and allowing the group to take the advantages offered in this local. A good legal advice can help the organization complies with the laws.

Another aspect of the legislation of each place is related to documents stored in electronic and optical media, which should be reviewed by each team. Just as the general law must be observed and can present diversity from place to place, there is a category of specific laws dealing with intellectual property, which may be different in each country that can often hinder the development of the software. It should be analyzed to see how the organization can guard against the theft of design information and source code of programs.

In an environment where there are several participants from different countries working is essential that the project manager worries about the issue of copyright and intellectual property of software or part thereof. It should be interesting seek legal advice and always be alert to changes in local laws involved with software development.

Besides being able to apply the penalties provided by law, managers can and should be aware to the sanctions for which employees must comply with in case of misuse of internal information or use of them outside the company. This action contributes to awareness of employees regarding the content of the projects developed by them or by third parties.

The software source code and its corresponding documentation is an intellectual resource that should receive the protection of law. It is the creation that should be protected, it is an intangible property whose owner has a right of ownership over it, and therefore an intellectual property right.

The intangibles resources are the fruit of intellectual creation that have high economic importance. Legal protection for resources is to ensure the creativity, to protect and to encourage the creativity and intellectual work to safeguard the rights of the creator from economic exploitation.

In Brazil, intellectual property can be guaranteed by copyright. The copyright protection ensures a work and have externalized the idea. It does not require registration, but it brings greater guarantees. However, copyright is not permanent, the lifetime for the author, parents, children and wife and other heirs lasts up to 60 years. The copy for purposes of comment, criticism, research and teaching is permitted, but in Europe, most countries recognize the moral character of the copyright while in the U.S. it does not. In order to have protection in other countries is necessary to search a signatory to the convention on the subject, and verify the effectiveness to guarantee those rights. The defense is made under penalty of copyright, it is necessary proof that the accused could not have access to the software so that it is possible condemnation. Another important aspect is that the software that was developed in the company belongs to the employer.

Therefore, access to products developed should be preserved only to those who need them to perform their tasks. Another branch of intellectual property is the industrial property in which the protection is effected to ensure of patents and trademark registration among others. The patent provides a monopoly on the creation, however, in Brazil is not recognized on the software. Even in the industrial property the trademark registration protect the merchant's goods and distinguishing them from others. In software the only protection is on the program (source code).

Time zone

Due to restrictions on working hours and, as well as of time zone, because they are in different locations, members of virtual teams may not be available for certain tasks or even to a synchronous communication with other members. There are also two other types of unavailability that are specifically related to the local context: one due to local holidays and other socially oriented. In addition to national holidays such as Christmas, Republic Day, Independence Day, there are also religious holidays. In this case, as there are diversity of religions in some country, it is also the larger the amount of holidays. In India, for example, they practice the Hindu, Islam, Christianity, Sikhism.

The socially oriented unavailability is due to needs of family and social obligations. Among the social obligations is, for example, the legal liability. The unavailability is a social concept culturally embedded. For example, China and India are countries focused on relationships, and norms. They care for elders at home, which requires a greater commitment to family.

However, it is possible to have flexible availability with accommodation of availability, in order to facilitate the temporal coordination in GSD. The flexible availability can be understood as the availability outside of working hours. In India, for example, there is a well defined boundary between work and private life, and plans can be changed flexibly to meet different demands. This can lead to situations where a person may not be available when it was expected, but that may be available when he/she would not be. In India, the work seems to never end, people even outside of work hours are availabe to compensate for holidays. Recently the flexible availability has been adopted as a way to gain advantages in competitive environments. On the other hand, in the United States, the balance between work and personal life is better balanced.

The accommodation of availability refers to the predisposition to shift work hours so that an overlay is established to encourage greater interaction among team member at these times of synchronous activities. Thus, if a meeting is scheduled for 8:00 am in the morning hours in Central America, corresponds to 9:00 pm in Beijing the same day. But for the Chinese team, it means that their working day will end only around 11:00 pm. Only after this time is that they go to home by train or bus, which might reflect on issues of personal safety. Thus, accommodate the meeting time to 7:00 pm in in Central America would correspond to 8:00 am the next day. This illustrates the accommodations that are negotiated based on the contextual needs.

Thus, GSD teams are exposed to challenges arising from these differences. The project manager should take it into consideration when distributing the activities of a project and also be tolerant and understanding when absences occur. Note, therefore it is necessary to care that this does not reflect a delay in a project schedule and budget no overflows. When the difference in time is small, has no major effect on quality, but the quality drops as the time difference increases.

4.4 Technical factors

Comunnication

Effective communication is vital in any organization. However due to the involvement of different places it is a great source of problems in GSD. Frequent communication is important to provide a constant confirmation that the members are still here and still working. The frequency and predictability of communication and the extent with that they are provided with feedback improves the effectiveness of communication leading to greater confidence and improving team performance. Inexperienced teams may experience anxiety and low confidence due to negative interpretations associated with silence or delay associated with the dispersion time.

Several practices have been proposed to mitigate the challenges related to communication: regular meetings, whether ad hoc or planned, or video conference organized as weekly sessions. Communication can be kept flowing swiftly through the use of wiki to document the discussions and decisions. These regular meetings can improve project definition, makes better socialization, increase trust, enhance respect among members and enhance the electronic communication subsequent.

The face to face meetings are crucial when the projects begin, because it offers the chance to answer important and urgent doubts. Teams can communicate using different tools, from cell phones, fax, chat, video conference, e-mail and groupware applications. These practices are used to support the communication needs in GSD: troubleshooting, reporting and monitoring, relationship building, decision making and coordination. However, success depends on the predisposition to adopt them and also of the project elaborated. Still, it is important that the tools are synchronized. For example, despite tools availability, if individuals forget to report changes or updates made during the day to other members it results in rework and lost time.

The trust and motivation have a direct impact on the level, content of communication and effective communication, and also about the use of tools. In general, when the software development occurs in the offsite model, communication is kept to a minimum, calls are not returned and emails are not getting answered. So many questions remain unanswered. When there is a direct communication, the speech is short and aggressive. This may indicate that online communication was being used as a means to limit and control the quantity and quality of information that was shared, which ultimately limit the establishment of personal relationships. It is easier to ignore someone that you do not know if he (she) is particularly one competitor.

Cooperation

Cooperation among team members is essential for the successful of virtual teams. The distance has a negative impact on the interaction intensity established among remote colleagues working collaboratively and effectively as a team (HERBSLEB AND MOCKUS, 2003). Yet, it is known, that it is not easy to successfully integrate geographically remote and culturally diverse individuals or groups into a single team (BATTIN *et al.*, 2001). Add the impact of fear and it is easy to understand why in these circumstances problems can and do arise.

In GSD environment to facilitate collaboration and cooperation among team members it is necessary that trust to be established. It is possible by knowing and building relationships between individual team members. When this is successfully achieved the results can be a motivated and cohesive team with a common purpose and shared goals and objectives.

The fear by itself undermines and inhibits the development of cooperation and trust. The studies have shown that in offsite software development, the local engineers mistrusted of offsite engineers. They see them as a potential threat for their future employment. In this instance trust was never established. Then, it results in communication problems, knowledge transfer limited, uncooperative behavior, and ultimately the failure of offsite strategy (CASEY and RICHARDSON, 2004); (CASEY and RICHARDSON, 2008).

Coordination

Malone and Crowston (1994) defined coordination as the management of dependencies between activities. The software development process, especially large scale systems development, is usually characterized as highly ambiguous, uncertain, and interdependent. Therefore, effective communication and coordination are critical to the success of software development projects, especially when they are globally distributed.

Espinosa *et al.* (2007) identified three major types of coordination needs in distributed software development, technical coordination, temporal coordination, and software process coordination. Temporal coordination refers to the mechanisms to schedule software development tasks, synchronize activities, and allocate resources in order to use optimally distributed resources and adhere to scheduled timelines (Espinosa *et al.*, 2007; Massey *et al.*, 2003; McGrath 1990). Herbsleb (2007) pointed out that the absence or disruption of many mechanisms (such as formal and informal communication) used to coordinate the work in co-located settings is the fundamental problem of globally distributed software development (SANGWAN et al., 2007). Regarding temporal coordination mechanisms, temporal separation restricts the synchronous communication, immediate information exchange, on-demand support, and real-time problem solving (CUMMING *et al.*, 2007). Temporal separation may cause problems in the workflow of globally distributed projects. So the time to deal with some problem can be longer, causing with this delay for coordination (ESPINOSA and CARMEL, 2003).

Global teams can adopt some tatics to minimize the effects of time separation and to facilitate coordination, such as: (i) sequencing or structuring activities for troubleshooting; (ii) using modular design to assign work to different locations in order to reduce the dependencies between tasks, and thus facilitate the needs of inter-local coordination; (iii) making working hours more flexible in order to create or expanding overlapping time, and thereby facilitating the synchronous communication. Similarly the distributed team members can rearrange their daily workflow, allocating the independent tasks on time slices overlapping and the dependent tasks in time slices without overlapping.

Process

The software process is the set of policies, organizational structures, technologies, procedures and artifacts needed to design, develop, deploy and maintain a software product (FUGGETTA, 2000). It involves steps consisting of a set of activities, methods, practices and technologies that are used throught development to maintenance and also either related products.

The process should enable the improvement of quality of service, engineering and design, reducing costs by increasing predictability and ability to mitigate risks and improve the efficiency and productivity of the organization.

In GSD environment a common process is essential. It directly assists all team members providing them with a common nomenclature for tasks and activities, and a common set of expectations. In GSD the variables and risks increase if there is not an appropriate methodology for the development process and so increasing chances of not meeting the initial planning.

A common process improves communication between teams and can minimize the ambiguity of artifacts. It provides support to the processes of communication, coordination and control by using a common nomenclature in the case of disciplines, roles, activities and artifacts to involve everybody.

However, more recently, due to the different business models present in GSD can be observed that participating organizations can have different process models. In order to meet this peculiarity, the software engineering area, particularly of collaborative systems have attempted to define techniques, mechanisms and strategies that provide the necessary support to make process more flexible during software development. An example of such mechanism could be a process engine that manages expertise of the different participating organizations with regard to the generation of artifacts during the development process. Still, the formal specification of tests can minimize the problems of ambiguity and also reduces the needs for communication (MULLICK et al., 2006), (AVRITZER et al., 2007) and (AVRITZER et al., 2008)).

Support tools

The geographic distribution and inter-organizational software development created the need for tools and techniques for coordination and cooperation in teams. In order to meet this need effort have been made to construct Distributed Software Development Environments (DSDE).

The DSDE have common requirements, such as integration, data management and process. However, it should be highlighted the need to provide appropriate support to enable cooperation among team members and an efficient allocation of resources. There are several approaches explored in the literature to define coordination and cooperation in DSDE: access control, information sharing, monitoring, support for communication board meeting (LIMA REIS, REIS, NUNES, 1998).

Since team members are geographically distributed, syncronous and assyncronous tools can be used by them to establish the effective communiction during activities development. So, chat, video conference are examples of synchronous tools. E-mails, discussin foruns and blogs are examples of asynchronous tools. Thus, the project activity developed by team members will determine the convenience and necessity to use one or other tool type.

The data generated from chats, forun or discussion list show the communication that there are among team members. Information concerned with coordination among team members in GSD can be obtained from tasks list and bugtracker. The cooperation that could be established among team members can be extracted from blogs or control version system logs. Nowadays effort have been made aiming at develop tools to storage and also to explore socio-technical information from organization repository. With this the idea is to offer an adequate support for an effective and efficient decision making by project manager and so turn the organization more competitive in a world so globalized.

Infrastructure

Technological advances have enabled an increasing number of people to have access to a large volume of information, whether textual, graphic or audio. To this end, it is not enough that tools to support different stages of development are available. It is necessary also made available a whole support infrastructure, including network infrastructure, availability of electricity, and adequate physical facilities.

The network infrastructure in some situations may include local or traditional underground cables or not. But it is also increasingly common to provide wireless networks. The continuous availability of electricity is of fundamental importance for the smooth progress of work, including interaction between the participants through different communication tools and / or interaction as mentioned above and also in situations where long transactions need to be processed. However, in some places, it may happen that in the workplace or business energy supplier interrupt or rationing energy. This can often lead to instability or even unsafe. In these cases should be, as far as possible, provide alternative ways such as a generator to ensure delivery and avoid situations that can often mean chaos.

Regarding to adequate physical facilities, it is expected that besides the size, the space has good lighting, ventilation and adequate furniture. The furniture associated with inadequate or incorrect posture can lead people to diseases that depart from the work.

It is worth noting, also, that when you try to maintain a standard technology infrastructure and operational in all units, suitable for carrying out the work, it is important to establish the collaboration, perform an effective control of documentation and version control of artifacts.

5. Example

Organizations in the search for better solutions and highly skilled professionals starts to expand their activities and partnerships with other companies around the world. Thus in its structure, organizations allocate their teams for projects considering skills and competencies.

Take the example of a team working on project development in the area of control earthquakes and volcanic inspections. This team is geographically distributed in three countries: Brazil, Japan and India. The project will be deployed in Japan.

In this scenario, the following solutions listed by Soares (2011), identifies some differences among the three countries regarding the development team. We highlight the local culture, and organizational culture as there are many differences among the three countries and local culture can influence the behavior of people working in organizations.

Thus, solutions must be sought to reduce the impact that differences could cause on project to be developed. The three elements outlined in Table 1, are socio-cultural, independent of the technical elements, which can impact the success or failure of the project if not properly managed. At managerial level, allocation of human resources in the distributed team must also be considered, the risks and the lack of integration and commitment of staff and additional costs arising from the creation of reporting structures and performance of training meetings must be reduced.

Regarding to education, specifically in the information technology area, it is expected that human resources allocated to the projects have the necessary training if team members are distributed in different places. Therefore, when access the selection process of human resources, the project manager must know the instituition where the people made undergraduate and graduate courses and verify how good is that education of students and future professionals.

The rivalry in the example cited, is not perceived in the three countries. So, when is considered Brazil and Japan remains the appreciation of Japanese immigration which results in both commercial and cultural exchanges. It is possible to see the influences of food, dancing, and miscegenation in the Brazilian states from Japanese immigrants. On the Indian religiosity it attracts Brazilian and therefore there is no apparent dispute between the two countries. There is, for most Brazilians, a mystical vision of India that is associated with the strong religiosity. In the Japan-India relationship does not detect rivalries that may impact the development of activities performed by team members.

	Brazil	Japan	India	Solution proposed (Adapted by Soares (2011)))
Language	Portuguese	Japanese	Indian	Standardization of language. Preference in hiring employees who are fluent in the languages involved. Courses and foreign language training within the company
Religion	Catholic Evangelical	Buddhism	Muslim	Instructions on the religious customs to other members. Respect for all religions of those involved in the project. Educate teams in order to avoid arguments and religious affairs.
Customs	Mixture of races and ethnicities. Strong regional customs.	Rigidity. Demand for high level behavior.	Devaluation of women. Strong family. Respect for animals.	Exchange of staff. Meetings and gatherings whenever possible.
Organizatinal culture	Relaxation Many holidays	Stiffness in the treatment. Stiffness in the schedule compliance.	Does not accept women in negotiations. Flexibility of hours.	Training and standardization.
Infrastructure	Continental country with large regional differences. Government programs to bridge gaps (broadband, telephony etc.). Problems in network infrastructure and energy.	Cutting-edge technology. Environment prone to seismic and climatic variations, which can cause problems in organizations.	Infrastructure problems that reflects the use of energy, and telephony networks. Bad roads.	Knowledge of reality to minimize impacts when problems occur.

Table 1. Differences among countries.

6. Final considerations

The growing search for greater competitiveness has led companies to adopt increasingly the GSD. Besides the physical distribution of teams, cultural differences, language, time zone, among others, increase the complexity of communication, coordination and control during software development process.

Software processes and their artifacts present perspectives: technological, social, psychological and others. The socio-technical perspective allows a deeper analysis on the relationship among methods, techniques, tools, development environment and organizational structure. The results of this type of analysis can be used to educate team members, disseminate best practices, improve process performance and quality of generated artifacts (DAMASEVIÈIUS, 2007).

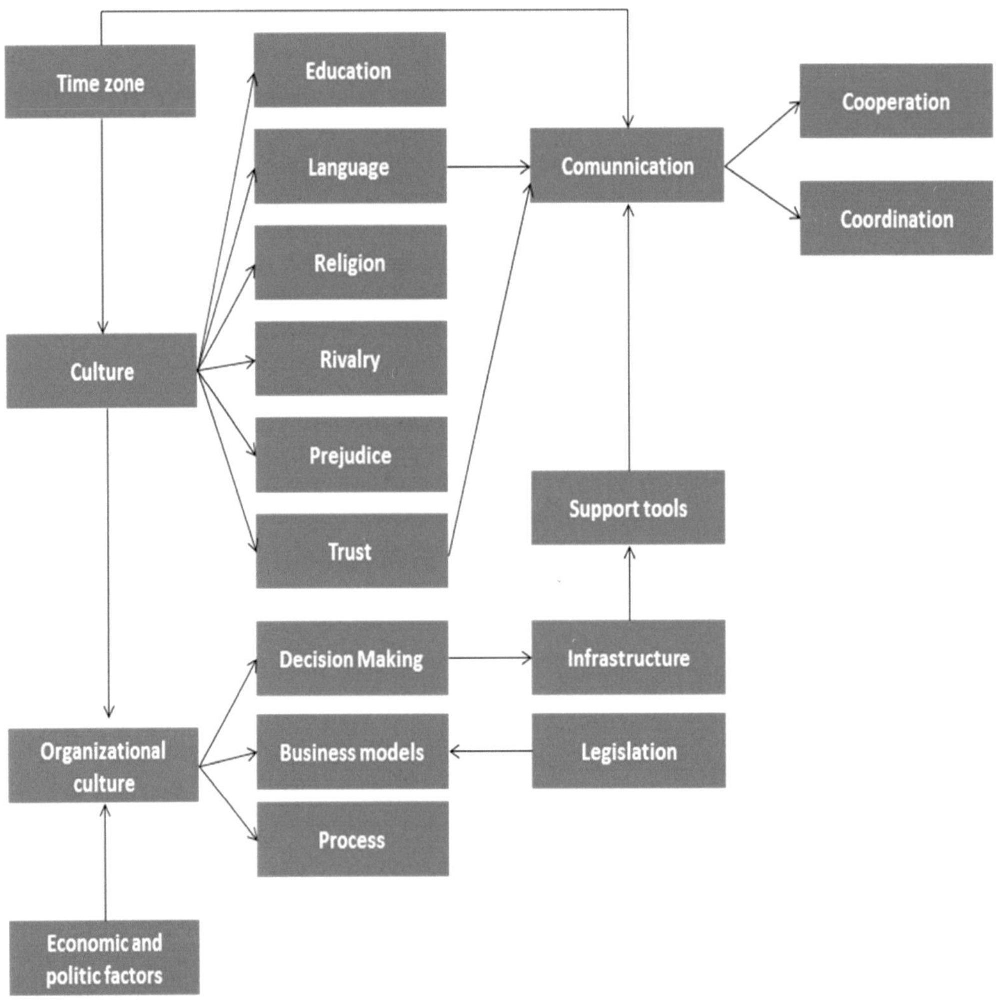

Fig. 4. Factors and relations.

The growing need to develop systems that meet the most different levels of decision making generate different types of information systems. Still, adoption of GSD makes increasingly clear that the differences caused by physical distance, social and time can affect the behavior of team members participating in the software development. The use of video conferencing and social networks as a means to improve communication are already increasingly popular. On the other hand data mining techniques have been increasingly exploited to improve the generation and knowledge sharing.

Thus, this chapter cast and discussed a set of elements stratified in people, organization, external factors and technical factors that constitute guidelines for better management of cultural, social and technical factors present in the global information systems development. Figure 4 present these factors and their relationship.

7. References

Aquino, J. G. (1998); *Diferenças e Proconceito - Alternativas teóricas e práticas.* Editora Summus - 8° Edição, 1998.

Avritzer, A.; Hasling, W.; Paulish, D. (2007) Process investigations for the global studio project version 3.0. In: ICGSE '07: Proceedings of the International Conference on Global Software Engineering, Washington, DC, USA: IEEE Computer Society, 2007, p. 247-251.

Avritzer, A.; Paulish, D.; Cai, Y. (2008) Coordination implications of software architecture in a global software development project. In: WICSA '08: Proceedings of the Seventh Working IEEE/IFIP Conference on Software Architecture (WICSA 2008), Washington, DC, USA: IEEE Computer Society, 2008, p. 107-116.

Audy, J.; Prikladnicki, R. (2008) *Desenvolvimento Distribuído de Software: Desenvolvimento de software com equipes distribuídas.* Rio de Janeiro, RJ: Elsevier, 2008.

Battin R. D.; Crocker, R.; Kreidler, J. ; Subramanian, K. (2001) Leveraging resources in global software development, IEEE Software, vol. 18, no. 2, pp. 70-77, 2001.

Begel, A. and Nagapan, N. (2008) Global software development: Who does it? In IEEE Internacional Conference on Global Software Engineering, pages 195–199, Los Alamitos, CA, USA.

Brenner, R. (1990) Rivalry: In Business, Science, Among Nations. Cambridge University Press, 1990.

Carmel, E. (1999) Global software teams: collaborating across borders and time zones. Upper Saddle River, NJ, USA: Prentice Hall PTR, 1999.

Casey, V.; Richardson, I. (2004) A practical application of the IDEAL model, Software Process Improvement and Practice, vol. 9, no. 3, pp. 123-132, 2004.

Casey, V.; Richardson, I. (2008) The impact of fear on the operation of virtual teams, in Proceedings of the 3rd IEEE International Conference on Global Software Engineering, Bangalore, India, 2008.

Cibotto, G. R. A. ; Pagno, R. T. ; Tait, T F. C. ; Huzita, E H M (2009). *Uma análise da dimensão sócio-cultural no desenvolvimento distribuido de software.* In: WOSES - Olhar sóciotécnico sobre a engenharia de software - SBQS, 2009, Ouro Preto - MG.

Clerc, V., Lago, P., and van Vliet, H. (2007) Global software development: Are architectural rules the answer? In ICGSE '07: Proceedings of the International Conference on

Global Software Engineering, pages 225–234,Washington, DC, USA. IEEE Computer Society.

Cukierman, H. L., Teixeira, C. and Prickladnicki, R. (2007) *Um olhar sociotécnico sobre a engenharia de software*. Revista de Informática Teórica e Aplicada, XIV.

Cummings, J.N., Espinosa, J.A., and Pickering, C. (2007) Spatial and temporal boundaries in global teams: distinguishing where you work from when you work. In Proceedings of the International Federation of Information Processing Working Group 8.2 on Information Systems and Organizations and 9.5 on Virtuality and Society: Virtuality and Virtualization, K. Crowston, S. Sieber, and E. Wynn (eds.), Portland, Oregon, USA, July 29-31, 2007, pp. 85-98.

Damasevieius, R. (2007) Analysis of software design artifacts for socio-technical aspects. INFOCOMP Journal of Computer Science, 6(4):07–16.

Damian, D. Workshop on global software development (2002) In: ICSE '02: Proceedings of the 24th International Conference on Software Engineering, New York, NY, USA: ACM, 2002, p. 667-668.

Eckhard B. (2007) Context-aware notification in global software development, Master's thesis, Institut fr Softwaretechnik und interaktive Systeme - Technischen Universitt Wien, 2007.

Enami, L.; Tait, T. F. C.; Huzita, E.H M (2006) A project management model to a distributed software engineering environment. In: ICEIS 2006 - International Conference on Enterprise Information Systems, 2006, Papus. Anais do ICEIS 2006, 2006.

Espinosa, J.A., Slaughter, S.A., Kraut, R.E., and Herbsleb, J.D. (2007) Team knowledge and coordination in geographically distributed software development," Journal of Management Information Systems (24:1), 2007b, pp. 135-169.

Espinosa, J.A., and Carmel, E. (2003) The impact of time separation on coordination in global software teams: a conceptual foundation," Journal of Software Process: Practice and Improvement (8:4), 2003, pp. 249-266.

Evaristo, J. R; Scudder, R; Desouza, K. C; Sato, O. (2004) A Dimensional Analysis of Geographically Distributed Project Teams: A Case Study. Journal of Engineering and Technology Management, vol. forthcoming. 2004.

Fuggetta, A. Software process: a roadmap (2000) In: ICSE '00: Proceedings of the Conference on The Future of Software Engineering, New York, NY, USA: ACM, 2000, p. 25{34.

Herbsleb, J. D.; Mockus, A.; Finholt, T. A.; Grinter, R. E. (2000) Distance, dependencies, and delay in a global collaboration. In: CSCW '00: Proceedings of the 2000 ACM conference on Computer supported cooperative work, New York, NY, USA: ACM, 2000, p. 319-328.

Herbsleb, J. D. ; Mockus, A. (2003) An empirical study of speed and communication in globally distributed software development, IEEE Transactions on Software Engineering, vol. 29, no. 6, pp. 481-494.

Herbsleb, J.D. (2007) Global software engineering: the future of socio-technical coordination. In: Proceedings of Future of Software Engineering (FOSE'07), IEEE, 2007.

Holmstrom, H., Conchuir, E. O., Agerfalk, P. J., and Fitzgerald, B. (2006) Global software development challenges: A case study on temporal, geographical and sociocultural distance. In Global Software Engineering, 2006. ICGSE '06. International Conference on, pages 3–11.

Kiel, L. (2003) Experiences in distributed development: a case study. The International Workshop on Global Software Development, ICSE, Portland, OR, 2003. May 9 pp. 44–47. 2003.

Kotabe, M. and Helsento, K. (1998) Global Marketing Management. Estados Unidos: Edit. John Wiley e Sons, Inc, 1998.

Laudon, K. and Laudon, J. (2011) Management Information Systems. 12. ed, Prentice Hall,2011.

Layman, L.; Williams, L.; Damian, D.; Bures, H. (2006) Essential communication practices for extreme programming in a global software development team. Information and Software Technology, v. 48, n. 9, p. 781-794, 2006.

Lima Reis, C.A.; Reis, R. Q.;Nunes, D. J. (1998) A Synchronous Cooperative Architecture For the Prosoft Software Engineering Environment. In: IV Congreso Argentino de Ciencias de la Computacion - Neuquen, Argentina.

Lings, B.; Lundell, B.; Agerfalk, P. J.; Fitzgerald, B. (2007) A reference model for successful distributed development of software systems. In: ICGSE '07: Proceedings of the International Conference on Global Software Engineering, Washington, DC, USA: IEEE Computer Society, 2007, p. 130-139.

Malone, T., and Crowston, K. (1994) The Interdisciplinary Study of Coordination, ACM Computing Surveys (26:1), 1994, pp. 87-119.

Massey, A.P., Montoya-Weiss, M., and Hung, C (2003) Because time matters: temporal coordination in global virtual project teams. Journal of Management Information Systems (19:4), 2003, pp. 129-156.

McGrath, J.E. (1990) Time matters in groups. In Intellectual Teamwork: Social and Technological Foundations of Cooperative Work, J. Galegher, R. Kraut, and C. Egido (eds.), Lawrence Erlbaum, Hillsdale, NJ, 1990, pp. 23-61.

Mockus, A.; Herbsleb, J. (2001) Challenges of global software development. In: METRICS '01: Proceedings of the 7th International Symposium on Software Metrics, Washington, DC, USA: IEEE Computer Society, 2001, p. 182.

Moscovici, F. (1993) *Renascença organizacional - a revalorização do homem frente à tecnologia para o sucesso da nova empresa.* 3.ed, José Olimpio Editora, Rio de Janeiro: 1993, 129 págs.

Motta, M.S.; Cukierman, H. L. (2009) *As resistências à implantação de um modelo de desenvolvimentode software em uma empresa pública.* V Workshop Um Olhar Sociotécnico sobre a Engenharia de Software - WOSES 2009.

Mullick, N.; Bass, M.; Houda, Z.; Paulish, P.; Cataldo, M. (2006) Siemens global studio project: Experiences adopting an integrated gsd infrastructure. In: Global Software Engineering, 2006. ICGSE '06. International Conference on, 2006, p. 203-212.

Olson J.S.; Olson, G.M. (2004) Culture Surprises in Remote Software Development Teams. ACM Queue, New York, v. 1, n. 9, p. 52-59, dec./jan. 2003-2004.

Pilatti, L.; Prikladnicki, R.; Audy, J. L. N. (2007) *Avaliando os Impactos dos Aspectos Não-Técnicos da Engenharia de Software em Ambientes de Desenvolvimento Global de Software: Um Caso Prático.* In: Anais III Workshop Um Olhar Sócio-Técnico sobre a Engenharia de Software (WOSES 07), pp. 85-96. Porto de Galinhas. 2007.

Prikladnicki, R.; Audy, J. L. N; Evaristo, R (2003) Requirements Management in Global Software Development: Preliminary Findings from a Case Study in a SW-CMM context. II International Workshop on Global Software Development at ICSE, Portland, Oregon. 2003.

Rigolon, F. J. Z. (1998) *O investimento em infra-estrutura e a retomada do crescimento econômico sustentável*, 1998. In: http://ppe.ipea.gov.br/index.php/ppe/article/viewFile/716/656

Sangwan, R., Bass, M., Mullick, N., Paulish, D. J., and Kazmeier, J (2007) Global Software Development Handbook, Auerbach Publications, Boca Raton, FL, 2007.

Schein, E. (2004) Organizational Culture and Leadership. San Francisco: Jossey,2004

Soares, P. H. (2011) *Uma Estratégia para Tratar os Aspectos Sócio - Culturais no Desenvolvimento Distribuído de Software*. Dissertação de Mestrado. Programa de Ciência da Computação, Universidade Estadual de Maringá, 2011.

Tait, T.F.C. Pacheco, R.C. S. (2001) Presentation of an Information Systems Architecture Model for Public Sector. International Conference on Enterprises Information Systems ICEIS (1) 2001: 275-278. Portugal.

Trindade, D. G. F.; Tait, T. F. C.; Huzita, E. H M (2008) A tool for supporting the communicantion in distributed environment for software development. Journal of Computer Science and Technology (La Plata), v. 8, p. 118-124, 2008.

Vidal, J. A. (2005) *Activismo e novas Tecnologias de Informação e Comunicação (TICs)*. Instituto Politécnico do Porto - 4º SOPCOM, 2005.

6

Mobile System Applied to Species Distribution Modelling

Álvaro Silva, Pedro Corrêa and Carlos Valêncio
Nokia Institute of Technology and University of São Paulo, University of São Paulo,
Instituto de Biociências, Letras e Ciências Exatas, UNESP – Univ Estadual Paulista
Brazil

1. Introduction

Species distribution based on ecological niche modelling has been used in several areas of ecology. It uses mathematics techniques which are applied to weather statistics and other physical factors which can affect the geographic extension of species in its ecological niche (Soberón& Peterson, 2005).

Based on known localization data (or absence) occurrences of individual species and relating them to environmental variables (such as relief, climate, humidity, etc), it is possible to predict the probability that a region will be favourable for those species survival.

This process depends on the quality of the gathered data in the field. Iwashita (Iwashita, 2008) presents a research concerning the errors influence on the collection point position. There are, however, human factors that can also influence the quality of these points. Here, the main problem is related to automate the presence and absence data gathering process and how to share that data with other scientists.

In order to solve these problems, this chapter presents a mobile system which supports the data gathering and modelling for the distribution of ecological niche. This solution involves Service Oriented Architecture applied to mobile systems. Beyond this, it proposes a new approach to help scientists choose an area to gather field data by previewing the models available for the researcher.

2. Distribution species modelling

Distribution species modelling is a way of analysing data applied mainly in biology which uses advanced geographic information systems (Peterson, 2001).

To understand what this modelling represents, it is necessary to understand the concept of ecological niche: according to Hutchinson (1957) ecological niche is defined as "a space with n-dimensional volume where each dimension represents the interval of environmental conditions or necessary sources for the species survival and reproduction".

In Peterson (2001), ecological niche is defined as a group of ecological condition in which a species is capable of maintaining population without immigration.

According to these concepts the ecological niche is nothing more than a determined region where the group of factors favours the species survival. Environmental features that influence species survival can be temperature, humidity, salinity, pH, feeding sources, luminous intensity, predatory pressure, population density, among others. Environmental factors are limited and remain relatively constant on the interval related to these animals timeline (Bazzaz, 1998).

The ecological niche is divided between realized and fundamental. Fundamental niche is defined as a group of environmental conditions necessary for species survival without considering the predators influence. Realized niche is where the species really occurs (Malanson et al., 1992). You can say that realized niche is a sub-group of the fundamental one.

Predictive modelling of species distribution is mainly concerned with the ecological niche modelling. It proposes a solution based on artificial intelligence for foreseeing a probable geographic species distribution of species.

The distribution modelling of ecological niche plays an important role in ecology. Among main applications is the environmental preservation areas planning (Austin, 2002; Guisan& Zimmermann, 2000; Sohn, 2009). Choosing a preservation area requires knowledge about a species ecological niche. With predictive modelling it is possible to identify statistically these areas.

Another area wherein modelling is a driving force, is in climate change research (Peterson et al., 2001; V. Canhos et al., 2005) which aims to identify how living creatures are affected by global warming.

More applications can be found: species replacement in nature, species and habitat management, biogeography and others (Guisan& Zimmermann, 2000).

One model visualization is shown on Figure 1, extracted from Sohn(2009) which made the modelling for cook-of-the-rock (*rupicolarupicola*) bird in the Brazilian Amazon region.

2.1 Collecting and modelling process

Basically, predictive modelling of ecological niche occurs in three phases: collecting, modelling and analysing the actual models. Figure 2 shows an IDEF0 diagram used to represent the business plan modelling. In this figure, it can be realized that to obtain a validated model, the sequence has to be followed: first collect the data, then use the entries in the model creation phase which are the data collected and the environmental variables, that are processed with the support of a number of predictive algorithms, thus generating the model and a set of indicators for this model. Based on these indicators it is possible to validate the generated model, evaluating its quality.

The first stage of the entire process is to obtain data about a species' presence or absence to be studied. Both are basically latitude and longitude.

Presence data represents the species' incidence or abundance outcomes in a given position or area. Absence data is given when there was a search for that species in some known region and even in an individual finding (Engler&Rechsteiner, 2004). Absences may occur due to the following (Philips et al., 2006):

- There was a species, but it could not be detected;
- The habitat is suitable, but for historical reasons the species is absent

- The habitat is not suitable.

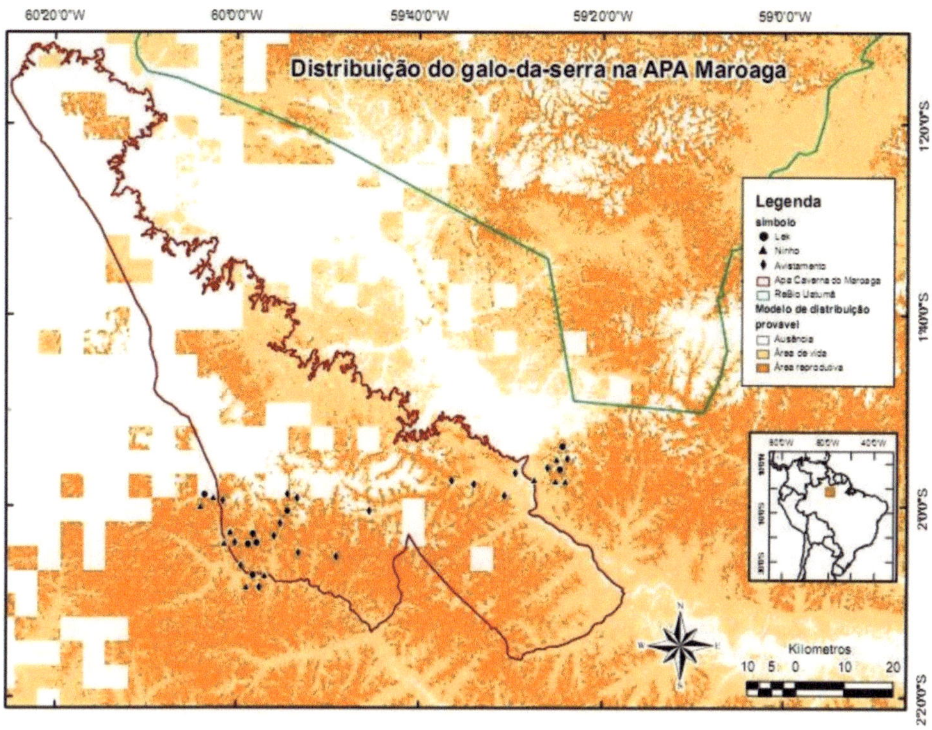

Fig. 1. Model visualization for cook-of-the-rock in Amazon area.

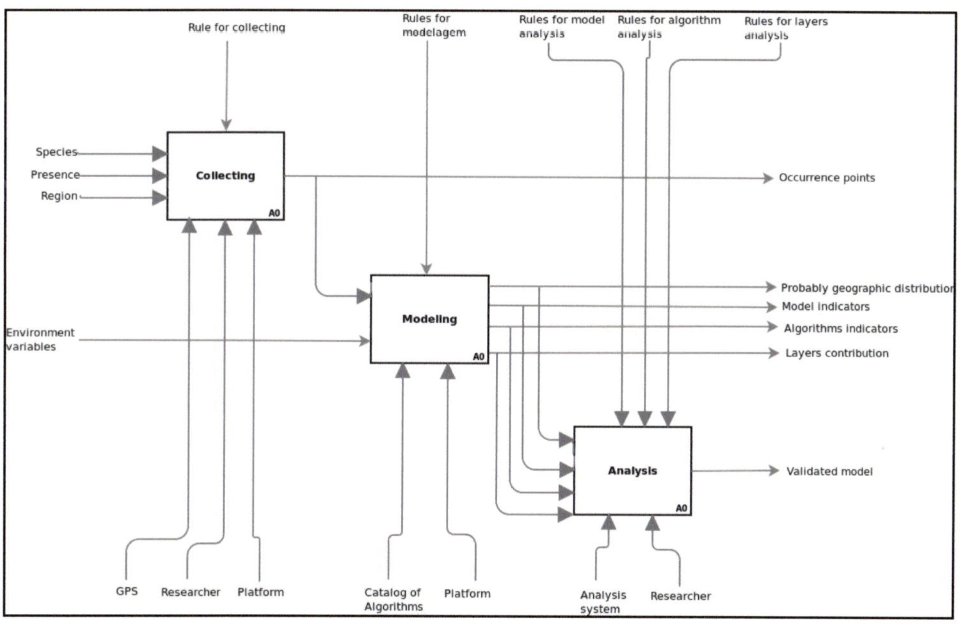

Fig. 2. IDEF0 diagram for modeling process.

The collecting can be separated into another process which follows the steps below:

1. Selecting the area to be studied: This is the stage where it determines the area used to collecting. The species is used as one of the inputs for this phase due to the fact that a species is usually found historically in a particular geographic region (Philips et al., 2006). This region can be, for example, the Amazon region or throughout Australia.
2. Choosing the spatial resolution: Spatial resolution is the scale used for the collection. This is an important step that needs to be emphasized. The choice of resolution can influence the model interpretation, since some patterns can occur in a given resolution, but on another scale may not be noticeable (Guisan&Thuiller, 2005). There are some techniques that help identify the best resolution to use in modelling as in Isaaks and Srivastava (Isaaks&Srivastava, 1989), which suggests the use of variograms to determine the sampling interval.
3. Restore occurrences in other data bases: It is about getting the data of the occurrence from other sources such as museums, zoos and environmental agencies. There are some entities that maintain a database with large numbers of environmental collections such as IABIN/PTN, GBIF, and Ornis.
4. Determination of observation points: Determine how many and where the points are positioned to observe the species. Based on the chosen spatial resolution and the known occurrence points, is intended to promote the best possible distribution of these points.
5. Determining the time of collection: It is the strategy to turn into a more efficient observation. Some species are nocturnal and others diurnal, and some climatic conditions affect these habits as intense heat, etc. Thus, it is necessary to determine these times.
6. Observation: In this phase, techniques are applied to the census of the species studied. These techniques aim to check both the presence and absence. The absence (or record scratch as it is called) (Engler&Rechsteiner, 2004)is a prominent factor due to the difficulty in obtaining such data (Philips et al., 2006). Depending on the species it can be used, for example, recorders that play back the sound of the female or male to attract a species that is in the region, as in Sohn(2009). It is also necessary to determine the time it will make the observation and the number of attempts.
7. Registration: The presence or absence data is stored electronically. Basically each record contains the following information: listener identification, latitude, longitude, type of observation (sighting, nest location, hearing, etc.) and registration date. Among these, the latitude and longitude are the ones that deserve greater emphasis. It uses a GPS to get these coordinates.

3. Architecture propose

With the modelling and collection processes being understood, an architecture can be elaborated to solve the problem described above. Here, it will be proposed and specified an architecture of a mobile system applied to species distribution modelling.

The architecture requires a generic basis to be used on any mobile application that needs to perform the species distributions modelling. Furthermore, it should also be able to adapt to constant changes in this area, such as allowing the use of new algorithms and data formats. Thus, the SOC paradigm is quite appropriate, and for this reason, this paper presents an SOA solution.

Basically, the process described in ANDREI, et al. (Andrei et al., 2004) was followed, which describes one for designing a service-oriented architecture, which combines the standards for e-business and concepts of service-oriented computing to solve problems encountered in industry. The steps are shown below:

1. Domain decomposition
2. Goal service-model creation
3. Subsystem analysis
4. Service allocation
5. Component specification
6. Structure enterprise components using patterns
7. Technology realization mapping

The steps above will be discussed on next sessions, except the steps 5 and 6. The step 5 will be performed on steps 1 and 3, while the step 6 suggests the use of standard IBM runtime, which are not applied to the pattern of collaboration.

3.1 Domain decomposition

From a business point of view, the domain consists on a series of functional areas. For this case one can observe two main areas: the system of collecting and modelling, as shown in Figure 3.

Fig. 3. IDEF0 diagram for modelling process.

For these functional areas, the following use cases can be identified, in general:

- UC1: Collect presence and absence data
- UC2: Create view for localization
- UC3: Create model
- UC4: View model

On Figure 4 is shown the use case diagram for this system.

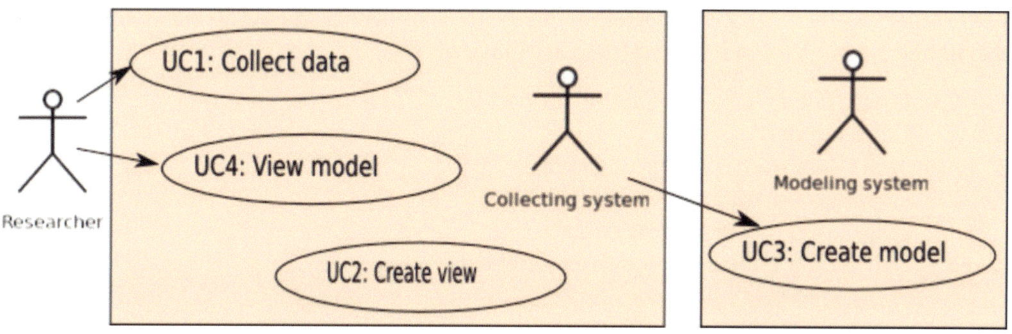

Fig. 4. Business use case diagram.

This business use cases are strong candidates for business services that will be exposed.

Once the business use cases are defined it is necessary to define the inputs and outputs of each service. As the project continues to be developed, the functional areas that were identified will be directed to a subsystem. It can be explained with the fact that the areas are a business sense, while subsystems are technology notions.

For each step described by ANDREI (Andrei et al., 2004), a set of IBM corresponding patterns are applied. Basically, these standards are divided into four parts: the highest standards, the application standards, runtime patterns and Product mappings.

This step will apply the highest standards. It is necessary to choose the pattern that best fits the system proposed on this paper. Since this system needs to provide an interaction among researchers from the field data collection and from other areas, the standard chosen was the Collaboration. Their application to the system proposed in this work can be seen in Figure 5.

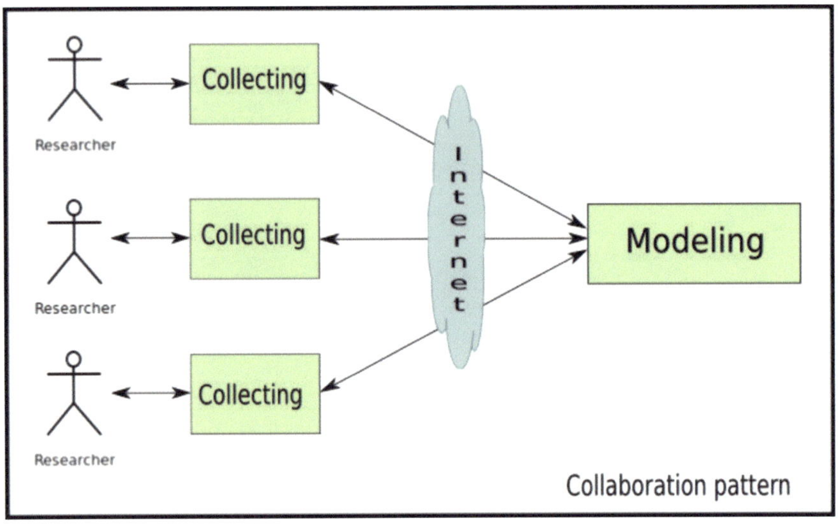

Fig. 5. Collaboration business pattern diagram.

3.2 Goal service-model creation

This second step is to create a model to identify how the services identified are complete with respect to the business. The following is the goal-service model in a nested notation, the mobile system for modeling species distribution:

1. Create accurate species distribution model
   a. Create model
2. Aggregate data from distributed teams
3. Collect data in an automated way
   a. Collect presence and absence data
   b. Provide a friendly interaction experience

      Manage project

      Generate view for localization

      View model

In this model the objectives are shown in regular text, service in italics and other necessary services that were not discovered during domain decomposition are shown in bold. It is observed that the services meet the main objectives of such system. At this stage it was also possible to identify a new service: managing the project. With this the user can add a new project for the species they are studying.

3.3 Subsystem analysis

At this stage of architectural design, business use cases are refined into system use cases. The subsystems are composed by business components and technical components.

High-level business use cases that have been identified in previous steps will be part of the subsystem components interface. The subsystems identified are Modelling and Collecting. The collecting subsystem is responsible for providing to the researcher the tools needed to create a species distribution model. The modelling subsystem is responsible for generating the model based on data provided by the collection subsystem. The components are shown in Figure 6.

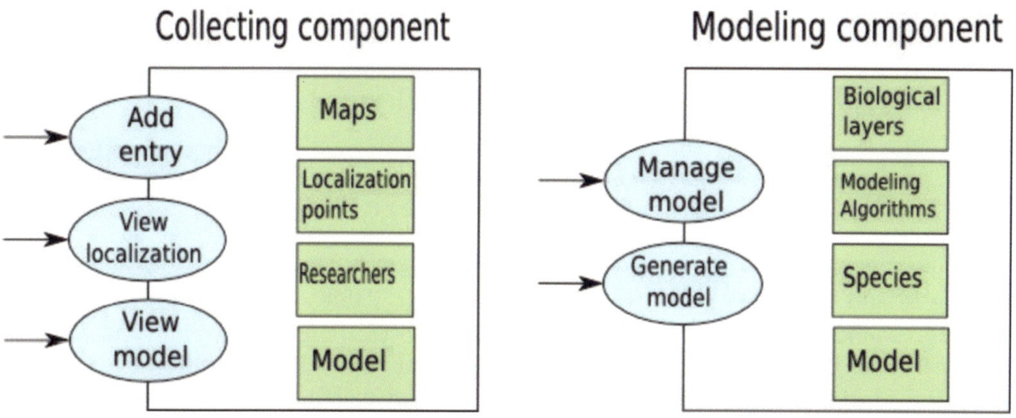

Fig. 6. Collect and Modelling components.

Based on this analysis the services below were identified:

- Localization service: Responsible for providing GPS data (latitude, longitude, altitude and so on).
- Maps service: Provides maps to be viewed on the mobile device. The answers are made in terms of small tiles of defined size. It means the service provides small sections of the map that the client wants. This service is responsible for storing maps to view offline. Provides both maps with satellite imagery, maps and biological layers.
- Occurrence points service: Provides an interface to store the presence or absence points by species.
- Species distribution modelling service: It is used to request the generation of the model for the desired species. In the case of mobile device, this service uses other remote services to generate the model.

The Figure 7 shows the IBM patterns applied to structure these services.

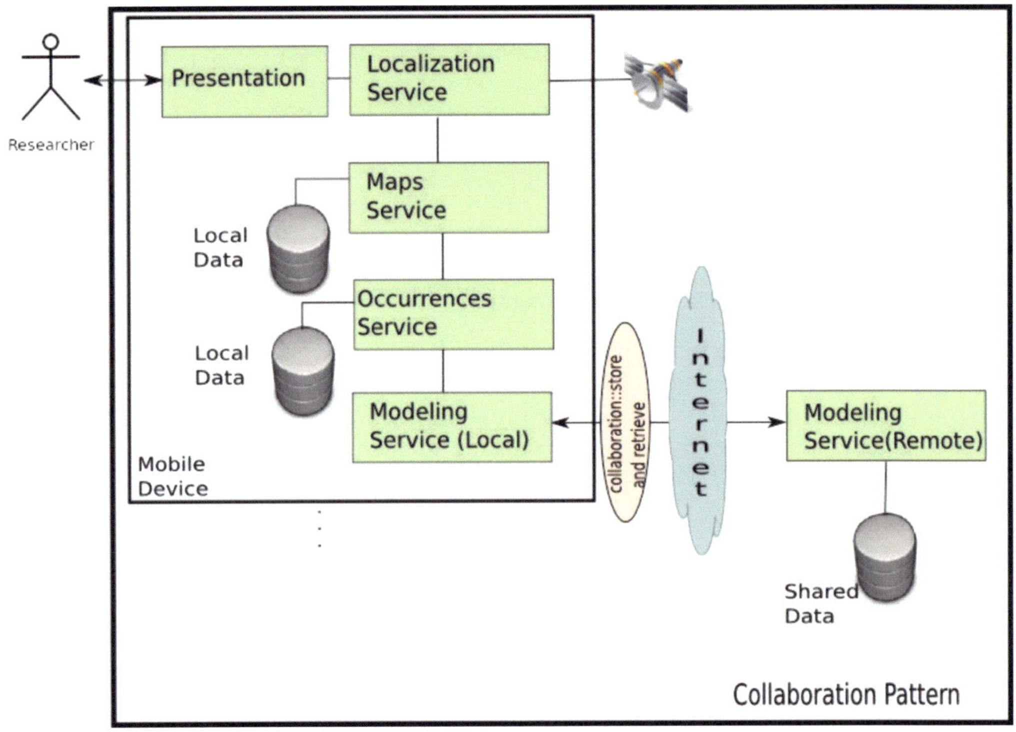

Fig. 7. Architecture with patterns applied and services for collaboration.

The type of collaboration that is used in this system is asynchronous, due to researchers only be able to add their data when there is a network available. According to the standard business collaboration of IBM, there are two types of application pattern: Store and Retrieve and Real-time. This system will use the first one, Collaboration:Store and Retrieve, because it meets the fact that the data does not need to be made available in real time.

This application pattern is further divided into two lines: community and directed. The first is used when data is available for a group of independent users who work together in some common interest. The second is used when data are available for a specific person or a closed and known group. The second one will be used due to, in certain cases, the presence data of some species should be kept in a secure and restricted access.

3.4 Service allocation

The purpose of this step is to ensure that all services will be hosted in a specific place and they all return a business value. The service allocation comes to who (what component) will provide and manage the implementation of each service.

For the proposed system all services will be available on mobile devices to be used by any application. Only the modelling service will be available on an external server with more processing power, however, there will be a customer-service model that will interface with this external service.

The main local services offer the following public interface:

- Location: Implement an easy way to retrieve the geolocation data. Abstracts the use of hardware resources so they are high level and simple. Simply, have the following methods: getLongitude, getLatitude, getAltitude.
- Maps: Service that provides maps to be displayed in applications. It also stores the maps when the device is online. It provides both satellite maps at various scales and biological layers. Provides through tiles (small parts of the map) to be lighter for the mobile device. Main methods are: getTile, and getLayerlistLayer. It also has some signs to notify the applications that are connected to them, such as the signal newLayerDownloaded.
- SpeciesDistributionModel Service: Provides an interface for any application to generate a species distribution model. This service is the one that connects the remote services to building the model, since it is not generated locally. If different models for the project registration in service. It also accesses other local service, which provides the points of presence and absence of a species to feed the model. Its main methods are: registerProject, getModel, addPresencePoints, addAbsentPoints, removePresencePoints, removeAbsentPoints, addServer, addLayer, removeLayer.
- Occurrence Points Service: responsible for storing the points of presence and absence of species. Main methods are: registerSpecies, add (bool presence, speciesId, location), remove (bool presence, speciesId, location).

3.5 Technology realization mapping

In this step, the technology used to implement the system will be specified. This technology can change according to other implementations.

On the server side, the services were implemented in C++, used as a CGI application that runs as a server in Apache Web Server. The interface is provided using SOAP (it could be another lightweight patterns). The library used to provide and manipulate data to generate a predictive species model is the Openmodeller running on a Linux machine.

The client side is an application developed in Python and uses the Qt graphics library, specifically the component QML (QtMarkup Language), which allows the creation of complex graphical interfaces using multiple facilitators to the developer. For the integration between Python and Qt, the library for python PySide was used, which lets the Qt Library be used, that is in C++, through Python. Another important library to be mentioned here is the QtMobility, which allows access to device resources such as access to the network card, GPS device, battery information, among others.

The services are registered on the client side services framework in Qt Mobility. These services are exported and available to use in any application, thus enabling its use by third-party applications. Once it uses only libraries provided by the Qt framework and the Qt Mobility, these services can run on any mobile or desktop device supported by the framework. Each service uses an XML that is used to register it as shown below:

```
<?xml version="1.0" encoding="utf-8" ?>
<SFW version="1.1">
<service>
<name>SpeciesDistributionModel</name>
<filepath>species_distribution_model</filepath>
```

```
<description>This service provides an easy way to load and generates an species distribution model, based on some location data.</description>
<interface>
<name>org.usp.sdmm.SpeciesDistributionModel</name>
<version>0.1</version>
<description>Interface to generate a species distribution modeling.</description>
</interface>
</service>
</SFW>
```

4. Client prototype

Below we present some features of the proposed system. The case study of the system has been performed in Amazonas state in partnership with National Institute for Researches of Amazon (INPA) (INPA, 2010).

4.1 The system importance

The usage of mobile phones for performing data gathering offers the following benefits to collecting and modelling ecological niche distribution:

- Collection automation: A user needs to select only a button on the geographic interface to identify a point of presence or absence of a species. Automatically the system calculates geographic coordination through GPS (Global Positioning System) and stores that data. The user will not have to take notes in other sources or electronic spreadsheet. This also guarantees reliability on the collected data.
- Accompanying changes in the model: With this system it is possible to follow the mobile phone through the model evolution and extent. More data can be added, including data from other field researchers.
- Better use of a researcher's distribution: With the simplification of the system more areas can be analysed by researchers. The researcher can work looking for species in different areas and still transfer data to all other researchers to access.
- Convenience: The mobile device is more compact thereby reducing the number of devices necessary to conduct the research.
- Usability: A more friendly and intuitive interface will be proposed in this document. With this system the user will gain some other facilities to perform data collection such as selecting only one button on the graphic interface to identify the presence or absence of species.
- Faster GPS in regions with GSM (Global System for Mobile Communications) networks: Modern phones do not use the traditional geo positioning system, but the Assisted GPS (A-GPS). It is a system that uses a server for helping to minimize the Time To First Fix (TTFF) and improving the robustness of the positioning. The accuracy of location is less than 3.1 meters and the TTFF are less than 5 seconds, working even in situation of critical satellite signs (Schreiner, 2007). The A-GPS uses any available networks such as the GSM network of the operator or even a wireless network in urban areas. This type of technology use case is important for species modelling which live in urban environments, such as rats and mosquitoes for example, when identifying possible diseases routs (Santana et al., 2008).

4.2 Technical restrictions

There are two main technical restrictions for the proposed system. They are:

- Network availability: One of the biggest challenges this project faces is the issue of communication between the cellular and the service provider. Most use cases for a system such as this involve communication networks with intermittent network access so the system shall work most of the time in off-line mode. The main objective of the application is automating the data collected and sending to the server. However it is not intended that data collection occurs at the point of collection, but as soon as there is an available network. Working in off-line mode, the application will be able to store the current coordinates, show saved models and analyse these models.
- Processing power of the devices: The predictive modelling of the species distribution requires high performance computing (Santana et al., 2008). The generation of a model can take between hours and days to prepare.

4.3 Business restriction

This type of research in Brazil needs to comply on some rules concerning the transfer of biodiversity data. This data needs, in many cases, to be kept secret. These measures are necessary for environmental property protection.

This kind of concern is important for Brazil, since 20% of the total number of species on the planet is in it. In august of 2009 the Ministry of Science and Technology published 'the concierge 693' which standardizes the manipulation and distribution of research data about biodiversity. This concierge makes the following observations:

- Management and authorship of data must be published.
- Usage condition and the access to data must be protected in the database.

4.4 Usability

The system needs to have easy browsing, be intuitive and have few steps necessary for performing tasks. The kind of device that is being proposed for use is a Smart phone, which has a limited screen size. It means that the icons need to be arranged in such to be very easy to use. Figure 1 shows the screen of this tool's main menu in a mobile device.

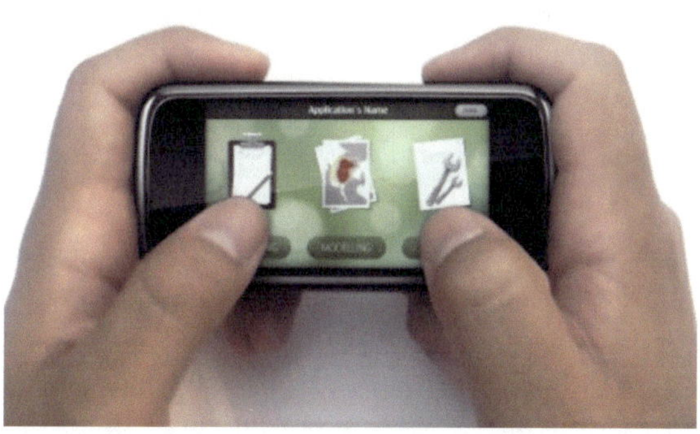

Fig. 8. Main Menu in a mobile device demonstrating the usability with the thumbs.

This interface shows how efficient it is for small devices that have touch screens. Usage of the thumbs allows more comfortable experience. Figure 2 shows the initial activities with the screens skeleton flowchart.

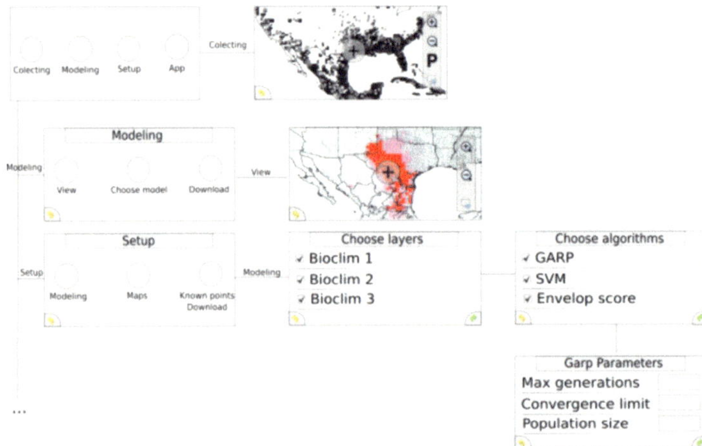

Fig. 9. Flowchart for some screens of the system.

5. Conclusion

This section presents the conclusions and final considerations based on the topics discussed in this chapter.

This article presented an architecture based on services to data collecting applied on species distribution modelling using mobile systems. In order to define the architecture, first of all, a follow up was made with researchers of the INPA Brazilian institute and it was based on real case. This phase made possible the process formalization for modelling and collecting data using IDEF0 diagrams. Based on this diagram, we can identify the collecting step really needs automation due to a lot of manual work.

Also, architecture was proposed. It uses a Service Oriented Architecture approach for mobile systems. This architecture is out to be satisfactory for species distribution modelling, since the data resources are by nature distributed. For the devices, an advantage using SOA is the ability for several applications to collaborate securely in collect and model species data. But, on the other hand the use of some standards in communication with the services can be expensive, as the patterns that use XML, which parser can be really expensive

This architecture can be used both to collect data for species distribution modelling, as for similar mobile systems. It is also due to the characteristics of SOA, as services decoupling.

Finally, was modelled a prototype for the application which takes under consideration a friendly user interaction. This prototype is simple to be used in field and reliable for the biological data. It proved very satisfactory to data collecting and generating models that can be used during the collecting phase. Another feature for this architecture is the collaboration that allows users from many sources share environmental data. One of the cons of this prototype is that the features are only basics, and it is necessary to add more features.

This area still has many computational challenges and they can become in future works. During this research it was identified some of those challenges. One of them is to use augmented reality and sensors network to improve the data collecting. Using the sensor networks is possible to identify the species while it is possible to use a mobile phone with a camera and using augmented reality to help the user to find the points and restore some data from the sensor.

6. References

Austin, M. P. (2002). Spatial prediction of species distribuition: an interface between ecological theory and statistical modelling, In:. Ecological modelling Elsevier , pp. 101-118.

Andrei, M., Ang, J., Arsanjani, A., Chua, S., Comte, P., Krogdahl, P., et al. (2004). Patterns: Service-oriented architecture and web services (1fs Edition ed.). New York: IBM WebSphere.

Bazzaz, F. A. (1998). Plants in changing environments: Linking physiological population, am community ecology. Am community ecology .

Engler, R., & Rechsteiner, L. (2004). An improved approach for predicting the distribution of rare and endangered species from occurrence and pseudo-absense data. Journal of Applied Ecology , 41 (2), 263-274.

Guisan, A., & Zimmermann, N. E. (2000). Predictive habitat distribution models in ecology. Ecological modeling , pp. 147-186.

Guisan, A., & Thuiller, W. (2005). Predicting species distribution: offering more than simple habitat models. Ecology Letters , 8 (9), 993-1009.

Hutchinson, G. E. (1957). Concluding remarks. Cold Spring Harbor Symposia on Quantitative Biology , pp. 415-427.

Isaaks, E. H., & Srivastava, R. M. (1989). Applied Geostatistics (2 ed.). Oxford, Oxford: University Press.

Iwashita, F. (2008). Sensibilidade de modelos de distribuição de espécies a erros de posicionamento de dados de coleta.

Malanson, G. P., Westman, W. E., & Yan, Y.-L. (1992). Realized versus fundamental niche functions in a model of chaparral response to climatic change. Ecological Modelling [ECOL. MODEL.] , 64 (4), pp. 261-277.

Peterson, A. T. (2001). Predicting species geographic distributions based on ecological niche modeling. Cooper Ornithological Society .

Peterson, A. T., Sánchez-Cordero, V., Soberón, J., Bartley, J., Buddemeier, R. W., & Navarro-Sigüenza, A. G. (2001). Effects of global climage change on geographic distributions of Mexican Cracidae. Ecological modelling , 21-30.

Philips, S. J., Anderson, R. P., & Schapire, R. E. (2006). Maximum entropy modeling of species geographic distributions. Ecological Modelling , 190 (3-4), 231-259.

Santana, F. S., Siqueira, M. F., Saraiva, A. M., & Correa, P. L. (2008). A reference business process for ecological niche modelling. Ecological informatics 3 , 75-86.

SCHREINER, K. (2007). Where We At? Mobile Phones Bring GPS to the Masses. IEEE Computer Graphics and Applications , 27, 6-11.

Soberón, J., & Peterson, A. T. (2005). Interpretation of models of fundamental ecological niches and species' distributional areas. p. 10.

Sohn, N. (2009). Distribuição provável, uso de hábitat e estimativas populacionais do galo-da-serra (Rupicola rupicola) com recomendações para sua conservação. Universidade Federal do Amazonas.

7

World Modeling for Autonomous Systems

Andrey Belkin[1], Achim Kuwertz[1], Yvonne Fischer[1] and Jürgen Beyerer[1,2]
[1]*Karlsruhe Institute of Technology (KIT), Institute for Anthropomatics (IFA), Vision and Fusion Laboratory (IES)*
[2]*Fraunhofer Institute of Optronics, System Technologies and Image Exploitation (IOSB)*
Germany

1. Introduction

Since ancient times mankind is building tools for facilitating survival and work. With time, the tools became complex and exquisite and even obtained consciousness and limited reasoning. The recent developments in computing and robotics led to creation of intelligent systems that are autonomous. The purpose of such *autonomous systems* is to function in different environments stand-alone according to some predefined strategy, e.g. protecting some areas or rescuing people in hazards. The intelligent autonomous systems were defined within the *IBM Autonomic Computing Initiative* in IBM (2001), Kephart & Chess (2003) with the following required abilities:

- *Self-Configuration* – ability to configure and reconfigure itself under internal and external changes;
- *Self-Optimization* – ability to optimize its working;
- *Self-Healing* – ability to discover and correct faults;
- *Self-Protection* – ability to identify and protect itself;
- *Self-Awareness* – ability to know its components, current status, ultimate capacity and connections to other systems;
- *Environment-Awareness* – ability to perceive and know the surrounding environment and context.

An operation of intelligent autonomous systems requires handling of *reactive* and *proactive* activities. The reactive behavior is required for immediate reactions on changes, such as bipedal locomotion balancing, avoiding direct hazards or grasping deformable items. The proactive analysis is required to perform planning and sophisticated decision making, e.g. helping people in a household. Such activities imply so-called constant *situation awareness* that demands perception of changes in the surrounding environment, comprehension of their meaning and projection of their status in the future as defined in Endsley (1995).

In practice, reactive and proactive handling involves complex information acquisition, processing and management. An example of a complete information workflow is presented in Fig. 1. At the beginning, a (heterogeneous) sensors system acquires data from the surrounding environment, called *world of interest* (WoI). The gathered data concerns WoI *entities*: topology features, things, persons, and relations. This data is processed by sophisticated extraction

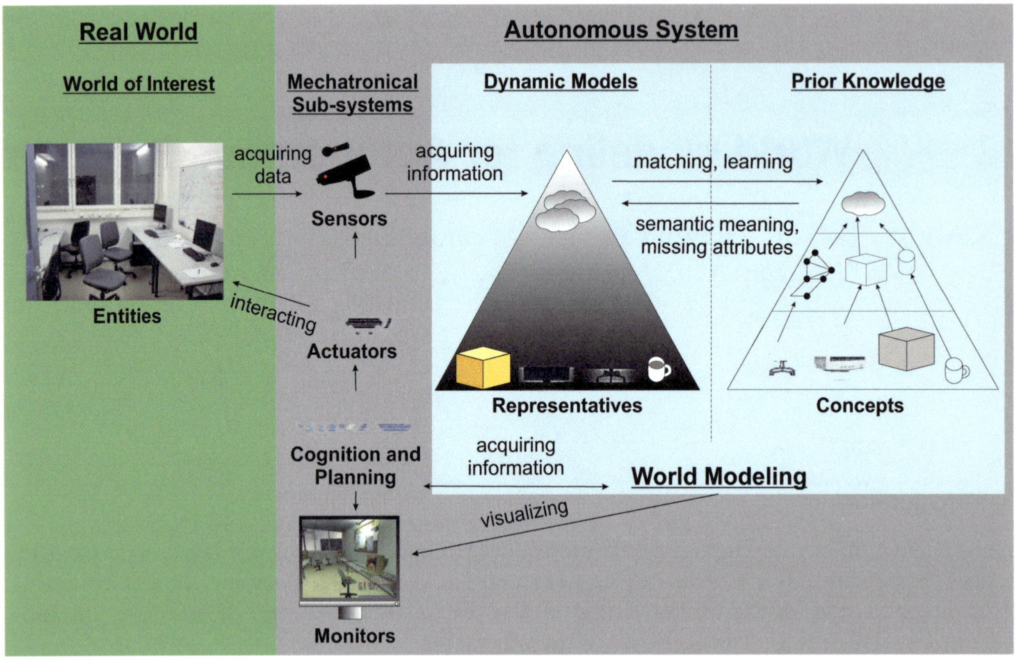

Fig. 1. Information workflow of autonomous systems.

methods in order to obtain as much information about the surrounding environment as possible and then fuse into *dynamic models* within the world modeling system. The world modeling system contains the knowledge about the environment and the autonomous system itself, necessary for the expected autonomous operation, and serves as a global information hub for all mechatronic sub-systems. The dynamic models contain up-to-date description of the WoI, expressing each real-world entity with virtual *representative*. Since such descriptions are created from sensory information, they lack semantic meaning and pre-defined characteristics expected for their type. In order to gain missing semantics and attributes, each representative can be matched and assigned to *prior knowledge concepts*. The content of the world modeling system is available to other mechatronic sub-systems, as, for example, monitors or cognition and planning modules. Based on the world modeling information cognition and planning modules assess the present situation and future states, make decisions and compound plans about future actions. These actions are then performed by actuators that interact with the world of interest. In the case of repeating properties or dependencies, the autonomous system can find out common patterns and try to extend the prior knowledge. The extension of prior knowledge is performed for automatic recognition of previously detected patterns and more efficient environment description. For this, a balance between description length of concepts and description length of dynamic models given prior concepts has to be empirically found.

The world modeling system serves as a virtual demonstrative model of the environment for the whole autonomous system. In order to perform efficiently, its following features are to be considered:

- Slim *symbolic representation* of the environment information;
- *Gathering station* for all the acquired information;

- *Interpretability* for humans and machines;
- *Object-orientedness;*
- Universal *probabilistic uncertainty handling;*
- Common *information hub* for all autonomous system components;
- Handling of *unknown objects;*
- Extensible concepts under *Open World* assumption.

More detailed operation of world modeling system is presented in the following sections: the Section 2 describes the relation between the environment and the autonomous system and defines the modeling domains. The Section 3 covers main aspects of fusing sensory information within the world modeling system. The detailed discussion of the world modeling system, including the mathematical concepts of parameter estimations is given in Section 4. Methods for autonomous prior knowledge extension are highlighted in Section 5. Some examples of practical realization of the described architecture and methods are given in Section 6 followed by conclusion and outlook.

2. Domains of the world modeling

During the operation of autonomous systems that have to make decisions, the process of acquiring and interpreting information from the environment forms the basis for the state of knowledge of such systems. As defined in Endsley (1995), this process is known as situation assessment. In today's autonomous systems, situation assessment is highly supported through various heterogeneous sensors and appropriate signal processing methods for extracting as much information as possible about the surveyed environment and its elements. Theories and methods of multi-sensor data fusion, e.g., as described in Hall & McMullen (2004), offer a powerful technique for combining information from different sources. The object-oriented world model (OOWM) is an approach to represent relevant information extracted from the sensor signals, fused into a single comprehensive, dynamic model of the monitored area. Bauer et al. (2009) developed a data fusion architecture based on the JDL (Joint Directors of Laboratories) data fusion process model, see Steinberg et al. (1999). An application of the OOWM for wide area maritime surveillance is presented in Fischer & Bauer (2010). Another application is to provide humanoid robots with a memory structure based on a complete Bayesian network, see for example Baum et al. (2010) or Belkin (2009).

However, the challenge of intelligent systems that act in an autonomous way is not only to collect as much sensor data as possible, but also to detect and assess complex situations that evolve over time. First ideas of modeling higher level entities like situations have been presented in Fischer et al. (2011). For the situation assessment process, probabilistic methods like hidden Markov models can be used (see Meyer-Delius et al. (2009)), but they are strongly dependent on training data. In Gheţa et al. (2010), a Bayesian method for the association of observations to objects is presented, and in Glinton et al. (2006), Markov random fields are used to model contextual relationships and maximum a posteriori labeling is used to infer intentions of the observed entities. In this section, we will clarify the separation of the real world and the world model represented in the system and introduce the concepts of objects, scenes, relations, and situations, which are necessary for the internal representation of the observed entities in the environment.

2.1 Information flow in autonomous systems

In applications where autonomous systems are used, a spatio-temporal section of the real world, the so-called world of interest. The general information flow inside such systems is visualized in Fig. 2, in which information aggregates, i.e. the stores of several information, are represented by boxes and processes are represented by circles. The information flow is as follows. The world of interest consists of entities and can be observed by sensors. Sensor systems can be of extremely heterogeneous types, e.g., video or infrared cameras, radar equipment, or RFID-chips. Even human beings can act as a sensor by observing entities of the real world. Observing the real world with sensors results in *sensor data*, for example a radar image or a video stream. Sensor data is then analyzed by means of existing knowledge and the resulting information is passed to the world model. The existing knowledge contains all information that is necessary for analyzing sensor data, for example specific methods and algorithms used for the detection and localization of people in video streams.

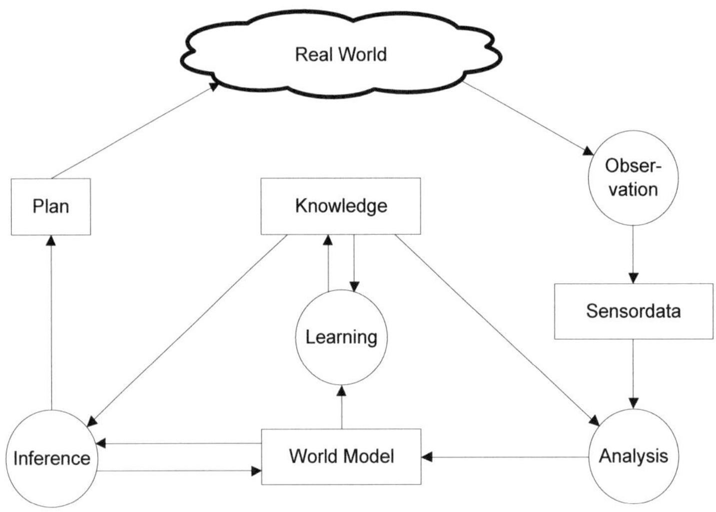

Fig. 2. General information flow in autonomous systems represented by information aggregates *(boxes)* and processes *(circles)*.

The *world model* is a representation of entities from the world of interest and contains representatives. Every representative has a corresponding entity in the real world. The mapping between entities in the world of interest and representatives in the world model is structure-preserving and can therefore be interpreted as a homomorphism. Specific mappings are termed as concepts and are part of the knowledge. Concepts are defined at several levels of abstraction, e.g., there are concepts for objects, scenes, relations, and situations. Concepts are used for example in the analyzing process by defining how an observed person is represented in the world model. As the world of interest is highly dynamic and changes over time, the history of the representatives is also stored in the world model. However, entities are not always directly observable. For example the intention of a person could also be an entity and be represented in the world model. As some entities cannot be observed directly, an inference process is reasoning about unobservable (and also unobserved) entities by means of knowledge. Therefore, the world model is always being updated and supplemented with new information by the inference process.

Summing up, knowledge contains all the information necessary for analyzing sensor data, updating the world model and supplementing it with new information. Concepts are used to describe the possible real-world entities in the world model. Characteristics of knowledge are of course extremely dependent on the application domain. Additionally, knowledge is not static. The content of the world model can be used for acquiring new knowledge by a learning process, for example structure or parameter learning in graphical models.

To close the loop of the information flow, the result of an inference process can also include a *plan*, of how to act further in the real world. This could be an action plan for an agent, e.g., to call the police, or a sensor management plan, e.g., a request for more detailed information from a specific sensor.

2.2 Concepts for world modeling

We will now introduce the concepts for objects, scenes, relations, and situations. The concept of an *object* is defined as a physical entity of the real world. An object can be (spatially) movable (e.g., a person) or stationary (e.g., a room). An object has several attributes, which can be divided into properties and states. Properties are time-invariant attributes, for example the height or the name of a person. State values can change over time and are therefore time-variant, for example the position or the velocity of a person. The representation of an object in the world model includes not only observed attributes, but also inferred ones. For example, the velocity can be inferred based on observed positions of a person. Furthermore, attribute values can be quantitative or qualitative. For example, the absolute position and the velocity of a person are quantitative attributes, and the attribute value that a person is smiling is a symbolic one.

By the concept of a *scene*, we define all observed and inferred object information at a point in time. A scene can therefore be interpreted as a time-slice, consisting of all objects and their attributes. To include the time aspect, we also speak of a sequence of scenes, when the scenes are considered at several discrete points in time. However, a scene does not include any type of relations. The concepts of a scene and a sequence of scenes are visualized in Fig. 3. By the concept of *relations*, we mean a statement about dependences between at least two different attribute values of one or more objects. Relational values can also be quantitative, e.g., the distance of two objects, or they can be qualitative, e.g., two objects are close to each other. Mostly, relational values are inferred, but some can also be observed, e.g., a distance measured by a laser. A relation can also exist between representatives of the same object in different scenes, e.g., the distance an object has covered between the two scenes.

The concept of a *situation* is defined only on the symbolic level. Thus, they have a higher level of abstraction, but the level of detail of the quantitative attribute values of objects and relations is getting lost. Situations are therefore characterized by symbolic attribute values. The simplest situation is a symbolic attribute value of an object, e.g., a person is smiling. There are also situations, which can only be inferred by observing the real world over a period of time, e.g., a person is dancing or two persons have a conversation. And, of course, situations can be inferred from other situations, e.g., if some persons are dancing and some persons are drinking beer, the inferred situation could be that there is a party going on. Although situations are also characterized by the information collected over a period of time

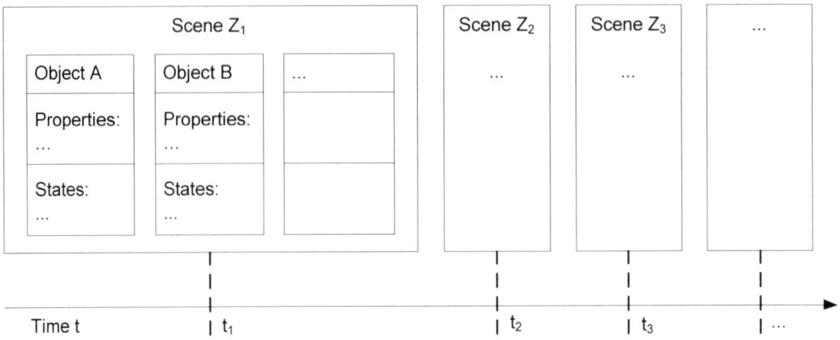

Fig. 3. The concepts of a scene and a sequence of scenes.

they only exist at a point in time. Their existence in the next time-point has to be verified again. However, the earlier existence and also the collection of further evidence over time can support the existence of a situation in the future. The concepts of a relation and a situation are visualized in Fig. 4.

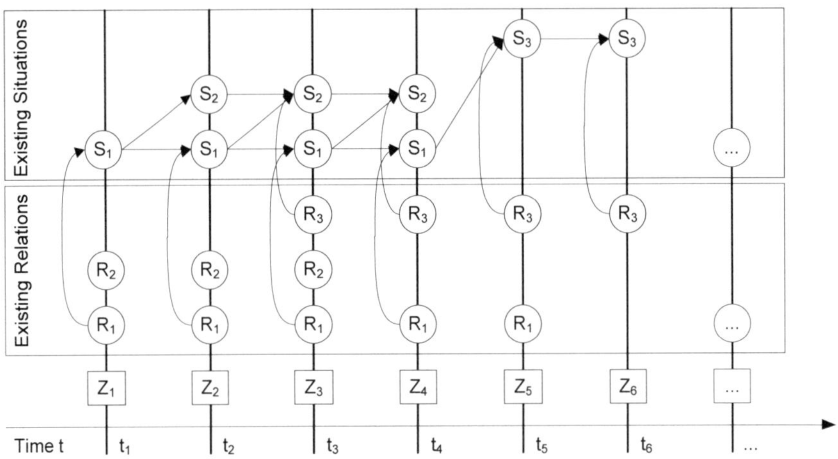

Fig. 4. The concepts of a relation and a situation.

3. Information fusion

An autonomous system perceives the surrounding environment with sensors. The acquired data are processed, analyzed and passed to a world modeling system, which contains a description of the current state of the environment. The new sensory information is fused into the existing environment description by matching and updating relevant representatives in the model. Since information from sensors contains uncertainty, this information matching and description update is not trivial. Before constructing such mechanisms, a suitable information and uncertainty representation has to be defined.

3.1 Information representation

There are many ways to represent information in the context of world modeling (see Belkin (2009)). The simplest way is to describe each parameter with a single numerical value (e.g. "*36.65*") or a fact value (e.g. "*Dog*"). However, this method does not reflect uncertainties, emerging from measurements always limited by sensor acceptance and efficiency. Accounting for uncertainty (e.g. keeping error values) allows for a more faithful representation of measured values. The next level of generalization of the information representation accounts for relations between parameters. The uncertainty, however, can be represented more accurately with probability distributions over possible values, e.g. by means of *Degree-of-Belief* (DoB). In the Fig. 5, there is a typical temperature DoB distribution of an object. The parameter relations can be incorporated into distributions by joint DoBs for groups of correlated attributes (e.g. joint DoB of type and temperature). In this case, the DoB combines discrete and continuous distributions into one common frame. The most general level of the information representation is then the joint DoB distribution for all modeling attributes that typically has combinatorially growing complexity and computational costs. The generalization hierarchy is shown in Fig. 6.

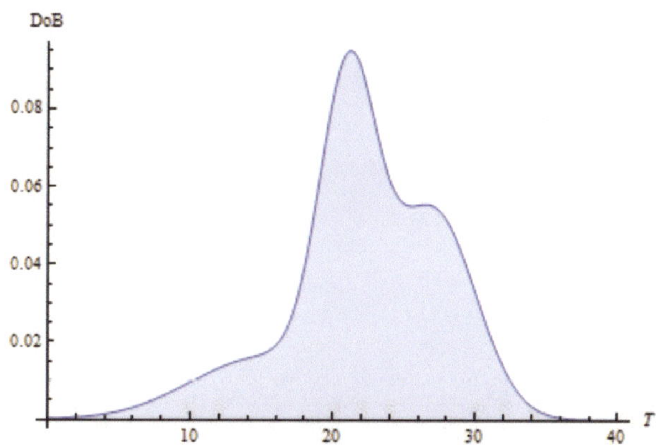

Fig. 5. A Degree-of-Belief distribution for the attribute "temperature".

3.2 Information life cycle

The sensory information has to be fused into the world model in order to update the current environment description. When a new entity is observed in the environment, a corresponding representative has to be created in the dynamic model. This can be achieved by the calculation of the posterior probability that from one hand a new entity has been observed at some time step and the other hand the observed entity exists, exceeding some *instantiation threshold*. If the entity is already present in the model with a representative, the new information is merged into the existing description by means of Bayesian fusion, raising the existence probability. In the absence of new measurements related to an entity, the aging mechanism changes the DoB distributions according to the *maximum entropy principle*, i.e. the uncertainty of the information increases. In particular, the uncertainty increase leads to the existence probability reduction. If the existence probability falls below some *reconfirmation threshold*, the world modeling system signals the need to re-observe the entity. The representative is deleted from the model, if the maximum of the DoB distribution for the existence goes below the *deletion threshold*, in order

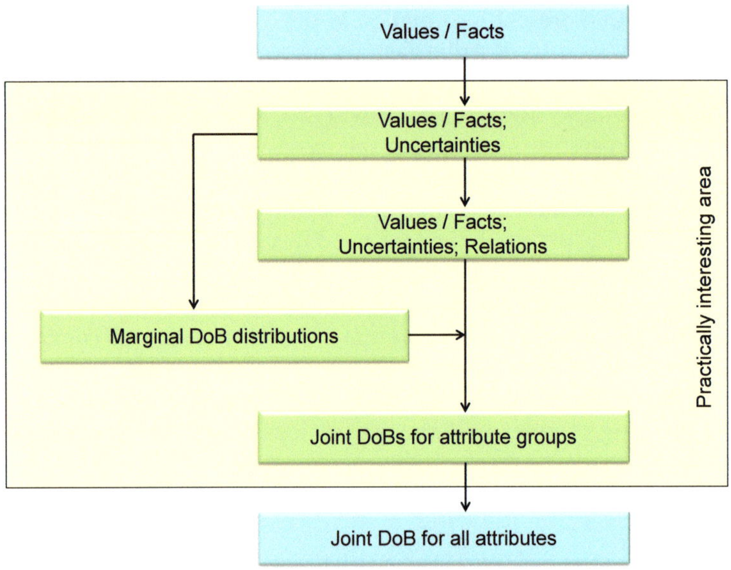

Fig. 6. The hierarchy of generalizing the representation of values.

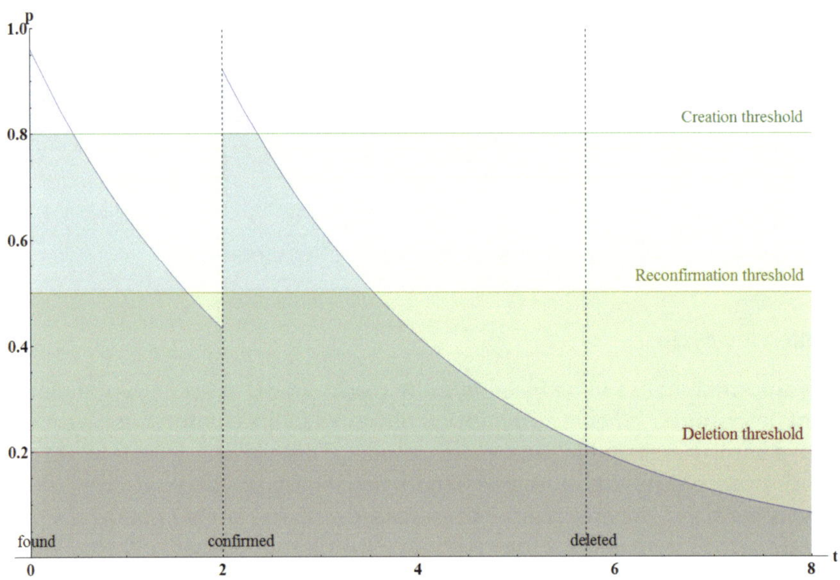

Fig. 7. An example of the existence probability life cycle.

to reduce the computational complexity of the whole model. The aging mechanism can be applied *on demand*: the existence probability of a representative is calculated as soon as the representative is requested by the system. The existence probability life cycle is presented in Fig. 7.

3.3 Bayesian framework

The management of the information life cycle requires the formal definition of observations, a mechanism to associate observations to representatives, and procedures to information update. Such a formal description is developed within the *Bayesian framework* presented briefly below and is given in details in Belkin (2010), Baum et al. (2010).

A modeled entity i at time step k is represented as a DoB distribution $p(e_k^i, \underline{a}_k^i)$, where $e_k^i \in \{0,1\}$ denotes whether the entity i exists and $\underline{a}_k^i := \begin{bmatrix} a_k^{i,1} & \dots & a_k^{i,n_a} \end{bmatrix}^{\mathrm{T}}$ denotes the vector of n_a descriptive attributes.

The fusion of an observation into the world model requires some *observation model*, which connects observations to representatives on some probabilistic basis. This connection can be described with the connection probability $p(d_k|\underline{e}_k)$, where $d_k \in \{0,1\dots,N_k\}$ denotes the representative, N_k is the number of representatives, and $\underline{e}_k := \left[e_k^1, \dots, e_k^{N_k}\right]^{\mathrm{T}}$.

The observation vector can be written as $\underline{y}_k^i := \left[\underline{y}_k^{i,1}, \dots, \underline{y}_k^{i,n_y}\right]^{\mathrm{T}}$ composed of observations for each given attribute (totally n_y).

After the association of observations, the existing description is updated in *the prediction and the update steps*. The prediction step propagates representatives from the time point $k-1$ to k, resulting in the predicted existence $p(e_k^i = 1|\hat{\underline{y}}_{1:k-1})$ and the predicted attributes $p(\underline{a}_k^i|e_k^i = 1, \hat{\underline{y}}_{1:k-1})$, where $\hat{\underline{y}}_k$ is an observation on the time step k and $\hat{\underline{y}}_{1:k-1}$ is a set of all observations till the time step $k-1$. This propagation increases the entropy of DoB distributions and, thus, the uncertainty. The predicted existence probability can be defined by a *Hidden Markov Model*

$$p(e_k^i = 1|e_{k-1}^i = 1) = \beta^i, \tag{1}$$

with $\beta^i \in (0;1]$.

The existence probabilities can then be predicted as

$$p(e_k^i = 1|\hat{\underline{y}}_{1:k-1}) = \beta^i \cdot p(e_{k-1}^i = 1|\hat{\underline{y}}_{1:k-1}). \tag{2}$$

The attribute probabilities can be predicted based on the *Chapman-Kolmogorov equation* as

$$p(\underline{a}_k^i|e_k^i = 1, \hat{\underline{y}}_{1:k-1}) = \int p(\underline{a}_k^i|\underline{a}_{k-1}^i) \cdot p(\underline{a}_{k-1}^i|e_k^i = 1, \hat{\underline{y}}_{1:k-1}) d\underline{a}_{k-1}^i, \tag{3}$$

with a propagation model $p(\underline{a}_{k+1}^i|\underline{a}_k^i)$ for entity attributes.

The update step merges the predicted state with the associated observation. The update attributes are given by

$$p(\underline{a}_k^i|e_k^i = 1, \hat{\underline{y}}_{1:k}) = \sum_{d_k} p(\underline{a}_k^i|e_k^i = 1, \hat{\underline{y}}_{1:k}, d_k) \cdot p(d_k|e_k^i = 1, \hat{\underline{y}}_{1:k}), \tag{4}$$

where the first factor is the posterior distribution

$$p(\underline{a}_k^i|e_k^i = 1, \hat{\underline{y}}_{1:k}, d_k) \propto p(\hat{\underline{y}}_k^{d_k}|e_k^i = 1, \underline{a}_k^i) \cdot p(\underline{a}_k^i|e_k^i = 1, d_k, \hat{\underline{y}}_{1:k-1}). \tag{5}$$

The updated existence is given by

$$p(e_k^i = 1|\underline{\hat{y}}_{1:k}) = \sum_{d_k} p(e_k^i = 1, d_k|\underline{\hat{y}}_{1:k}). \tag{6}$$

3.4 Kalman filter and its extensions

In the case of linear dependence of attributes on observed parameters and Gaussian measurement noise, modeling attributes can be updated by the *Kalman filter* (KF) (cf. Bar-Shalom & Fortmann (1988)) and its extensions. The KF takes multiple sequential measurements of some parameters and combines them in order to evaluate the entity's state at that time instant, resulting in a better estimate than obtained by using one observation alone. During the fusion of multiple measurements, a system's dynamics model (e.g. physical laws of motion), known control inputs, and covariances (a measure of the estimated uncertainty) are considered in the prediction step. In the update step, the filter averages a prediction of an entity's state with a new observation based on a weighted average. The weights are calculated from the covariance, estimated on the prediction step, and assure that the more exact values (i.e. with lower uncertainty) have a greater influence on the state estimate.

More specifically, the Kalman Filter model assumes the following evolution of the (unobservable) true state of the system $\underline{\tilde{a}}_k$ (index i is omitted for clarity) from time step $k-1$ to step k and the description of the observed values $\underline{\hat{y}}_k$ at time step k:

$$\underline{\tilde{a}}_k = F_k \underline{\tilde{a}}_{k-1} + B_k \underline{u}_k + \underline{w}_k, \tag{7}$$

$$\underline{\hat{y}}_k = H_k \underline{\tilde{a}}_k + \underline{v}_k, \tag{8}$$

where F_k is a propagation matrix, B_k is a control-input model matrix, $\underline{u}_k$ is a control vector, $\underline{w}_k \propto N(0, Q_k)$ is a process noise with a covariance Q_k, H_k is an observation model, and $\underline{v}_k \propto N(0, R_k)$ is an observation noise with a covariance R_k.

The prediction step gives an estimate $\underline{\hat{a}}_{k|k-1}$ of the attributes and its covariance matrix $\hat{P}_{k|k-1}$ according to:

$$\underline{\hat{a}}_{k|k-1} = F_k \underline{\hat{a}}_{k-1|k-1} + B_k \underline{u}_{k-1}, \tag{9}$$

$$\hat{P}_{k|k-1} = F_k \hat{P}_{k-1|k-1} F_k^T + Q_{k-1}. \tag{10}$$

The update step corrects the prediction using the information observed at step k:

$$\underline{\hat{a}}_{k|k} = \underline{\hat{a}}_{k|k-1} + K_k \left(\underline{\hat{y}}_k - H_k \underline{\hat{a}}_{k|k-1} \right), \tag{11}$$

$$\hat{P}_{k|k} = (I - K_k H_k) \hat{P}_{k|k-1}, \tag{12}$$

where $K_k = \hat{P}_{k|k-1} H_k^T S_k^{-1}$ is the Kalman matrix with pre-calculated residual matrix $S_k = H_k \hat{P}_{k|k-1} H_k^T + R_k$ and I is the appropriate unit matrix.

In practical application, it is useful to simplify the attributes vector. For example, in entity tracking one can describe the movements with the constant velocity model (see Das (2008)), assuming accelerations as random evolution of the process.

In the case of multiple targets being tracked in clutter by multiple sensors, an extension to Kalman filter is required. For example, the Probabilistic Data Association (PDA) filter weights the association hypotheses according to their probabilities (Bar-Shalom & Tse (1975), Bar-Shalom & Fortmann (1988)). The further development, called Joint PDA (JPDA), analyzes joint events in order to track closely located entities (Fortmann et al. (1983)). The Integrated PDA (IPDA), proposed in Mušicki et al. (1994), introduces creation and deletion of tracked entities on a probabilistic basis. One of the most advanced methods, called Joint Integrated Probabilistic Data Association Filter (JIPDAF), combines all above mentioned ideas and considers all combinations of the observation to entity assignments and the creation and deletion mechanisms of modeling entities (Mušicki & Evans (2002)).

4. World modeling architecture

The world modeling represents the complete knowledge that is required for the operation of an autonomous system. The dynamic models contain up-to-date description of the world of interest, expressing each real-world entity with a virtual representative, and are similar to short-term memory. The prior knowledge contains pre-defined information about known particular entities or generalizations of entity classes, thus representing a long-term memory. The modeling system serves as a global information hub for all other mechatronic sub-systems. Hence, the structure of the world modeling is organized in a consistent, robust and efficient way, enabling fast search over representatives and attributes on a probabilistic basis. Moreover, there are mechanisms for consistency checks, correcting improbable states, e.g. flying cups or spatially overlapping representatives. Before introducing these advanced mechanisms, we demonstrate here the practical realization of attributes.

4.1 Modeling attributes

Since modeling information, in particular attributes, can be updated by different mechatronic sub-systems (e.g. perception and cognition modules) there has to be a global scheme or protocol for the information interchange. This global scheme defines attribute and relation concepts: which attributes are allowed, which possible values do they have, their semantic meaning, units, coordinate system, prior probability distribution (e.g. prior size distribution for kitchen tables), and so on. After defining attributes, the specific Degree-of-Belief description has to be introduced.

In practice, a continuous Degree-of-Belief distribution can be conveniently given via a Gaussian mixture model (GMM) approximation. The GMM represents a weighted sum of M component Gaussian densities as given in Eq. 13. The parameter M is empirically selected to find a balance between the computational complexity and the approximation precision. As new sensor information is fused into the dynamic model, the number of components in the mixture usually increases. In order to sustain the predefined number of M densities in the mixture, reduction techniques can be applied as discussed in Williams (2003).

$$p(\underline{x}|\omega, \underline{\mu}, \Sigma) = \sum_{i=1}^{M} \omega_i g\left(\underline{x}|\underline{\mu}_i, \Sigma_i\right), \tag{13}$$

where $\underline{x}$ denotes a D-dimensional continuous data vector, ω_i are the normalized mixture weights with $\sum_{i=1}^{M} \omega_i = 1$, and $g\left(\underline{x}|\underline{\mu}_i, \Sigma_i\right)$ are the component Gaussian densities. Each component density is a D-variate Gaussian function as given in Eq. 14:

$$g\left(\underline{x}|\underline{\mu}_i,\Sigma_i\right) = \frac{1}{(2\pi)^{D/2}\,|\Sigma_i|^{1/2}}\exp\left\{-\frac{1}{2}\left(\underline{x}-\underline{\mu}_i\right)^T\Sigma_i^{-1}\left(\underline{x}-\underline{\mu}_i\right)\right\}, \tag{14}$$

where $\underline{\mu}_i$ denotes mean vectors and Σ_i covariance matrices.

4.2 Progressive mapping

After modeling attributes are clearly defined, it is important to introduce a common mechanism for attribute groups management. It is convenient to group attributes, which correspond to the same entity in the real world. It is natural then to describe representatives within the object-oriented (OO) methodology. It is important though to distinguish the OO approach in the most common sense and OO programming paradigm, which limits many modern world modeling systems to one application field. The OO languages have a clear inheritance structure of classes that is inapplicable for modern autonomous systems due to many arising problems. One of the problems is the arbitrariness of measured attribute sequences, e.g. color before size or vice versa, which prevents creation of one clear hierarchy of concepts. Another problem is the *open world* assumption, vital for intelligent autonomous systems. In the absence of clear inheritance hierarchy of classes, modeling entity is represented by a growing conglomerate of attributes and relations, created from incoming sensory information. Each observation is associated with the sets of attributes and relations and fused on a probabilistic basis. The update of such growing unclassified information containers is called *progressive mapping* (cf. Belkin (2009), Kühn et al. (2010)).

The progressive mapping can be visually described by the *abstraction level pyramids* (cf. Gheţa et al. (2008)). The dynamic model can be viewed as a hierarchy of abstraction levels, which contain *blank representatives* at the top and more specific representatives downside the hierarchy. The blank representative is an empty *information container* that marks the existence of "something", e.g. the existence of an entity that has not yet been measured. Each observation associated with the entity is iteratively fused into the information container, lowering the representative in the abstraction hierarchy. The idea of dynamic extension of information containers allows for an arbitrary information flow and an abstract information management. In order to understand these kind of attribute sets, they can be at any time matched to known concepts in the prior knowledge.

4.3 Prior knowledge

In order to classify each attribute container, e.g. assign a type, it can be at any time matched to the prior knowledge as shown in Fig 8. The prior knowledge contains general concepts as well as information about specific entities. This match, made on a probabilistic basis, provides the missing semantics and deduces the deficient attributes. The contents of the prior knowledge database can be predefined and then extended during the operation by concepts and entities via a learning process, as described in Section 5. Since prior knowledge contains a global information compendium about the environment, it is reasonable to store it outside the autonomous system (e.g. on a computer cluster) and provide a remote connection. In a case of remote connection failure, it is possible to operate the autonomous system without prior knowledge, though, without complex cognition abilities.

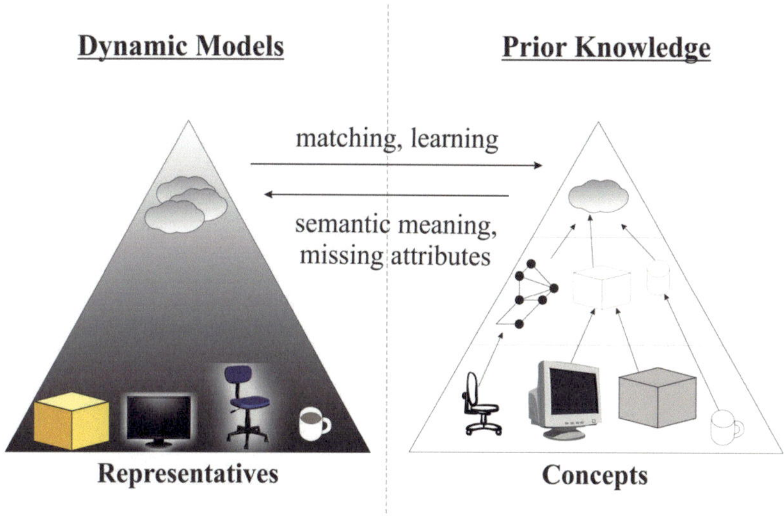

Fig. 8. World modeling architecture.

The concrete realization of matching between a dynamic representative and a class concept or specific entity is not trivial. It is possible to perform a deep search through one given tree-organized concepts hierarchy. Each node can be compared to the representative by two criteria: the structural similarity of attributes and the DoB distributions similarity. The structural similarity implies counting attributes that were observed and added to dynamic description to prior attributes described in ontology. Mathematically, such comparison can be performed by sets metrics, e.g. Tanimoto distance (Rogers & Tanimoto (1960)), Sørensen index (Sørensen (1957)) or other discussed in the overview article Jackson et al. (1989). The DoB distribution similarity between a representative attribute and the prior DoB can be calculated based on Gaussian mixture model metrics, such as Kullback-Leibler distance (Kullback & Leibler (1951), Cover & Thomas (1991)) or Wasserstein L^2 metric (Hazewinkel (2001), Jensen et al. (2007)).

4.4 Quantitative evaluation of the model

The information coming from sensors or stored in the world model can be evaluated numerically. For example, each observation or attribute vector can be characterized by some *information entropy*, that is a measure of uncertainty of a random variable (see Cover & Thomas (1991)). The difference between entropies before and after the observation and dynamic model fusion can give estimation on the information gain.

The numerical estimation of a given attribute can be quantified through the information entropy formulas:

$$H(A) = -\sum P(a) \log_2 P(a), \tag{15}$$

where A denotes some attribute and a is its discrete value and

$$h(A) = -\int p(a) \log_2 p(a) da, \tag{16}$$

in case a is continuous.

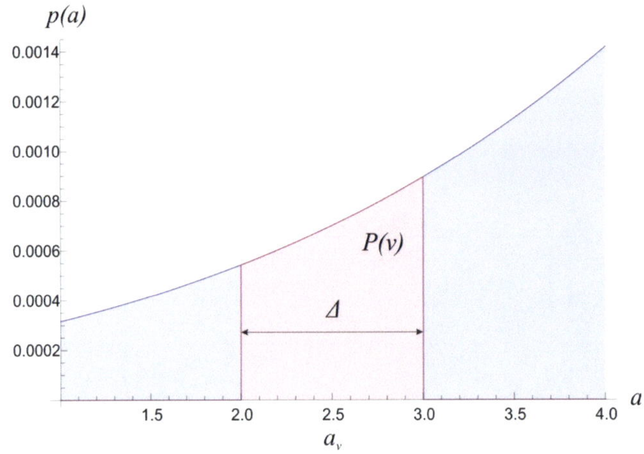

Fig. 9. Discretization of a Degree-of-Belief distribution to Least Discernible Quantum.

In order to numerically estimate a representative as a whole, one has to analyze the entropies of all its attributes. Thus, one needs a unified framework for handling discrete and continuous distributions uniformly. However, by discretizing attribute A to A^* with smaller and smaller steps, so that $P(a^*) \rightarrow p(a)$ the corresponding entropy diverges from the continuous as $\lim_{a^* \rightarrow a} H(A^*) \neq h(A)$. One of the possible ways to overcome this problem is the introduction of the *least discernible quantum* (LDQ) (cf. Oswald (1991)), which specifies the utmost precision of any operation over the given attribute.

The least discernible quantum Δ defines the precision of each considered attribute. It is natural to set Δ equal to the accuracy of sensors. The discretization to LDQ can be performed by dissecting the distribution into sections as shown in Fig. 9 and integrating each section as in Eq. 17:

$$p(a) \rightarrow P(v) := \int_{a_v - \frac{\Delta}{2}}^{a_v + \frac{\Delta}{2}} p(a)da, \tag{17}$$

where $a \in [a_v - \frac{\Delta}{2}, a_v + \frac{\Delta}{2}]$ and $v \subseteq \mathbb{N}$.

The discretized entropy is defined then as

$$H_\Delta(A) := H(v) = -\sum_{v} P(v) \log_2 P(v). \tag{18}$$

5. Concept learning

For autonomous systems, concepts contained in its *knowledge* characterize the mapping from real world *entities* to *representatives* in the world model in a homomorphic way (Sydenham (1982)). The main purpose of the mapping is to share a meaningful set of symbols with its environment: on the one hand this mapping allows classification and even identification of the observed entities based on measurements of their attribute values. On the other hand, concepts allow to interoperably exchange meaningful information, e.g., when receiving requests from humans. Based on the mapping of representatives to concepts, human requests and sensor data can be interrelated and furthermore represented entities can be enhanced with rich semantics not derivable from pure observations (Heizmann et al. (2010)).

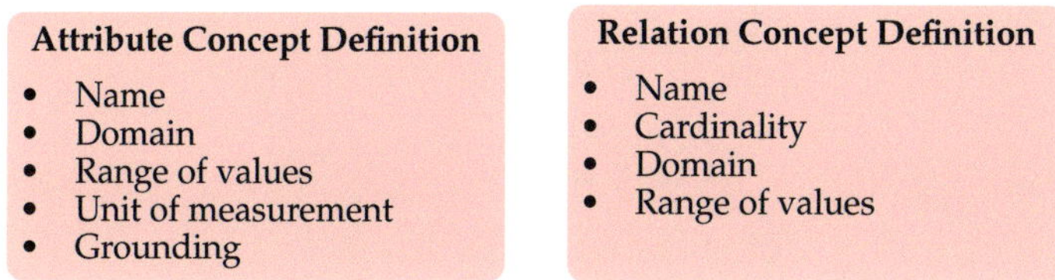

Fig. 10. Definition of attribute concepts and relation concepts.

Within a world model for autonomous systems, *semantics*, i.e. the meaning of symbols received from sensors or humans, have to be introduced in one or another way (Lim et al. (2011)). When preparing a system for operation, it is possible to equip the system with definitions of all the relevant concepts that are supposed to be encountered within its operational tasks. Since these concepts are defined prior to operation, they constitute *a priori* knowledge. By relying on a priori knowledge, an autonomous system is able to interrelate, classify and semantically handle only the entities occurring in a closed world. When operating in a real-world environment, however, modeling tasks often go beyond closed worlds towards an open-world modeling task: representing and handling a dynamic and changing environment which consists of entities of possibly unforeseen types (Kennedy (1998)). To cope with open-world modeling, an autonomous system must be able to extend its knowledge beyond a priori information by *acquiring new concept definitions*. Another purpose of knowledge is thus to store information *learned from experience* during operation.

The task of dynamically expanding the knowledge of an autonomous system constitutes an extension to the classical concept learning problem, i.e. learning Boolean valued functions (over attributes) from a given set of (training) data (Mitchell (1997)). In order to extend the knowledge of an autonomous system, new entity concepts must be learned. In concept learning, the process of learning can be regarded as a search within concept space (Mitchell (1997)), i.e. the space of all representable concepts. The structure of this space constitutes the bias to the concept learning problem and thus determines how concepts are learned and which concepts can be learned at all (Mitchell (1980)).

Within our presented approach to world modeling for autonomous systems, the structure of concept space is loosely defined by the object-oriented world model. In the following, this structure shall be further formalized to enable structured concept learning. Besides structuring concept learning, this formalization extends the general applicability of object-oriented world modeling by formally abstracting entity representation from the sensor data, thus making sensor components exchangeable and acquired knowledge interoperable.

Entity concepts we are interested in generally comprise a set of attributes. An attribute thereby is associated with an *attribute concept*. Attribute concepts describe the domain of an attribute (e.g., a height value, a position, a color, the number of wheels, the kind of fuel, etc.), its allowed range of values, its unit of measurement and the information on how instances of this attribute concept are grounded in the real-world (e.g., modeled a priori, measured by a sensor system, related to an effector interaction or to communication with humans). When instantiating attribute concepts within an entity concept, the expected attribute value(s) have to be specified in the form of a probability distribution interpreted in a DoB sense. Fig. 10 shows the definition of an attribute concept. Besides their attribute values, real-world entities can be characterized by their relations to other entities. Relations are associated with *relation concepts*. As shown in Fig. 10, a relation concept includes a name, the cardinality of the

Object Concept Definition

- Name
- Attributes
- Class relations

Fig. 11. Object concept definition

relation, its domain and its range of values. Relation concepts define the relations occurring between entity concepts as well as relations existing between single concept instances, i.e. representatives, or even attributes. The domain in attribute concepts and domain and range of values in relation concepts are specified by appropriate entity concepts, e.g., a concept for color. The unit of measurement in attribute concepts can take values from a predefined hierarchy of unit concepts, e.g., specifying length units like meter or centimeter and their conversions. By abstracting the range of values and the unit of measurement from the domain to be represented within attribute concepts, sensors of different type can define different attributes (e.g., differing in unit and range of measured quantities) associated with the same attribute concept. Thus, these sensors are either interchangeable or can consistently interoperate.

The most basic entity concepts for world modeling are *object concepts*, which map physical real-world entities to representatives. Object concepts are defined based on attribute concepts and relation concepts. They consist of a name, a set of attributes and a set of class relations to other entity concepts (which apply to all representatives of a given concept). Fig. 11 shows the definition of object concepts. More abstract entities like roles (e.g., a customer), groups of objects, situations, etc. can be modeled by extending the given definition for object concepts. Following the definitions for entity concepts given above, *concept learning* within object-oriented world modeling allows for learning new object concepts as well as new attribute and relation concepts. By learning new attribute concepts, for example, the entity concept space is changed, thus extending beyond classical concept learning.

As with the syntactical aspects of concept representation, the *semantics of entities* and the semantics of their attributes also play an important role in concept learning. When an autonomous system for example faces the task of representing an encountered real-world entity, its learning component has to choose the relevant attributes from all available attributes (e.g., through sensor measurements or human input). To make an elaborate choice, the system has to base its decision on the semantics of the considered attributes and relate them to its general purpose. When defining a priori knowledge for an autonomous system, an ontology-like structure organizes conceptions as interrelated symbols. Within our object-oriented world model, attributes are used to further describe these conceptions, like a car having four wheels or a cup being cylindric and 9 cm tall. Nevertheless, for an autonomous system none of these conceptions has a meaning by itself. Furthermore, they do not reference any real-world entities. Thus, all concepts in the knowledge have to be grounded in either the real world or the human thought (for human-machine-interaction) (Harnad (1990)).

For the grounding of entity concepts, their attributes are considered. *Attribute concepts* in world modeling can be divided into three groups:

- perceptual,
- effector,

- and semantic attributes.

Perceptual attributes (like the height, color or speed of an entity) are grounded within the sensor components providing value information for these attributes. *Effector* attributes are grounded within the actuators used to manipulate real-world entities based on values represented by these attributes (Kennedy (1998)). An effector attribute for example can be the weight and the shape of a cup supposed to be grasped, lifted and moved. As can be seen from this example, there is no sharp boundary between perceptual and effector attributes (the weight could also be measured, e.g., by a scale). Which attribute is grounded by which sensomotoric component of an autonomous system thus in general depends upon the task currently at hand. Perceptual attributes are used for classifying and identifying of the observed real-world entities, while effector attributes assist in manipulating these entities.

Furthermore, there are attributes in the knowledge that can be directly associated with neither a sensor component nor an actuator component. Examples of such attributes may include information about if and how an entity can be moved (e.g., something is fixed to a wall and cannot be moved at all, or a door can only be rotated on its hinges), where an object is usually located (e.g., a cup in the cup section of a cupboard), etc. These attributes constitute *semantic* attributes as they are not directly stemming from either acquired knowledge or long-term experience (like long-term observation of a specific situation in conjunction with reasoning about it). Semantic attributes include the physical properties, behavior and capabilities of real-world entities. These attributes are useful in modeling the human grasp of the meaning of entities for autonomous systems, e.g., a cup as a drinking vessel, and thus enable human-machine understanding. Furthermore, they allow the semantical enrichment of the represented entities after mapping them to a known concept. By deriving information not obtainable by the pure use of sensomotoric components, they serve thus as a basis for higher-level information processing, like reasoning or planning.

After having defined a structure for entity concepts and the examined attribute semantics, we now move on to learning new entity concepts. *Concept learning* for autonomous world modeling can be structured as a task consisting of two interconnected subtasks:

- a deductive inference task on concepts in the knowledge, and
- an inductive learning task on sensor data.

The first subtask performs deductive inference on concepts already present in knowledge in order to either add new semantic properties or even learn whole new concepts (e.g., generalizations) in order to gain a better understanding of the world of interest (by a more appropriate or efficiently organized concept hierarchy). For example, a new super class drinking vessels could be created by deductive inference based on the common properties of the classes of cups and glasses. For extracting the semantic properties and hidden relations, the deductive subtask compares the concepts and their attributes for similarities, employing a variety of conceivable measures ranging from probability distribution metrics (like Kullback-Leibler divergence (Kullback & Leibler (1951))) to methods based on vector space models for entity concepts. After having found sufficiently similar concepts, one possible inference is to extract the matching parts and transfer them into a new concept, which then subsumes the deduction result within its set of inferred semantic properties, and the necessary conditions for these properties to hold in its set of attributes.

The second subtask in concept learning constitutes an inductive inference problem: learning new concepts from observations, which in case of the world modeling are given in the form of a set of representatives. A world model enhances the observed real-world entities with semantics by mapping them to the known concepts. If a given representative cannot be properly assigned to the concepts stored in the knowledge, no useful semantics can be derived. Thus, the quality of the concept assignment is crucial for the overall quality of the world model. To ensure high-quality modeling, measures based on Shannon Entropy (Shannon (1948)) or Minimum Description Length (Rissanen (1978)) methods can be employed to evaluate the assignment of observed representatives to concepts. If a poor concept assignment is detected for some representatives, changes to the current set of concepts stored in the knowledge can be performed, including the creation of additional concepts and adaption or even deletion of the existing concepts. Created new concepts can subsequently be enriched with semantics by the deductive subtask.

6. Experimental set-up

The described theoretical analysis, as well as the complete system architecture for the world modeling has been tested in the three experimental set-ups:

- The German Science Foundation (DFG) project Collaborative Research Center (SFB) 588 "Humanoid Robots – Learning and Cooperating Multimodal Robots", see DFG SFB 588 (2001-2012);
- The Fraunhofer Institute of Optronics, System Technologies and Image Exploitation (IOSB) project "Network Enabled Surveillance and Tracking" (NEST), see Moßgraber et al. (2010);
- The Fraunhofer IOSB project "Wide Maritime Area Airborne Surveillance", see WiMAAS (2008-2011).

The main goal of the SFB 588 project is to create household assisting anthropomorphic robots (the three developed generations of such robots are presented in Fig. 12) with the following features:

- Autonomous operation;
- Humanoid shape;
- Multimodality;
- Cooperation;
- Learning capabilities;

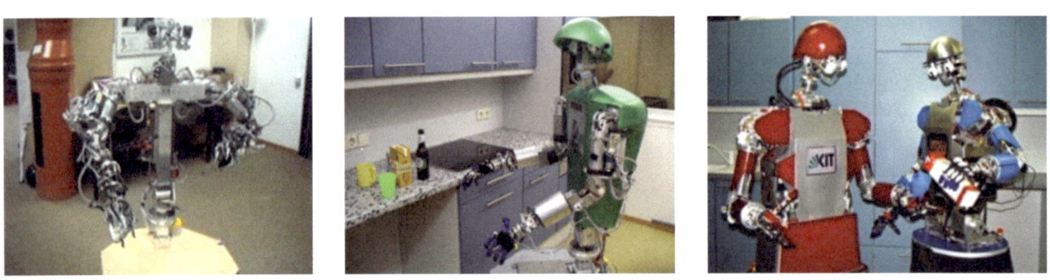

(a) ARMAR-I (b) ARMAR-II (c) ARMAR-III

Fig. 12. The three generations of the humanoid robot ARMAR (DFG SFB 588 (2001-2012)).

In fact, self-sufficient humanoid robots represent androids that are one of the ultimate goals of engineering and natural sciences. The multimodality implies that the communication

(a) Object detection in video streams

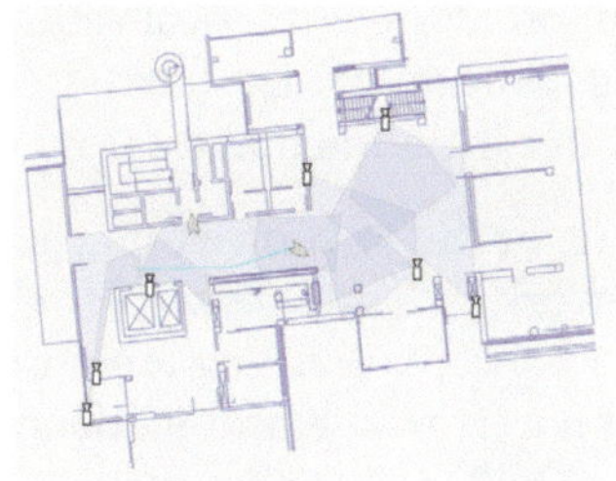

(b) World model of observed persons in indoor surveillance

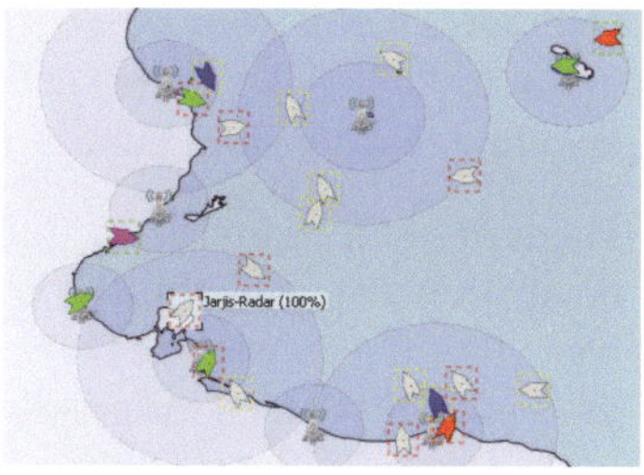

(c) World model of observed vessels in maritime surveillance

Fig. 13. Applications of world modeling surveillance systems.

is intuitive for humans and machines, using speech, gestures, mimics, and haptics. The cooperation between humanoid robots and humans with support of intentions and context recognition techniques and safety regulations allows for collaborative activities. At the top of the robot's cognition abilities is the capability to learn. During the interactive explorations the new entities, concepts and even motions can be learned with an aid from a human. Due to complexity of the given tasks, such humanoid robots need a comprehensive state of knowledge on their environment. The required mechanisms and principles for the knowledge processing and management are implemented within the object-oriented world modeling system developed within the SFB 588 project (see Belkin (2009), Kühn et al. (2010), Belkin (2010), Baum et al. (2010), Gheţa et al. (2010)).

In the NEST research project, the proposed world modeling system has been employed as a virtual information hub between the evaluation and analysis services of an intelligent video-assisted security and monitoring system. In the context of indoor surveillance, detection of moving persons was performed in the video streams, see Fig. 13(a). Observations from several cameras are fused into a consistent representation and the resulting world model can be visualized, see Fig. 13(b). In the WiMAAS-project, the focus was on observing the maritime vessel behavior. Detections of vessels are coming from several different sources, e.g., navigational radar or signals from the automatic identification system (AIS). The resulting world model is visualized in Fig. 13(c). Based on the content of the world model, several methods for behavior analysis of the moving vessels can be applied.

7. Conclusion

This chapter outlines the state of the art of world modeling for autonomous systems and introduces several novel methods. First, we overview the world modeling problem, introduce the nomenclature and discuss the common concepts and methods used in the problem area. Then the global structure of the information workflow is specified along with the definition of the modeling domains. Next, each step of the information workflow is discussed in detail: the fusion of the incoming information from the sensors, the real-time autonomous modeling of the surrounding environment, the prior knowledge employment and the learning of new concepts. We also describe modern methods of the information fusion, including the information representation techniques, the information life cycle within the autonomous system, the Bayesian framework for information association and fusion and the Kalman filter. The dynamic modeling is discussed by presenting methods for modeling attributes and entities, followed by the definition of the numerical estimate of the information content in the model. A separate section is dedicated to the learning of new concepts and the prior knowledge extension. Finally, the three experimental set-ups are described.

There are still many open questions in the area of world modeling. For example, there is no appropriate probabilistic framework for joint Degree-of-Belief distributions, many issues regarding the consistency checks or concepts learning are unsolved. In spite of many stated problems, first steps for creation of a universal world modeling for autonomous systems are carried out and the modeling system will evolve with the time, becoming more complex and intelligent.

8. References

Bar-Shalom, Y. & Fortmann, T. E. (1988). *Tracking and data association*, Academic Press.

Bar-Shalom, Y. & Tse, E. (1975). Tracking in a cluttered environment with probabilistic data association, *Automatica* 11.

Bauer, A., Emter, T., Vagts, H. & Beyerer, J. (2009). Object oriented world model for surveillance systems, *Future Security: 4th Security Research Conference*, Fraunhofer Press, pp. 339–345.

Baum, M., Gheţa, I., Belkin, A., Beyerer, J. & Hanebeck, U. D. (2010). Data association in a world model for autonomous systems, *Proceedings of IEEE 2010 International Conference on Multisensor Fusion and Integration for Intelligent Systems*.

Belkin, A. (2009). Object-oriented world modelling for autonomous systems, *Technical report*, Institute for Anthropomatics, Vision and Fusion Laboratory, Karlsruhe Institute for Technology.

Belkin, A. (2010). Information management in world modeling, *Technical report*, Vision and Fusion Laboratory, Institute for Anthropomatics, Karlsruhe Institute of Technology (KIT).

Cover, T. M. & Thomas, J. A. (1991). *Elements of Information Theory*, Wiley-Interscience.

Das, S. (2008). *High-Level Data Fusion*, Artech House Publishers.

DFG SFB 588 (2001-2012). Humanoid robots – learning and cooperating multimodal robots. URL: *http://www.sfb588.uni-karlsruhe.de*

Endsley, M. R. (1995). Towards a theory of situation awareness in dynamic systems, *Human Factors* 37(11): 32–64.

Fischer, Y. & Bauer, A. (2010). Object-oriented sensor data fusion for wide maritime surveillance, *2nd International Conference on Waterside Security*.

Fischer, Y., Bauer, A. & Beyerer, J. (2011). A conceptual framework for automatic situation assessment, *2011 IEEE First International Multi-Disciplinary Conference on Cognitive Methods in Situation Awareness and Decision Support (CogSIMA)*, pp. 234–239.

Fortmann, T. E., Bar-Shalom, Y. & Scheffe, M. (1983). Sonar tracking of multiple targets using joint probabilistic data association, *IEEE Journal of Oceanic Engineering* OE-8: 173–183.

Gheţa, I., Heizmann, M., Belkin, A. & Beyerer, J. (2010). World modeling for autonomous systems, *Proceedings of the KI 2010: Advances in Artificial Intelligence*, Springer Lecture Notes in Computer Science, pp. 176–183.

Gheţa, I., Heizmann, M. & Beyerer, J. (2008). Object oriented environment model for autonomous systems, *in* H. Boström, R. Johansson & J. van Laere (eds), *Proceedings of the second Skövde Workshop on Information Fusion Topics*, Skövde Studies in Informatics, pp. 9–12.

Glinton, R., Giampapa, J. & Sycara, K. (2006). A markov random field model of context for high-level information fusion, *Proceedings of the 9th International Conference on Information Fusion*.

Hall, D. L. & McMullen, S. A. H. (2004). *Mathematical Techniques in Multisensor Data Fusion*, Artech House, Inc.

Harnad, S. (1990). The symbol grounding problem, http://cogprints.org/3106/. URL: *http://cogprints.org/3106/*

Hazewinkel, M. (ed.) (2001). *Encyclopaedia of Mathematics*, Springer, chapter Wasserstein metric.

Heizmann, M., Gheta, I., Puente León, F. & Beyerer, J. (2010). Information fusion for environment exploration, *in* F. Puente León & K. Dostert (eds), *Reports on Industrial Information Technology*, Vol. 12, KIT Scientific Publishing, pp. 147–166.

IBM (2001). Autonomic computing: Ibm's perspective on the state of information technology, Manifesto. URL: *http://www.research.ibm.com/autonomic/manifesto/*

Jackson, D. A., Somers, K. M. & Harvey, H. H. (1989). Similarity coefficients: Measures of co-occurrence and assosication or simply measures of occurrence?, *The American Naturalist* 133: 436–453.

Jensen, J. H., Ellis, D. P., Christensen, M. G. & Jensen, S. H. (2007). Evaluation of distance measures between gaussian mixture models of mfccs, *Proceedings of the International Confeference on Music Information Retrieval*, Vol. 2, Citeseer, pp. 107–108.

Kennedy, C. M. (1998). Anomaly driven concept acquisition. URL: *http://citeseerx.ist.psu.edu/viewdoc/summary?doi=10.1.1.38.7360*

Kephart, J. O. & Chess, D. M. (2003). The vision of autonomic computing, *Computer* 36(1): 41–50.

Kühn, B., Belkin, A., Swerdlow, A., Machmer, T., Beyerer, J. B. & Kroschel, K. (2010). Knowledge-driven opto-acoustic scene analysis based on an object-oriented world modelling approach for humanoid robots, *Proceedings of the 41st International Symposium on Robotics and the 6th German Conference on Robotics*.

Kullback, S. & Leibler, R. A. (1951). On information and sufficiency, *Annals of Mathematical Statistics* 22: 49–86.

Lim, G. H., Suh, I. H. & Suh, H. (2011). Ontology-Based unified robot knowledge for service robots in indoor environments, *IEEE Transactions on Systems, Man and Cybernetics, Part A: Systems and Humans* 41(3): 492–509.

Meyer-Delius, D., Plagemann, C. & Burgard, W. (2009). Probabilistic situation recognition for vehicular traffic scenarios, *Proceedings of the 2009 IEEE international conference on Robotics and Automation*, pp. 4161–4166.

Mitchell, T. M. (1980). The need for biases in learning generalizations, *Technical report*.

Mitchell, T. M. (1997). *Machine Learning*, 1st edn, McGraw-Hill Education (ISE Editions).

Moßgraber, J., Reinert, F. & Vagts, H. (2010). An architecture for a task-oriented surveillance system: A service- and event-based approach, *Fifth International Conference on Systems (ICONS 2010)*.

Mušicki, D. & Evans, R. (2002). Joint integrated probabilistic data association - jipda, *Proceedings of the International Conference on Information Fusion*.

Mušicki, D., Evans, R. & Stankovic, S. (1994). Integrated probabilistic data association, *IEEE Transactions on Automatic Control* 39.

Oswald, J. R. (1991). *Diacritical Analysis of Systems: a Treatise on Information Theory*, Ellis Horwood Limited.

Rissanen, J. (1978). Modeling By Shortest Data Description, *Automatica* 14: 465–471.

Rogers, D. J. & Tanimoto, T. T. (1960). A computer program for classifying plants, *Science* 132: 1115–1118.

Shannon, C. E. (1948). A mathematical theory of communication, *Bell system technical journal* 27.

Sørensen, T. (1957). A method of establishing groups of equal amplitude in plant sociology based on similarity of species and its application to analyses of the vegetation on danish commons., *Biologiske Skrifter, Kongelige Danske Videnskabernes Selskab* 5: 1–34.

Steinberg, A. N., Bowman, C. L. & White, F. E. (1999). Revisions to the jdl data fusion model, *Sensor Fusion: Architectures, Algorithms, and Applications, Proceedings of the SPIE Vol. 3719*.

Sydenham, P. H. (1982). *Handbook of Measurement Science: Theoretical fundamentals*, Vol. 1, Wiley.

Williams, J. L. (2003). *Gaussian mixture reduction for tracking multiple maneuvering targets in clutter*, Master's thesis, Graduate School of Engineering and Management, Air Force Institute of Technology, Air University, USA.

WiMAAS (2008-2011). Wide maritime area airborne surveillance. URL: *http://www.wimaas.eu*

8

Analysis of Interactive Information Systems Using Goals

Pedro Valente and Paulo N. M. Sampaio
University of Madeira
Portugal

1. Introduction

The high competitiveness in the world markets lead enterprises to provide their clients with the best services and products as possible in order to obtain important advantages over their opponents. These services and products are result of the enterprise's business processes (BPs) which, therefore, need to be improved.

The improvement of BPs can be achieved, both by, reorganizing their tasks, or by automating (completely or partially) these BPs by means of the development of interactive information systems (IISs) which articulate the work of every actor, thus improving speed and reliability of the goal(s) (of the BP) to be achieved.

ISSs are computer based software systems (Land, 2002) that have the ability to manage structured information which can be manipulated by humans by means of user interfaces in order to perform their tasks within the enterprises' BP. Since numerous BPs need automation, the development of IISs must be planned in order to best schedule the deployment of new and existing improved services and products, according to the needs of every stakeholder and available resources.

The successful development of IISs is usually a complex and demanding task that can only be achieved if a project is organized in such a way that every stakeholder is able to negotiate its intentions in terms of functional (and also non-functional) requirements. Once these requirements are implemented in an acceptable price, they will bring an added value to the enterprise, enhancing its overall business effectiveness and efficiency, and therefore contributing to ensure its wealth and survival in a demanding market.

The precise identification of functional requirements (FRs) is a crucial task for the fluent development of a project, and can be carried out during the organization of new or existing BPs if every stakeholder is able to express its point of view over the problem and if a final agreement is achieved. Following the identification of FRs, the implementation effort should be estimated, the requirements analysed and the system designed in such a way that future developers have no doubts on its implementation, improving the probability that the system is produced on schedule and with the fewer mistakes as possible.

The work presented in this chapter is based on Goals (Valente, 2009), a software engineering (SE) process proposed in order to provide the needed tools to define the precise conception of an IIS. Goals' first phase (requirements) defines the FRs of the IIS based on the design of the automated BP using Process Use Cases (PUC) (Valente & Sampaio 2007a). Goals' second phase (analysis) consists in the analysis of these requirements producing use cases design and a comprehensive architecture, using MultiGoals (Valente & Sampaio 2007b), which can be used to define implementation precedences and development tasks assignment. The artifacts produced by both requirements and analysis phases can be integrated with Interactive Use-Case Points (iUCP) (Nunes, 2010) to estimate project effort. MultiGoals can be further applied to complete the design (third phase) of the complete IIS including support for multimedia design.

1.1 Goals' requirements and analysis phases

Goals is a (business) process for the production of the correct IISs and can be applied for the resolution of a specific information problem. This process is defined into 6 different phases following a standard construction process: (i) requirements definition, (ii) analysis of the problem, (iii) design of the solution, (iv) development, (v) test and (vi) installation of the finished IIS. Goals also predicts that the software will need maintenance following two possibilities: (i) introduction of new requirements, in which situation the complete process will be followed again, and, (ii) corrective maintenance in which case the process is verified from the beginning in order to identify where the mistake took place during the conception.

The first three phases of the development process, which are the phases defined by Goals (requirements, analysis and design) are presented in Figure 1.

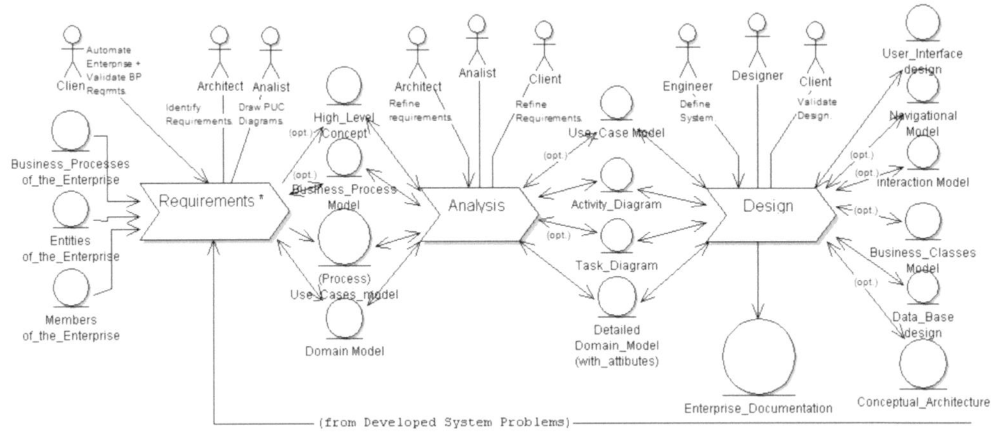

Fig. 1. Goals' phases of Requirements, Analysis and Design.

Each phase of Goals is a business process itself in which a different methodology should be applied to produce information for the construction of the IIS. Although the Goals process is independent from the methodologies used, some restrictions should be observed in order to achieve the minimal quality for the global process and assure that full advantage is taken from the available inputs and that the needed outputs are also produced. Also, each phase defines: the human intervenient and their objectives, the minimal set of information inputs, and the outputs for the next phase.

The next sections describe the development and integration of the first two phases: (i) requirements, in order to produce functional requirements, and (ii) analysis, in order to produce the system´s architecture and effort estimation.

1.1.1 Requirements phase

The methodology chosen for the phase of requirements should be: (i) use case-oriented, in order to identify (essential) use cases (Constantine, 2002), and (ii) information-oriented, in order to produce a Domain Model (Nunes, 2001).

This phase is triggered by the client with the intention of automating the enterprise regarding the resolution of some information problem, and can take advantage of artifacts that might already exist in the enterprise such as: business processes; information entities, or; organization of the enterprise.

The following artifacts are defined as the minimal set of information to achieve functional requirements definition: (i) Use Cases Model (or equivalent, identifying all use cases) - the use cases of the system, and; (ii) Domain Model - information entities of the enterprise. Optionally a High-Level Concept (Kreitzberg, 1999) and a Business Process Model (Eriksson & Pencker, 2001) identifying the enterprises' goals can be elaborated.

In Process Use Cases, the methodology suggested by Goals for the requirements phase, architect, analyst and client work in order to produce the needed output elements: High-Level Concept; Domain Model; Business Process Model, and; Process Use Cases Model.

1.1.2 Analysis phase

The methodology chosen for the analysis phase should be: (i) use case-driven, in order to detail the previously identified use cases, and; (ii) information-oriented, in order to detail the previously identified entities.

The following artifacts are defined as the minimal set of information to achieve comprehension of the problem: (i) an Activity Diagram (or equivalent) of the decomposition of the use cases into user intentions (or equivalent, representing user tasks) and system responsibilities (or equivalent, representing system behaviour), and; (ii) a Domain Model. Optionally a Use Cases Model, a Task Model (Paternò et al., 1997) can be elaborated, and an implementation effort estimation method applied.

In MultiGoals, the methodology suggested for the analysis phase, architect, designer and client work to produce: (i) a Use Cases Model; (ii) Activity Diagrams; (iii) an Interaction Model, (iv) an Application Domain Model, and (v) a System Architecture.

iUCP, the method presented in this chapter in order to estimate project effort, takes advantage mainly from the use cases and actors identified in the requirements phase and the System Architecture produced in the analysis phase to calculate the number of man-hours needed to finish the construction of the IIS.

This chapter presents a comprehensive illustrated example of the application of the previous methodologies to define, in a straight lined process: the project's concept, the BPs design, the information entities (in a domain model), the use cases design, the systems' architecture and the effort estimation (integrating with iUCP). To support the understanding of these contents the following definitions should be observed:

- activity - action performed by humans within an enterprises' organization, carried out or not, in interaction with a system. Activities are a generalization of the concept of use case (actions performed in interaction with a system).
- (essential) use case - specially structured form of a use case that represents a single, discrete and well defined task over a system that is complete and meaningful. Use cases should be described in abstract, simplified, and implementation-independent terms using the language of the domain understood by the users (Constantine & Lockwood, 2000).
- actors - humans that play a role in an enterprises' organization, performing at least one activity.
- interaction space - class that represents the space within the user interface of a system where the user interacts (...) to carry out some particular task or set of interrelated tasks (Nunes, 2001).
- task – class that models the structure of the dialogue between the user and the system in terms of meaningful and complete sets of actions required to achieve a goal (Nunes, 2001).
- entity - a class used to model perdurable information (often persistent). Entity classes structure domain (or business) classes and associate behavior often representing a logical data structure (Nunes, 2001).

The methods presented in this chapter are directed to software engineers and business process managers and have been developed based on its application in real projects mainly in the Software Applications Development Office at University of Madeira, a software development environment characterized by demanding terms, high information accuracy and usability user standards.

2. Requirements phase

The precise identification of functional requirements and its acceptance by all the stakeholders of a project is a key factor for the correct conception and success of an IIS, and user participation in the development life cycle can be seen as critical to achieve usable systems and has proven its efficacy in the improvement of systems appropriateness.

This section presents Process Use Cases (PUC) (Valente & Sampaio, 2007a), a methodology that defines the steps to achieve the identification of functional requirements in terms of use cases as a sequence of the organization of new or existing BPs and also identify the initial information entities and actors involved in an IIS.

2.1 Process use cases steps for requirements definition

PUC is a methodology defined within Goals, and is a Requirements Enginnering (RE) solution to bind the phases of requirements and analysis rapidly through the identification of use cases and information entities during the organization of BPs.

In order to achieve automation of the BP, PUC covers partially the lifecycle of Business Process Management (BPM) (Figure 2) (Webinterx, 2006) assuring that the BPs are analyzed, improved and modeled before they are automated (monitoring is out of the scope of PUC). The "analysis" is understood as the inspection of the current workflow of the BP, the "improvement" is the reorganization of the BP in a way that it becomes more efficient and/or more effective. After the "improvement", the BP is "modeled" and finally it is "automated" by a SE process that leads to the development of an IIS.

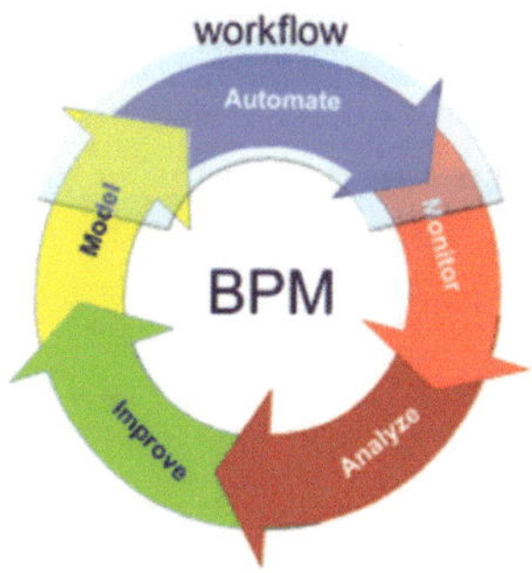

Fig. 2. Business Process Management lifecycle.

PUC describes the development of 4 artifacts: 1 statement and 3 models (respectively High-Level Concept, Domain Model, Business Process Model and Process Use Cases Model) using an information-oriented strategy for the identification and association of the components generated: business processes, information entities, actors and use cases.

Consider Table 1 which enumerates the steps of PUC. Each step has a name (Interiorize Project, Information Identification, etc...) and produces one artifact (High-Level Concept, Domain Model, etc...) that is manipulated by an intervenient (architect, analyst and/or client) towards components definition (entities, business processes, etc...).

Step	Step Name	Model Name	Components Manipulated	Intervenient
1	Interiorize Project	High-Level Concept	N/A	Architect, Client
2	Information Identification	Domain Model	entities	Analyst, Client
3	Business Processes Identification	Business Process Model	business process, entities, actors	Analyst, Client
4	Use Cases Identification	Process Use Cases Model	tasks, use cases	Architect, Analyst, Client

Table 1. Steps of Process Use Cases methodology

In order to illustrate PUC, a project ("Gastronomy Project") developed for a small enterprise is presented. This (non-profitable) enterprise related to a local governmental library (in Madeira, Portugal), is responsible for the bibliographic investigation on gastronomy. The idea of the director is to divulgate the gastronomic events promoted by the enterprise and the existing gastronomic recipes in a website. However, the budget for the project is reduced and the software development should be kept to its minimal.

The enterprise had three informal units, besides the business manager, responsible for the execution of its main activities: the secretary (responsible fot the contact with the clients), the investigation unit (responsible for aquiring and cataloging recipes), and the events unit (responsible for the organization of events). After a first approach, in which an attempt was made to understand the main activities of the enterprise, it was possible to understand that the enterprises' main products were: the identification and cataloging of gastronomic recipes and the organization of gastronomic events.

The application of the steps of Process Use Cases to this project and the more relevant artifacts produced are presented in the next sections.

2.1.1 PUC Step 1 – Interiorize project

The High-Level Concept (HLC) (Kreitzberg, 1999) is a technology independent paragraph that describes the part of the system (or full system) that is going to be implemented. The HLC must be understood by all the stakeholders (the community) of the project promoting a shared vision that will help the project community to keep focused on the product development. The Interiorize Project is the only unstructured part of PUC.

In this step client and architect agree on a HLC for the project. To do this, it is important to understand the scope of the project within the enterprise's global activity, so, it is necessary to understand how the enterprises' activities lead to the production of its main product(s) and what is the strategic reason that leads to the need of automation. Artifacts such as the enterprise's hierarchical organization and legislation may provide important information.

In the example project presented in this section the HLC agreed with the client was: "**Capture the attention of potential and actual clients for the gastronomic patrimony and events of the enterprise**.". The HLC expressed the intention of the enterprise to enlarge the number of clients and promote client fidelity by providing a quality service of information that combined the traditional historical recipes and the events that promoted those recipes.

2.1.2 PUC Step 2 – Information identification

Information is very stable within an enterprise. Mainly, information manipulated by core business processes is persistent from the birth of the enterprise until its closure and is independent from the technology used to manipulate it. Information is usually manipulated by several BPs of the enterprise, that once correctly identified (both information parts and BPs) will produce valuable artifacts for the Business Process Mangagement and Software Engineering activities.

In this step, the analyst identifies the main "concepts of information" defined in the HLC. These information concepts are transformed into entities that will be the first ones in the Domain Model, the output of this step. Entities represent information (not actions, actors, nor business processes; but the name may coincide) and relate to each other by the composition of a meaningful structure. This structure has relations of hierarchy (inheritance), dependency (composition) and possession (association) and is called Class Diagram as defined in UML (Object Management Group, 2003). In PUC, the entity stereotype is used instead of the class stereotype which at this stage is a more accurate concept of information.

The Domain Model can be used along all the Software Engineering process. At implementation stages, it is often used to generate database tables and (programmed) classes to manipulate these entities. The Domain Model must be updated at any stage in the process when new entities are revealed.

The Domain Model is defined based on the information entities identified in the HLC statement. These information entities are placed in the Domain Model relating to each other according to the natural relation between information entities using the relations of the UML's Class Diagram, being their cardinality also defined. Within PUC, and after this first step, the Domain Model will be updated whenever new information entities are identified, speccially during the modeling of the Business Process Model (Step 3).

In the example project presented in this book, the first entities derived from the High-Level Concept concepts of information were: "client"; "recipe" and "event". The entity "client" existence, although implicitly related to the events, was reinforced when we noticed that the business process for recipe capture also involved donation of recipes by "clients". The first entities identified were then combined with other entities ("Advertisement", "Producers" and "Recipe Submitted for Approval") identified in Step 3 (Business Processes Identification) to compose a single information structure as presented in Figure 3. It is suggested that the analyst describes the Class Diagram in natural language to the client in order to achieve diagram validation.

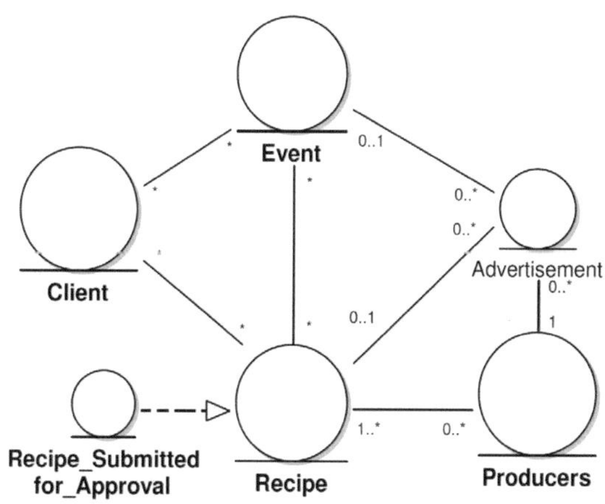

Fig. 3. PUC Step 2 - Domain Model.

2.1.3 PUC Step 3 – Business processes identification

The objective of this step is to identify business processes (BPs) for possible automation based on the information entities identified until this stage. At the same time, valuable information that can serve as documentation for future Business Process Management activities is being produced.

BPs exist in an enterprise to achieve a certain objective, a goal, a product, that can be described by information (associated with this product). BPs happen as many times as the need to give response to the needs of some enterprise member or third party (e.g. client) with some responsibility (active or passive, with some relation to the enterprise) within the activity of the enterprise. Many enterprise members can interact with these processes by carrying out some complete, unitary task, in which many different entities can be manipulated (consumed or produced). In order to be able to control (e.g. reorganize) these BPs, it is important for an enterprise to maintain complete and detailed information of relations among BPs, their inputs, outputs, actors and triggering events.

In this step, analyst and client will identify, relate and detail BPs. The identification of BPs should take place, at least, from the business unit (in an enterprise organization hierarchical perspective) "directly" responsible for the information being managed, i.e. unit(s) that consume or produce this information to achieve complete and meaningful tasks. BPs that relate "directly" to the information identified until this stage must be documented, if within the scope of the project defined in the High-Level Concept, in order to provide the understanding of all the manipulation made over the identified information.

BPs are named according to their goal, i.e., the product of the BP, whether it is a service, information or a material product (e.g. product "television", BP name "build TV"). The outputs and inputs (information, resource and output in the Business Process Model (Eriksson & Pencker, 2001)) are represented by entities. When the flow is towards the BPs it represents an input (and generates an event) and the contrary direction represents an output. Associations can be bi-directional representing event, input and output. Actors are associated with BPs using "associations" and their objectives are written in natural language (e.g. "approve recipe") separated by a plus signal (+) naming the association. When an actor triggers the BP, an event is generated and its relation with the BP is represented with a flow (arrow form). BPs can be related to each other, i.e., the outcome of a BP (which is an event) serves as the income to the next one.

In the example project presented in this section, four BPs that directly manipulated the entities "client"; "recipe" and "event" (Step 2) were identified: (i) the "Obtain Recipe" BP in which donators and investigators donate recipes that are evaluated by a gastronomy consultant; (ii) the "make event" BP that generates information for the entity "event", in which business manager and the event organizer interact to create a new event using the "producer" and "recipe" entities; (iii) the "advertise" BP which was created in order to produce information for the enterprises' future website, in which the business manager delivers advertisements to the advertiser about recipes, events or generalized news; and, (iv) the "obtain gastronomic information", which is a new BP that will exist as a consequence of the new website and represents the usage of that website by the clients of the enterprise. The relations between the identified BPs, the actors involved and information entities manipulated are illustrated on Figure 4.

2.1.4 PUC Step 4 – Use cases identification

The documentation of BPs in a language that every intervenient (stakeholders of a project) understands is important to enable correct dialogue over the actors, activities and goals of the BP. BPs can be partially or completely automated or not automated at all.

The identification of use cases is the purpose of this step. The BPs identified in the previous step will now be detailed using an Activity Diagram (Object Management Group, 2003) in which the activities that need automation will be transformed into use cases providing the projects' functional requirements.

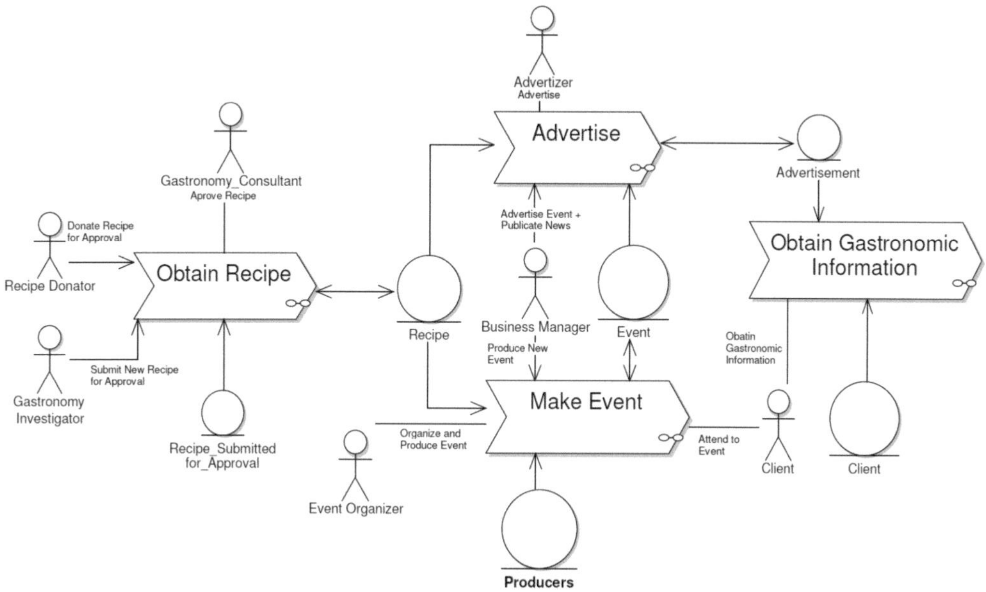

Fig. 4. PUC Step 3 - Business Process Model for the Gastronomy Project.

In this step, analyst and client model the activities and use cases of the BP which will be performed by the actors until achieving the targeted goal. The BP is designed with the Process Use Cases Model, through the use of an UMLs' Activity Diagram with swimlanes. The UML's activity stereotype is used to represent actions of the BP which are not use cases. Fork and Decision can be used to represent parallel activities and decision points, respectively.

Once all activities are identified, it is important that the architect (with the client) decides which activities should be automated. When this happens, a use case (stereotype change) takes the place of that activity.

In the example project presented in this section, four Process Use Case models were designed following the identification of the four BPs relevant for the project identified in Step 3, from which we chosen the "Obtain Recipe" to illustrate the Step 4 of PUC in Figure 5.

2.2 Process use cases basis and related works

Different abstractions provided by different techniques are used to represent the information acquired within PUC. These techniques are: UML (Object Management Group, 2003) that provides the modeling notation; Wisdom (Nunes, 2001) that provides the basic concepts for the RE process, by means of the "Requiremens Workflow"; the High-Level Concept (Kreitzberg, 1999) a concept used in PUC without changes; the Business Process Model (Eriksson & Pencker, 2001) that provides the (adapted) notation used in PUC for modeling BPs and their interaction with users and information, and Usage-centered design (Constantine, 2006) that provides the definition of (essential) use case and the basis for the definition of actor.

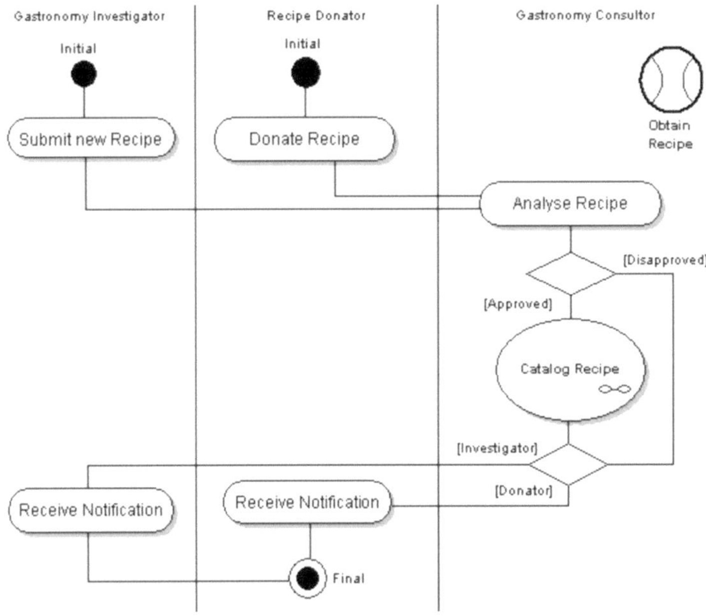

Fig. 5. PUC Step 4 - Process Use Cases Model for the "Obtain Recipe" BP.

The following RE related works also identify use cases as a result of the analysis of business processes: (González & Díaz, 2007) proposes an extensive approach which defines business strategy, business and IT infrastructure to produce a Business Process Goal Tree from which the goals that need automation (use cases) are derived; (Shishkov & Dietz, 2005) that derives use cases from the description of business processes based on the construction of norm sentences; Usage-centered design (Constantive, 2006) that represents the relevant activities (BPs) and interrelationships among them (Activity Map), caracterizes each activity (Activity Profiles) and identifies each participant (Participation Map) and their relationships with each other and with the various artifacts involved in the activity, and then extracts (Activity-Task Map) the task cases (essential use cases) from the activities previously identified; (Dijkman & Joosten, 2002) that proposes a detailed procedure to transform business process models into use case diagrams by mapping roles to actors, steps to use cases, and tasks to interactions; Wisdom (Nunes, 2001) that comprehends the steps of "Interiorize Project" producing an High-Level Concept, "Understand System Context" producing a Domain Model and/or a Business Model, "User Profiling" producing a Role Model and "Requirements Discovery" that encompasses finding actors and essential use cases; and (Štolfa & Vondrák, 2006) that proposes that business processes are designed using Activity Diagrams and that a mapping is made between the activities of the business process and use cases, which can be "one-to-one" or "mapping several actions to use cases" by applying the Sequential pattern or the Optional pattern respectively. For a more comprehensive analysis and comparision of the related works on RE please refer to (Valente, 2009).

3. Analysis phase and effort estimation

Following the identification of the functional requirements, it is important that these, which represent development problems, are further analysed in order to better understand user needs and the components that will be needed to support the construction of the IIS (for these users), and how much time will be needed to develop it.

MultiGoals (Valente & Sampaio, 2007b) is a User-Centered Design (UCD) based methodology that inherits from Usage-Centered Software Engineering and Interactive Multimedia Documents (IMDs) design the concepts and techniques needed in order to understand the user, simplify conception of the usage, and conceptually conceive the user interfaces, system functions and information entities that will compose the IIS with support for Multimedia, covering the phases of analysis and design. Interactive Use Case Points (iUCP) (Nunes et al., 2010) is a method that estimates the effort needed to develop an IIS based on the information produced from the phases of requirements and analysis.

This section presents the analysis phase of MultiGoals and how it uses the artifacts produced in the requirements phase, in order to detail the usage of the system, identify system functions and information entities and their dependencies, and how these objects can be complementarily integrated with iUCP to estimate the effort of the implementation of the IIS, therefore allowing the scheduling of the project within the enterprises' activities.

3.1 MultiGoals for system analysis

MultiGoals is a methodology that defines 11 steps for both analysis and complete detailed design of an IIS. Although it was conceived in order to be comprehensive and cover all the aspects of the conception of an IIS, it also provides the flexibility to be partially applied.

This section will illustrate the application of the simplified analysis steps (Steps 1 and 2, highlighted using and *) of MultiGoals (by means of the example "Gastronomy Project" previously used to illustrate PUC), plus Step 3 - Interaction Model, and Step 11 - System (Conceptual) Architecture that defines the dependencies between the objects identified in the previous steps, i.e. User Interfaces, System Functions and Information Entities.

Consider Table 2 that presents the steps of MultiGoals. Each step adopts a different modeling technique (Use Case, Activity Diagram, Interaction Model, etc...) to produce the appropriate component (actor, task, system responsibility, etc...), within a standard Software Engineering (SE) phase and IMD design level, that will lead to the design of the application.

3.1.1 MultiGoals Step 1 – Use cases model

The Use Cases Model in MultiGoals follows the classical semantics and notation for the UMLs' Use Case Diagram (Object Management Group, 2003). In order to specify the Use Case Model, it is necessary to associate actor(s) to the use cases that they perform.

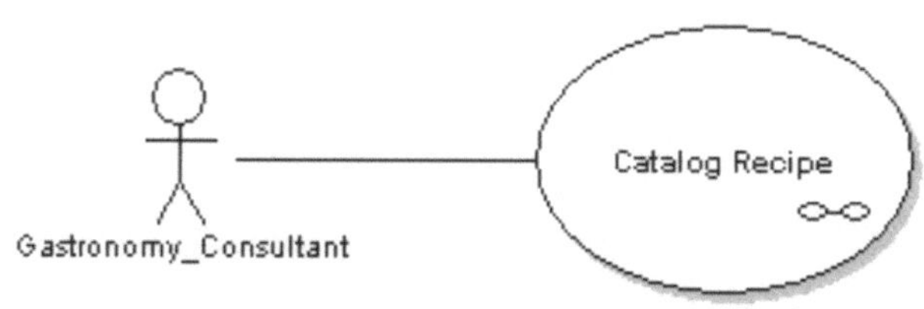

Fig. 6. MultiGoals Step 1 - Use Cases Model (partial) for the "Gastronomy Project".

Step	Step/Model Name	Components Manipulated	SE Phase	IMD Design Level
1*	Use Cases Model	actor, use case	Analysis	Requirements
2*	Activity Diagram	interaction space, task, system responsibility	Analysis	Requirements
3	Interaction Model	task, system responsibility	Analysis, Design	User Interaction
4	Navigation Model	interaction space	Design	Presentation
5	Presentation Model	interaction space, task	Design	Presentation, User Interaction
6	Application Domain Model	entity	Design	Presentation, Content
7	Application Object Model	entity object	Detailed Design	Presentation, Content
8	Conceptual Model	interaction space, task, system responsibility, entity, entity object	Detailed Design	Conceptual, Content
9	System Behavior Model	system responsibility	Detailed Design (Multimedia)	Conceptual
10	Temporal Model	task, system responsibility	Detailed Design (Multimedia)	Conceptual
11	System Architecture	interaction space, task, system responsibility, entity, entity object	Analysis, Detailed Design	Conceptual

Table 2. Steps of MultiGoals methodology

Following the application of the PUC methodology, the Use Cases Model can be directly deduced from the Process Use Cases Model by connecting the actor and use cases that are on the same swimlane. In the example presented in Figure 6, the "Gastronomy Consultant" actor and the "Catalog Recipe" use case were directly derived from the Process Use Cases Model presented in Figure 5 of section 2.1.4 PUC Step 4 – Use Cases Identification.

3.1.2 MultiGoals Step 2 – Activity Diagram

The Activity Diagram will specify how the interaction between the user and the system will lead to the accomplishment of the use case by means of its decomposition into user intentions and system responsibilities, described in abstract, technology-free, implementation independent terms using the language of the application domain and of external users (Constantine & Lockwood, 2000).

The user intentions are represented by the task stereotype and the system responsibilities are represented by the control stereotype. User intentions are tasks that the user wants to accomplish on the system, being most of the times a high level task representing what the user is doing at this step in order to complete his goal (e.g. "Reserve Room"). System responsibilities are the response of the system to the task carried out by the user (e.g. "Confirm Room Reservation").

The Activity Diagram can begin in either side, system or user. Usually, in common cases, 2 to 6 tasks are enough to the user accomplish what he needs. Of course, the number of tasks depends on the complexity of the overall use case purpose. After the Activity Diagram is completed with tasks and system responsibilities, the interaction spaces (user interfaces) in which the tasks will be performed, ant the entities on which the system responsibilities depend must be identified. Notice that one interaction space can support one or more tasks.

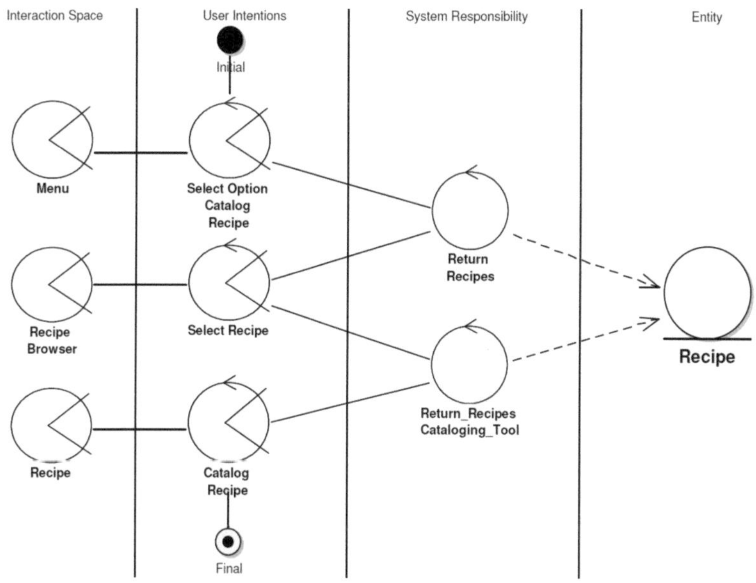

Fig. 7. MultiGoals Step 2 - Activity Diagram for the "Catalog Recipe" use case.

For instance, consider the Activity Diagram depicted in Figure 7. In this diagram, the user intentions initially describe the intention of the user to "catalog a recipe" which is expressed in the "menu" interaction space and immediately carried out by the system returning the recipes in the "Recipe Browser" interaction space so that the user can select the recipe to edit or select a new recipe. After selecting the recipe, the system will return the recipe cataloging tool ("Recipe" interaction space) to the user where the edition of the recipe will be made. The "Return Recipes" and "Return Recipes Cataloging Tool" system responsibilities depend on the "Recipe" entity.

3.1.3 MultiGoals Step 3 – Interaction Model

The Interaction Model details the user interaction necessary in order to perform a user task and specifies which will be the response of the system to each one of the user (sub) tasks, relating these tasks to the interaction spaces where they occur.

The Interaction Model details (decomposes) tasks into sub-tasks, and the corresponding system responsibilities into sub-system responsibilities. The higher level of an Interaction Model is a combination task -> system responsibility taken from the Activity Diagram. Thus, a task is decomposed by means of a ConcurTaskTrees' Model (Fábio Paternò et al., 1997) up to the representation of a physical interaction on the user interface. Similarly, corresponding system responsibilities (which are controls, system functions) are decomposed into lower level controls, which are executed whenever that user task takes place. The sub- tasks are then associated with the corresponding sub-system responsibilities, interaction spaces where the tasks occur are also associated with these tasks, and entities on which the system responsibilities depend are also identified.

The decomposition of tasks into sub-tasks is carried out using aggregation, e.g. "Reserve Room" decomposes into "Select Room", "Select Customer" and "Select Duration". Moreover, an operator also must be specified among the sub-tasks in order to determine their order. These operators can be: Choice (T1 [] T2); Independent concurrency (T1 ||| T2); Disabling (T1 [> T2); Enabling (T1 > T2); Suspend/Resume (T1 |> T2); Order independent (T1 |=| T2). For further information on these operators see (Fábio Paternò et al., 1997).

3.1.4 MultiGoals Step 11 – System Architecture

The System Architecture is the representation of all the relevant components for implementation of the system, and the relations of dependency among them. These components are: interaction spaces (User Interfaces), system responsibilities (System Functions) and entities (Information Entities).

From Steps 2 and 3 of MultiGoals it is possible to extract the interaction spaces, controls and entities of the system, and from the Step 2 of PUC is possible to extract the entities that are directly manipulated by the controls. A relation of dependency is used to relate the components, meaning that an component only works correctly if the other component exists and also works correctly.

From Step 2 of MultiGoals (Activity Diagram), illustrated in Figure 7, it is possible to deduce that one interaction space depends on a control when this control provides valid information for that interaction space, in this case "Recipe Browser" depends on "Return Recipes", and "Recipe" depends on "Return Recipes Cataloging Tool" system responsibility. From Step 3 of MultiGoals (Interaction Model) it is possible to extract directly the relation of dependency from the interaction space to system responsibility to entity.

In the "Catalog Recipe" use case the "Return Recipes" and "Return Recipes Cataloging Tool" system responsibilities will depend on the entities "recipe" and "recipe submitted for approval". These dependecies are represented in Figure 8.

Moreover, it is possible to define precedences of implementation based on the existing dependencies. The components on wich more components are dependent on must be developed first since they will be evoqued by the dependent components. It is also possible to isolate the components that are relevant for a specific use case by means of the existing dependency relations, therefore allowing the possibility to choose which use case to develop first.

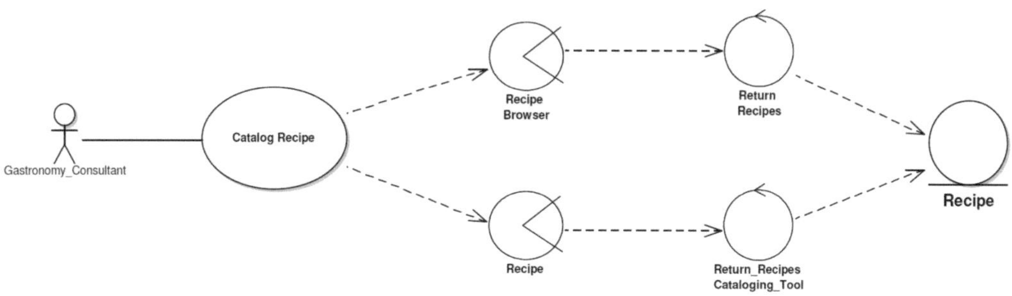

Fig. 8. System Architecture for the "Catalog Recipe" use case.

3.2 MultiGoals basis and related works

Different abstractions provided by different techniques are used to represent the information acquired within MultiGoals. These techniques are: UML (Object Management Group, 2003) that provides the modeling notation, Wisdom (Nuno Nunes, 2001) that provides the main SE process, Usage-centered design (Constantine, 2006) that provides the definition of (essential) use case and the Canonical Abstract Prototypes (Constantine, 2003) for user interface design, and ConcurTaskTrees (Paternò et al., 1997) that provides the technique for user-task modeling.

The following SE related works are also UML based and use case-driven, and support the design of Interactive Information Systems with support for Multimedia:

- UML-based Web Engineering (UWE) (Koch et al., 2008) which is a methodology for the analysis and design of internet application, that produces in five steps the following artifacts: (i) Requirements Specification - (that produces the) Use Cases Model and for each use case an Activity Diagram; (ii) Content - Content Model; (iii) Navigation Structure - Navigation Model and Process Flow Model (for each identified navigation class); (iv) Presentation - Presentation Class and Presentation Model, and; (v) Aspect Modeling - Model Aspect, Link Traversal Aspect and Flow Aspect.
- W2000 (Baresi et al., 2001) is an Hypermedia methodology recognized as the ancestor of a family of several design methodologies, composed of the following steps: "Requirements Analysis", that produces a Use Cases Model, and the "navigation" capabilities associated with each user; the "State Evolution Design" that analyses the state of the information usign an UML StateChart diagram; the "Hyperbase Information Design" that models the domain classes and their attributes; and, the "Hyperbase Navigation Design" that defines the "navigational nodes" and "navigational links" which are derived based a set of rules and design decisions.
- OMMMA (Sauer & Engels, 2001) is a methodology for the development of IMDs that models: the domain (both information and media) using a Class Diagram; interaction using a Collaboration Diagram, temporal and logical system behavior (including navigation) using Statechart and Sequence diagrams, and presentation using the stereotypes of of the identified classes to represent their spatial location in the use interface. OMMMA covers all the design aspects of IMDs (modeling presentation, content and conceptual levels).

For a more comprehensive analysis and comparision of the related works on SE methods for analysis and design with support for Multimedia please refer to (Valente, 2009).

3.3 Interactive use case points for effort estimation

Interactive Use Case Points (iUCP) (Nunes et al., 2010) is a method for effort estimation at early stages of a project based on the weighting of the functional requirements (as use cases) and identified actors, following the phases of requirements and analysis.

iUCP takes advantage of the additional information that can be withdrawn from Usage-centered design (Constantine & Lockwood, 1999) techniques to produce an improved weighting of: actors, specially by means of the concept of user role (an abstraction that represents a relationship between an user and a system that can be described by the context in which is performed); and (essential) use cases by means of the simplification introduced by this concept when compared to the notion provided by the traditional use case as provided by UML (Object Management Group, 2003), and the accurate definition of programmable classes and entities manipulated by each use case that can be retrieved from a system architecture, in order to produce an enhanced calculation of traditional UCPs (Karner, 1993).

Users are weighted in iUCP according to the following criteria in order to calculate the unadjusted actor weight (UAW):

- Simple system actors (a factor of 1) communicate through an API (Application Programming Interface).
- Average system actors (a factor of 2) communicate through a protocol or data store.
- Simple human actors (a factor of 3) are supported by one user role.
- Complex system actors (also a factor of 3) communicate through a complex protocol or data store.
- Average human actors (a factor of 4) are supported by two or three user roles.
- Complex human actors (a factor of 5) are supported by more than three user roles.

Use cases are weighted in iUCP according to the following criteria in order to calculate the unadjusted use case weight (UUCW):

- Simple use cases (a factor of 5) involve a simple UI or simple processing and only one database entity.
- Average use cases (a factor of 10) involve moderately complex UIs and two or three database entities.
- Complex use cases (a factor of 15) involve complex UIs or processing and three or more database entities.

The Unadjusted Use-Case Points (UUCP) is the sum of the previous variables, i.e., UUCP = UAW + UUCW.

The UUCP is then further modified trough the weighting of the technical (Technical Complexity Factor, TCF) factor that reflects how difficult will it be to construct the system, and environmental (Environment Complexity Factor, ECF) factor that estimates how efficient the project is. Both TCF and ECF are the result of similar formulas that include two constants (C_1 and C_2), and a set of 13 and 8 factors (F_1 to F_{13} and F_8), each multiplied by its own weight (W_1 to W_{13} and W_8) respectively and classified (each F_i) from 0 to 5.

The TCF is computed according to the following formula:

$$TCF = C_1 + C_2 \sum_{i=1}^{13} W_i \times F_i$$, where $C_1 = 0{,}6$ and $C_2 = 0{,}01$.

The complexity factors and each corresponding weight are depicted in Table 3.

F_i	**Factors Contributing to Complexity**	W_i
F_1	Distributed systems.	2
F_2	Application performance objectives, in either response or throughput.	1
F_3	End user efficiency (on-line).	1
F_4	Complex internal processing.	1
F_5	Reusability, the code must be able to reuse in other applications.	1
F_6	Installation ease.	0,5
F_7	Operational ease, usability.	0,5
F_8	Portability.	2
F_9	Changeability.	1
F_{10}	Concurrency.	1
F_{11}	Special security features.	1
F_{12}	Provide direct access for third parties.	1
F_{13}	Special user training facilities	1

Table 3. Technical complexity factores and corresponding weights.

The ECF is computed according to the following formula:

$$ECF = C_1 + C_2 \sum_{i=1}^{8} W_i \times F_i$$, where $C_1 = 1{,}4$ and $C_2 = -0{,}03$.

The environmental factors and each corresponding weight are depicted in Table 4.

F_i	**Factors Contributing to Efficiency**	W_i
F_1	Familiar with Objectory.	1,5
F_2	Part time workers.	-1
F_3	Analyst capability.	0,5
F_4	Application experience.	0,5
F_5	Object oriented experience.	1
F_6	Motivation.	1
F_7	Difficult programming language.	-1
F_8	Stable requirements.	2

Table 4. Environmental complexity factores and corresponding weights.

The final calculation of UCP follows the formula UCP = UUCP x TCF x ECF

In order to estimate the number of man.hours of a project the UCP should be multiplied by a productivity factor (PF) that reflects the number of man.hours needed to implement one UCP (the lower in cardinality is the PF, the higher is the productivity), i.e., the total development man.hours of a project would be UCP x PF. For further information on the PF and application of the original UCP consult (Clemmons, 2006).

4. Case study

This section illustrates with a case study based on a project ("Creditations") developed at a professional level in the Software Applications Development Office of the University of Madeira (UMa), the application of the methods described in the previous sections.

In a simplified description, the "Creditations" project consisted in providing the UMa's IIS with the automation of the creditations business process, that involved a request from students of creditations for their actual degree based on courses previously approved in degrees of other universities or UMa. For each course the degree's director would then give a creditation in a given quantity of ECTS (European Credit Transfer and Accumulation System) that would contribute for the conclusion of the student's current degree.

The requirements phase for the "Creditations" project consisted in the application of the PUC methodology, and the analysis phase consisted in the application of analysis steps (1, 2, 3 and 11) of the MultiGoals methodology. After the analysis phase, the effort estimation method iUCP was applied. The diagrams and calculations produced by PUC, MultiGoals, and iUCP will now be presented and described.

4.1 Requirements definition: PUC Step 1 – Interiorize project

The elaboration of the High-Level Concept (HLC) was based on the project description provided by the client, the Rectory of UMa, and the available documentation on the creditations business process. The HLC for the project was:

"Provide students the possibility of requesting creditations for the current degree based on past courses, and the degree's director with the possibility of crediting the request. The student will be able to appeal, in which case the process will be reviewed by the rectory."

4.2 Requirements definition: PUC Step 2 – Information identification

In order to accomplish this step the initial main concepts of information, transformed into entities, derived from the HLC (high-lighted in light-green) were: Student; Creditation; Course; Degree; and Director. The remaining entities (in dark-green): Registration; Degree Plan; Conclusion Plan; Institution; and Files, were ellicited later during the analysis process and then added to the diagram and associated with the previous entities. The final Domain Model is depicted in Figure 9.

4.3 Requirements definition: PUC Step 4 – Process use cases model

The third step of PUC, Step 3 - Business Processes Identification, identifies BPs that relate to each entity if within the scope of the project defined in the HLC. Although many BPs existed that relate to each identified entity such as: registration process; degree publication; director election, among many others, only the creditation BP was within the scope of the HLC, and therefore, was the only one documented, yet, not in Step 3 for schedule reasons, but in Step 4, what would be sufficient to attain the primary goal of the requirements phase, the identification of the use cases for the project.

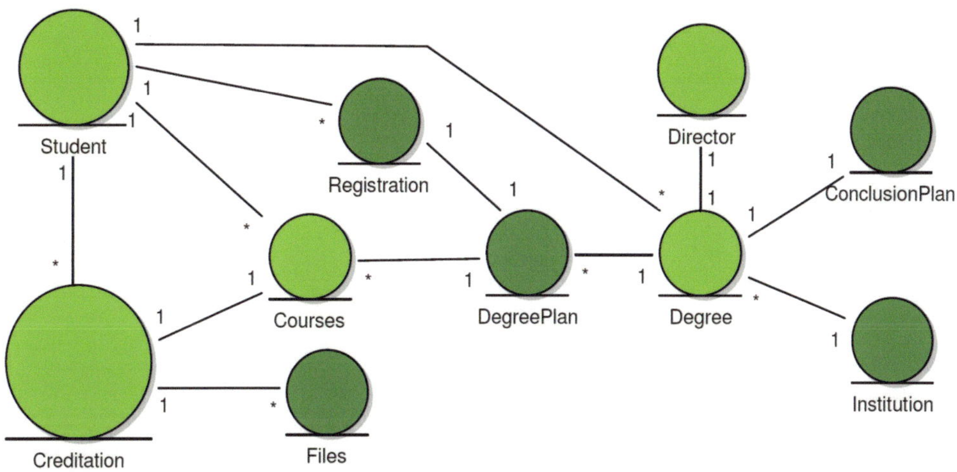

Fig. 9. PUC Step 2 - Domain Model for the "Creditations" project.

The elaboration of Step 4 – Use Cases Identification was made with the client of the project, the Rectory, that provided all the documentation and information necessary to elaborate the sequence of steps that would lead to finishing the creditation BP, and with the Academic Issues Unit (UAA), that accumulated the experience of hundreds of processes.

The previous creditations BP, based in excel files, was first analyzed, and then improved, introducing new activities, for inspection of the initial requests from the students, and appeal to the rectory. The BP was then modeled and decided which activities would be automated (transformed into use cases). The final result of the revized and translated (from portuguese to english) BP is illustrated in Figure 10.

4.4 Analysis: MultiGoals Step 2 – Activity Diagram

Following the identification of the use cases in Step 4 of PUC, the next step would be gathering all the use cases in a single diagram (the Use Cases Model) and relate them to the identified actors. However, since the Process Use Cases Model already establishes those relations, and the "Creditations" BP is the only BP for the project, there is no need to repeat the same information in another diagram, therefore Step 1 of MultiGoals was omitted.

Following the identification of the use cases for the project, the next step consists in analyzing the tasks that each actor has to carry out in the system in order to accomplish its activity. Each use case was decomposed into user tasks and system responsibilities in a sequence of steps, and each task was related to the interaction space in which it would be performed, and each system responsibility to the entities that would provide the information necessary to its functioning.

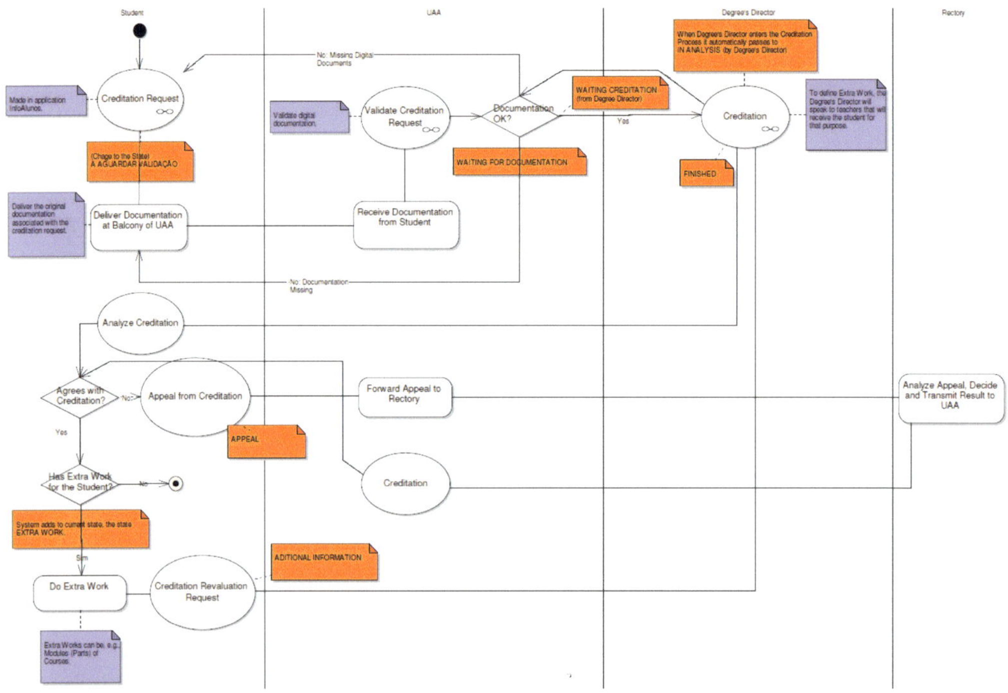

Fig. 10. PUC Step 4 – Process Use Cases Model for the "Creditations" project.

From the six use cases identified, we chose to present one of the most representative, "Creditation". In this diagram all the tasks that the user needs to carry out in order to accomplish the use case were identified and the appropriate responses from the system were defined. Complementarily, the interaction spaces where the user interactions occur, and the entities on which the system responsibilities depended were identified. The Activity Diagram for the "Creditation" use case is depicted in Figure 11.

4.5 Analysis: MultiGoals Step 3 – Interaction Model

The Interaction Model is used to specify interaction between the user and the system that was not already specified in the Activity Diagram. Following the example given in Step 2, Figure 11, the "Specify Scientific Area and Level", "Specify Classification" and "Specify State of Creditation Request" tasks, specific to a single course (a creditation request can gather several past courses), were associated with the system responsibilities that supported the information needed to the task, as well as the association between the tasks and the interaction spaces where they occur and the entities on which the system responsibilities depended.

The Interaction Model for the tasks derived from the "Creditation" use case are depicted in Figure 12.

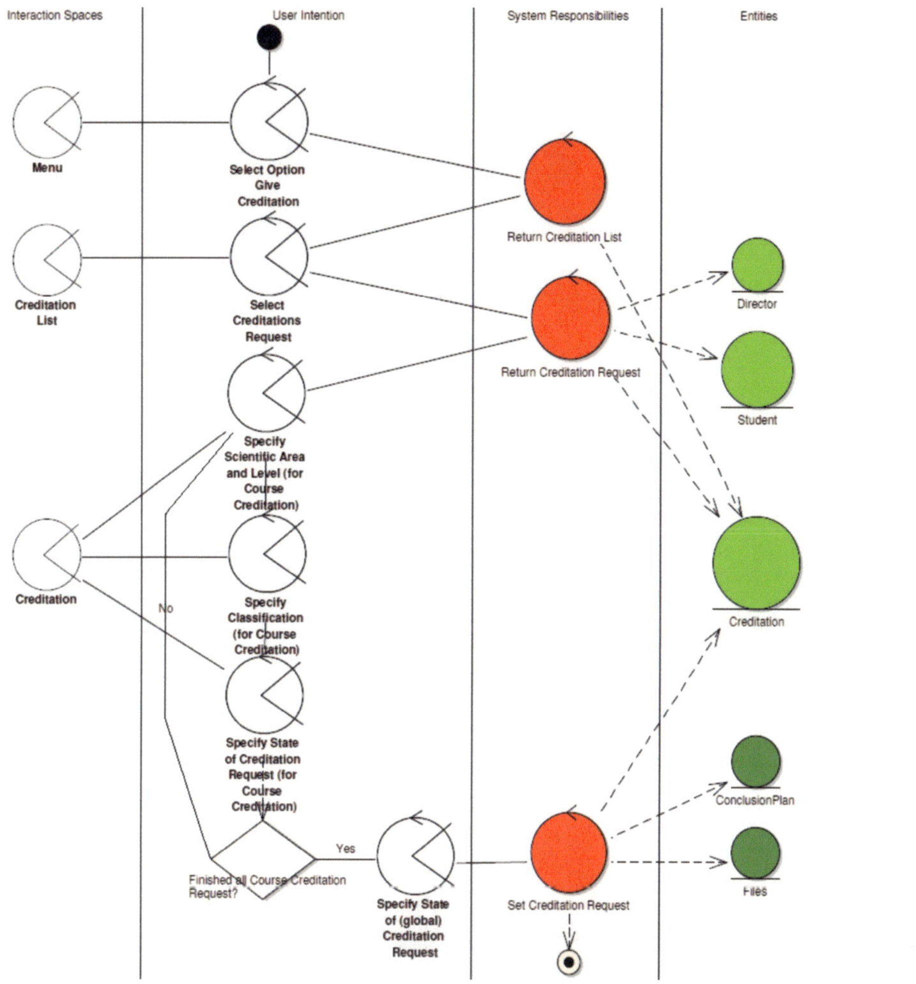

Fig. 11. MultiGoals Step 2 - Activity Diagram for the "Creditation" use case.

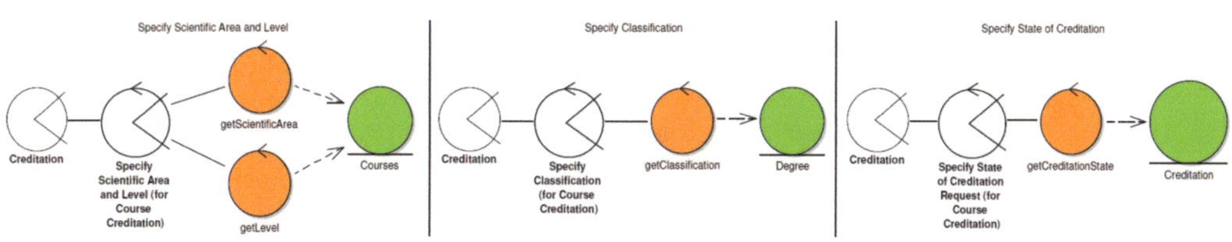

Fig. 12. MultiGoals Step 3 - Interaction Model.

4.6 Analysis: MultiGoals Step 11 – System Architecture

The elaboration of System Architecture is based on the definition of the existing dependencies between the identified components. The composition of the diagram follows the sequence: placing of the interaction spaces, placing of the system responsibilities on which the interaction spaces depend; placing of the entities on which the system responsibilities depend on. The System Architecture is presented in Figure 13.

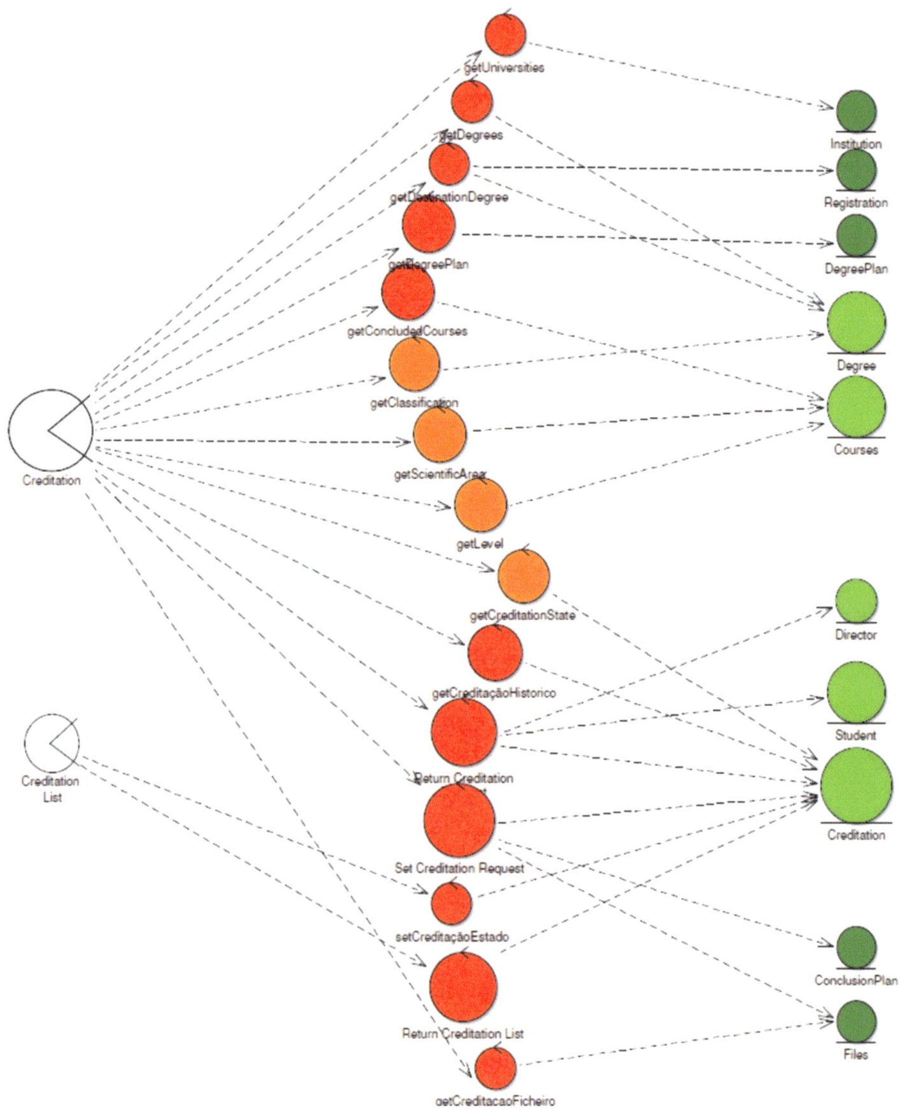

Fig. 13. MultiGoals Step 11 - System Architecture Creditations project.

4.7 Effort estimation: Interactive use case points

The calculation of the effort estimation for the "Creditations" project was based on the information included in the diagrams presented in this section.

The first step for the application of the iUCP method was the definition of the Unadjusted Actor Weight (UAW). Since Goals does not distinguish actor from role, i.e., every actor is actually a role, and since there was no possible generalization regarding a common actor considering the identified roles: Student; UAA; and Degree's Director (the Rectory role did not interact with the system), every actor was considered a simple human actor. Thus, 3 simple human actors multiplied by a factor of 3 resulted in a UAW of 9.

The next step was the calculation of the Unadjusted Use Case Weight (UUCW). In this case, since all the use cases interacted with 10 database entities all the use cases were considered complex once all of them interacted with the "Creditation" and "Creditation List" interaction spaces. Thus 6 use cases multiplied by a factor of 15 resulted in and UUCW of 90.

The calculation of the technical complexity factor (TCF) consisted in assigning a classification between 0 and 5 to the technical factors (F_1 trough F_{13}) and multiply each factor for each weight (W_1 trough W_{13}) and sum each result, situation that is depicted in Table 5.

Factor (F_i)	F_1	F_2	F_3	F_4	F_5	F_6	F_7	F_8	F_9	F_{10}	F_{11}	F_{12}	F_{13}	**Sum**
Weight (W_i)	2	1	1	1	1	0,5	0,5	2	1	1	1	1	1	
Classification	0	4	3	5	5	3	4	0	4	3	3	0	3	
Classification*W_i	0	4	3	5	5	1,5	2	0	4	3	3	0	3	33,5

Table 5. Base parameters for the calculation of the TCF.

The result was then multiplied by the constant C_2 = 0,01 and summed to the constant C_1 = 0,6 resulting in a TCF of 0,935.

The calculation of the environment complexity factor (ECF) consisted in assigning a classification between 0 and 5 to the technical factors (F_1 trough F_8) and multiply each factor for each weight (W_1 trough W_8) and sum each result, situation that is depicted in Table 6.

Factor (F_i)	F_1	F_2	F_3	F_4	F_5	F_6	F_7	F_8	**Sum**
Weight (W_i)	1,5	-1	0,5	0,5	1	1	-1	2	
Classification	3	0	4	3	4	4	0	3	
Classification*W_i	4,5	0	2	1,5	4	4	0	6	22

Table 6. Base parameters for the calculation of the TCF.

The result was then multiplied by the constant C_2 = -0,03 and summed to the constant C_1 = 1,4 resulting in a TCF of 0,74.

For the calculation of the UCP for the project the formula UCP = UUCP x TCF x ECF (in which UUCP = UAW + UUCW) was applied with the result of 68,4981. Applying a productivity factor (PF) of 21,57 (a PF moderated by the previous application of the iUCP method), a final estimation of 1476,82 man.hours was obtained.

5. Conclusions

Goals defines a set of restrictions and main guidelines regarding the requirements, analysis and design phases that are crucial for the correct conception of an IIS, resulting in artifacts that can be used in the remaining phases of the construction to minimize development errors. The application of the phases of requirements and analysis is sufficient to produce valuable results, such as a system conceptual architecture and an effort estimation, that can be crucial for the success of the complete project.

The requirements phase, completed by means of the application of the PUC methodology, resulted in the correct identification of the functional requirements, entities and actors for the project based on the reorganization of the base BP for the project, in which the Process Use Cases Model played a central role in the discussion between the software development team, the client and other stakeholders of the project.

The analysis phase, completed by means of the application of the MultiGoals methodology, complemented the results of the previous phase with the identification of the user interfaces, the system functions and entities for the project, therefore producing sufficient information so that the system could be design in detail in the following design phase. Moreover, the system architecture provides an overview of the dependencies between the objects of the project allowing development tasks assignment.

The application of the iUCP method for effort estimation, integrated by means of the compatibility of the definition of actor (MultiGoals) and role (iUCP) and by the identification of the entities manipulated by each use case, proved to be a consistent tool, since the deviation from the 1476,82 man.hours was only of (plus) 9%.

In spite of the need to accomplish 7 steps in order finish the complete analysis of the problem behind the project and estimate its effort in terms of man.hours, they provide the analyst with enough information to easily bridge its efforts towards the correct design of the solution (only steps 4, 5 and 6 of MultiGoals for non-Multimedia projects), therefore increasing implementation efficiency and minimizing future need for maintenance of the completed IIS.

6. References

Baresi, L., Garzotto, F. & Paolini, P. (2001). Extending UML for Modeling Web Applications. In: Proceedings of 34th Hawaii International Conference on System Sciences, Maui, Hawaii. Vol. 3.

Clemmons, R. (2006). Project estimation with Use Case Points, In: CrossTalk - The journal of Defence Software Engineering, Diversified Technical Services Inc., Vol. 19, Issue 2, pp. 18-22.

Constantine, L. (2002). Usage-Centered Engineering for Web Applications, In: IEEE Software, Vol. 19(2), pp. 42-50.

Constantine, L. (2006) Human Activity Modeling: Toward a Pragmatic Integration of Activity Theory and Usage-Centered Design. In: Human-Centered Software Engineering II, Seffah, A., Vanderdonckt, J., and Desmarais, M. (eds.), NY: Springer-Verlag, 2009.

Constantine, L. & Lockwood, L. (1999). Software for Use: A Practical Guide to the Models and Methods of Usage-Centered Design, Addison-Wesley Longman. ISBN: 978-0201924787.

Constantine, L. & Lockwood, L. (2000). Structure and Style in Use Cases for User Interface Design. In Object Modeling and User Interface Design. Boston: Addison Wesley. ISBN: 978-0201657890.

Dijkman, R. & Joosten, S. (2002). An Algorithm to Derive Use Cases from Business Processes. In: Proceedings of the 6th IASTED International Conference on Software Engineering and Applications (SEA), M.H. Hamza (ed.), Boston, MA, USA, pp. 679-684.

Eriksson, H. & Pencker, M. (2001). Business Modeling With UML: Business Patterns at Work (1st ed.), John Wiley & Sons, ISBN: 0471295515.

González, J. & Díaz, J. (2007). Business process-driven requirements engineering: a goal-based approach. In: Proceedings of 8th Workshop on Business Process Modeling, Development, and Support (BPMDS'07), Trondheim, Norway.

Karner, G. (1993). Resource Estimation for Objectory Projects. Objective Systems SFAB.

Koch, N., Knapp, A., Zhang, G. & Baumeister, H. (2008) UML-based Web Engineering: An Approach based on Standards. In: Web Engineering: Modelling and Implementing Web Applications. pp. 157-191, chpt. 7. Springer, HCI, Vol 12, 2008. ISBN: 978-1-84628-922-4.

Kreitzberg, C. (1999). The LUCID Framework (Logical User Centered Interaction Design) (Pre-Release Version 0.4). Retrieved December 19th 2007: http://www.cognetics.com

Land, R. (2002). A Brief Survey of Software Architecture, In: Mälardalen Real-Time Research Centre (MRTC) Technical Report, ISSN 1404-3041.

Nunes, N. (2001). Object Modeling for User-Centered Development and User Interface Design: The Wisdom Approach, Phd Thesis, Universidade da Madeira, Madeira, Portugal.

Nunes, N., Constantine, L. & Kazman, R. (2010). iUCP - Estimating interactive software project size with enhanced use-case points, In: IEEE Software, Vol. 28, pp. 64–73, ISSN: 0740-7459.

Object Management Group. (2003). Unified modeling language superstructure, version 2.0. final adopted specification.

Paternò, F., Mancini, C. & Meniconi, S. (1997). ConcurTaskTrees: A Diagrammatic Notation for Specifying Task Models, In: Proceedings of INTERACT '97, IFIP TC13 International Conference on HCI, pp. 362-369.

Sauer, S. & Engels, G. (2001). UML-based Behavior Specification of Interactive Multimedia Applications. In: Proceedings of IEEE Int'l Symposium on Human-Centric Computing Languages and Environments (HCC), pp. 248—255, Stresa, Italy.

Shishkov, B. & Dietz, J. (2005). Deriving Use Cases from Business Processes. In: Enterprise Information Systems V, S. Netherlands (Ed.), Vol. Computer Science, pp. 249-257. ISBN: 978-1-4020-1726-1 (Print) 978-1-4020-2673-7 (Online).

Štolfa, S. & Vondrák, I. (2006). Mapping from Business Processes to Requirements Specification. Universitat Trier.

Valente, P. (2009). Goals Software Construction Process, VDM Verlag Dr. Müller, ISBN: 978-3639212426.

Valente, P. & Sampaio, P. (2007a). Process Use Cases: Use Cases Identification, In: Proceedings of ICEIS´2007 - 9th International Conference on Enterprise Information Systems, Vol. Information Systems Analysis and Specification, pp. 301-307, Funchal, Madeira, Portugal.

Valente, P. & Sampaio, P. (2007b). Goals: Interactive Multimedia Documents Modeling. In: Lecture Notes in Computer Science, K. Luyten (Ed.), Vol. 4385/2007, pp. 169-185, Springer Berlin/Heidelberg, ISBN: 978-3-540-70815-5, Hasselt, Belgium.

Webinterx. (2006). Services. Retrieved December 19th 2007: http://www.webinterx.com/services/

9

A Scheme for Systematically Selecting an Enterprise Architecture Framework

Agnes Owuato Odongo, Sungwon Kang and In-Young Ko
Kenya Electricity Generating Company (KENGEN), Kenya

1. Introduction

EAF is "a logical structure for classifying and organizing the descriptive representations of an enterprise that are significant to the management of the enterprise as well as to the development of the enterprise's systems" [17]. EAF is also defined as "a set of assumptions, concepts, values, and practices that constitute a way of viewing reality" [27]. It establishes data element definitions, rules, and relationships and a baseline set of products for consistent development of systems, integrated, or federated architectures. These architecture descriptions may include Families of Systems (FoSs), Systems of Systems (SoSs), and net-centric capabilities for interoperating and interacting in the Net-Centric Environment" [6]. Various EAFs have been developed such as Zachman Framework (ZF) [13][14], Department of Defense Architecture Framework (DoDAF) [6], The Open Group Architecture Framework (TOGAF) [36][35], Federal Enterprise Architecture Framework (FEAF) [10][11], Treasury Enterprise Architecture Framework (TEAF) [8], and The Command, Control, Communications, Intelligence, Surveillance, and Reconnaissance (C4ISR) [29]. However, their unique limitations and dissimilarities make it impossible to use any of them in isolation to completely solve a specific problem. In short, no single existing EAF in isolation is capable of providing a complete solution to an Enterprise Architecture system design problem [31][12][19] [3].

Comparisons of EAFs have been done in the past in order to select the best EAF for system or Enterprise Architecture (EA) development [3][32][31][27][28][24][22][26]. However, none of the past comparisons have focused on EAFs usages and related perspectives and aspects in comparing and selecting EAF based on how they support the various usages. A complete EA system design problem solution may encompass various usages and choosing the right EAF that best supports each usage is of paramount importance. Research has revealed that the existing EAFs have weaknesses and strengths. This is to say that none of them in isolation can offer complete EA design support solution [2][19][17]. EAFs may overlap by addressing similar views, however, they are developed for particular needs, and they differ in the stakeholders they support and their domain. In regard to the above statement, EAFs is used in EA design in order to manage system complexity and to align IT to business [27]. The organizations not using EAFs in EA design spend more in building IT systems which are costly to maintain and offer little business value. It is a fact to say that failing to use EAFs in EA design that aligns IT with business needs makes it expensive and difficult to organize and align IT systems with business needs later after realizing the alignment was not met initially. Comparing and selecting the best EAF that best supports a specific usage is meant to reduce complexity in system management and to allow alignment of IT systems to business needs at initial stage.

This chapter is unique in that it has identified the various usages and considered them to select the best EAF for each. Usages have not been used in selecting EAF In comparing and selecting EAF in past, therefore, this is a new step to improve the selection of EAF for use. All existing EAFs in isolation cannot offer complete EA design solution to an enterprise problem [27] and neither is any of the existing EAF in isolation can support all the listed usages in our chapter as has been demonstrated by the two examples given in section 5. The chapter, therefore, makes a step further by proposing an EAF selection scheme and uses the scheme in selecting an EAF for each usage based on how it addresses the perspectives and aspects relevant to the usage. By selecting the relevant usages to the specific situation and selecting the best EAFs supporting them provides the best solution to the EA systems design. This new scheme has not been availed by the researchers in the past.

To select the best EAF for system or EA development, EAFs have been compared in the past [2][11][24]32]. Past comparisons did not focus on EAF usages and related them to perspectives and aspects. Perspectives are comparison criteria and aspects are the criteria attributes. The chapter proposes an Enterprise Architecture Framework selection scheme (EAFSS) focusing on usages and uses it to select the best EAF for each usage. The scheme has four steps as shown in Fig. Step 1 is split into Fig.1. step 1 is split into 1A and 1B. 1A focuses on identifying usages and 1B searches for comparison perspectives and aspects.

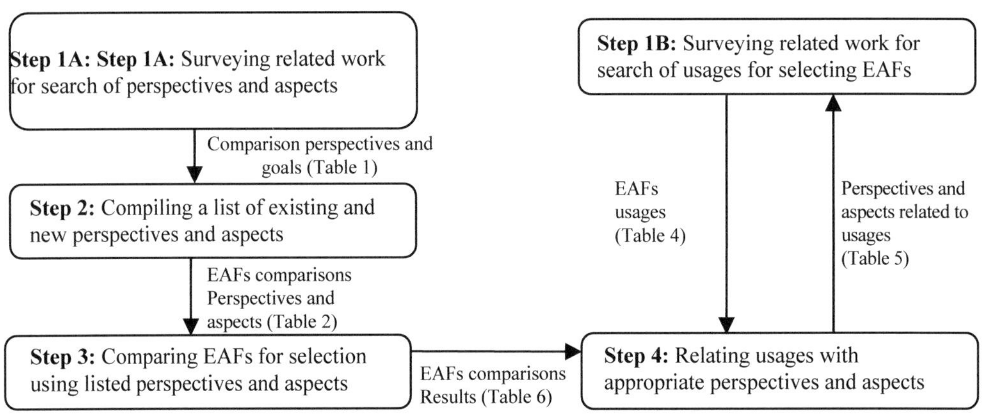

Fig. 1. The chapter approach steps

The focus of the steps is as explained. Step 1A focuses on surveying related work in search of perspectives and aspects. Step 1B conducts the survey on related work with the aim of determining EAF usages. Step 2 compiles the list of perspectives and aspects identified in Step 1A. Step 3 compares the EAF using the listed perspectives and aspects. Step 4 relates the usages to the perspectives and aspects. All these steps have their results in the form of tables to be shown later in this chapter.

The remainder of the chapter is structured as follows: Section 2 describes related works on EAFs comparisons and other EAFs related work. Section 3 focuses on steps toward comparing EAFs. Section 4 introduces our proposed Enterprise Architecture Framework Selection Scheme (EAFSS). Section 5 is the comparisons of EAFs. Section 6 gives examples of application of EAFSS. Section 7 concludes the research and outlines our contributions towards EAFs selection. Section 8 gives the references used in the chapter.

2. Related works

This section surveys related works. It is divided into two parts. The first part covers related works on comparison of EAFs. The second part covers other related works which we thought would contribute positively towards the chapter's goal.

2.1 Related Works on EAF comparison

Comparison was conducted on EAF to develop a method of selecting EAF for system or EA development in specific environments [3]. Furthermore, EAFs are used in designing EA to see the whole enterprise as well, in order to identify the commonality as well as recognize the dimension of entirety and of depth [16]. The comparison focused only on characterizing EAFs by vital elements they need to contain to satisfy the system or EA development. EAFs were compared using ZF as a benchmark, views, abstractions and system development life cycle. The goal was to provide a means of selecting the best fitting EAFs [22]. To determine the current state of EAFs, [31] compared the EAFs using the same perspectives as [3] but considered very few aspects under the three perspectives. He focused his comparison on selecting or tailoring or adapting an EAF [31]. Comparison on EAFs was conducted to determine the contributions each EAF has made to improve EA efforts [26]. The results show that EAFs contribution varies.

Architecture Framework Ontology (AFO) was used to compare EAFs with the goal of characterizing them to determine their overlaps [24]. The goal was to identify certain features that separate artifacts from products they produce to be able to asses EAF for suitability for system or EA development. Comparison was conducted on EAFs by recognizing features of the EA discipline and their principles as relevant; by focusing on structures and methodologies [27]. This was to enable a blending method of developing EAF or selecting the best for specific use. Comparison was conducted on EAFs using requirements that EAF should meet to develop, describe and maintain EA, and determine EAFs capabilities in supporting EA [32]. Commonly used EAFs were compared using some quality aspects to identify relationship among views and the usage growth of EAFs [28].

2.2 Other critical related works

A survey was conducted on papers touching on EAF and the result was that adoption is the major topic [19]. Other topics included benefits of using EAFs, common modeling techniques, summarizing and using EAFs and enterprise environmental change design principles. Assessment of EAFs was conducted to develop an extended EAF by identifying EAFs products to form extended EAF [12]. The topics intended to improve EA effort and is eagerly awaited for. Companies in diverse industrial domains own very complex Enterprise Software Systems (ESS) that has become a challenge to manage and so a utility-based approach was proposed to replace Chief Information Officer (CIO) to manage complexity in ESS [23].

Survey on EA trends revealed that EA is used worldwide in industries, minor and sizeable organizations, and in government organizations [15]. The stormy subjects include delivering road maps for change; managing IT portfolio and complexity; and supporting system development. Modeling EA using BPML standard business methods is widely acknowledged, however, the current accepted Information Systems (IS) modeling standards are OMG's Model Driven Architecture and UML OMG's [18]. An assessment was conducted on EAFs to determine the status of EAFs in regard to industry and government IT; to identify an EAF definition that can be commonly used as a reference [25]. Architecture-centric concept was provided to model the enterprise to address complete concerns.

2.3 Summary of the related work

Related work on comparisons covered various perspectives and aspects. A perspective focuses on a specific interest on an object. It is used to classify content of an object by categorizing them into groups that have related aspects. Aspects are the contents connected to the perspective. Comparison goals are Are the outcomes of research work. Table 1 is a summary of the related works on EAFs comparison. In the last column we have perspectives and aspects, for example, [3] used three perspectives for comparison, i.e. P1, P2 and P3 and the P1 perspective has the aspects P1.1, P1.2 and etc. In the table, when the same perspective or aspect is repeated in the following papers the same ID for it is repeatedly used.

Paper	Comparison Goal	EAFs Compared	Comparison perspectives and aspects
[3]	Selecting and tailoring EAF for system or EA development.	RM-ODP 4+1 View TOGAF FEAF ZF	P1. Goals P1.1 Architecture definition and understanding P1.2 Architecture development process P1.3 Architecture evolution support P1.4 Architecture analysis P1.5 Architecture models P1.6 Design rationale P1.7 Design tradeoff P1.8 Standardization P1.9 Architecture knowledge base P1.10 Architecture verifiability P2. Inputs P2.1 Business drivers P2.2 Technology inputs P2.3 Business requirements P2.4 Information system environments P3.5 Current architecture P2.6 Non functional requirements

Paper	Comparison Goal	EAFs Compared	Comparison perspectives and aspects
			P3. Outcomes P3.1 Business model P3.2 System model P3.3 Information model P3.4 Computation model P3.5Software configuration model P3.6 Software processing model P3.7 Implementation model P3.8 Platforms P3.9 Non functional requirements design P3.10 Transition design P3.11 Design rationale
[22]	Selecting and determining best fit of EAFs.	DoDAF ZF TEAF FEAF TOGAF	**P4. Views** P4.1 Planner P4.2 Owner P4.3 Designer P4.4 Builder P4.5 Subcontractor P4.6 User **P5. Abstractions** P5.1 What P5.2 How P5.3 Where P5.4 Who P5.5 When P5.6 Why **P6. System development life cycle** P6.1 Planning P6.2 Analysis P6.3 Design P6.4 Implementation P6.5 Maintenance
[32]	Identifying requirements to be met by EAFs for EA development, determining EAF capability support to EA building, and developing EA descriptions.	ZF ARIS C4ISR DoDAF FEAF MDA TEAF TOGAF	**P7. Guide** P7.1 Meta model P7.2 Procedure model P7.3 Modeling technique P7.4 Role P7.5 Specification document

Paper	Comparison Goal	EAFs Compared	Comparison perspectives and aspects
[27]	Developing EAFs by blending method, as well as selecting an EAF for use	ZF FEAF GEAF TOGAF	**P7. Guide** P7.6 Process completeness P7.7 Maturity model P7.8 Reference model guidance P7.9 Practice guidance P7.10 Governance guidance P7.11 Partitioning guidance P7.12 Prescription catalog **P8. Quality** P8.1 Taxonomy completeness P8.2 Vendor neutrality P8.3Time to value P8.4 Information availability P8.5 Business focus
[28]	Evaluating relationship among the views and the EAFs usage growth.	DoDAF FEAF TOGAF	**P8. Quality** P8.6 Alignment P8.7 Integration P8.8 Value creation P8.9 Change management P8.10 Compliance
[26]	Identifying appropriate EAF and incorporating best practices to enhance EA effort.	FEAF TOGAF TEAF DoDAF	**P7. Guide** P7.6 Guidance on EA development process P7.7 Maturity/status **P9. Miscellaneous** P9.1 Basic organizational approach and views P9.2 Integrated EA product specifications descriptions P9.3 EA strategic vision and goals P9.4 Architecture principles provision P9.5 Product for specifying standards P9.6 Security considerations in EA P9.7 Tool support P9.8 EA repository issues
[24]	Identifying EAFs features for EA suitability, selecting the best framework and identifying similarities in EAFs	FEAF DoDAF TEAF TOGAF ZF GERAM	**P1. Goals** P1.3 Architecture evolution support **P3. Outcomes** P3.10 Transition strategy and plan definition **P8. Quality** P8.11 Explicit detail of products **P9. Miscellaneous** P9.9 Explicit specification

Paper	Comparison Goal	EAFs Compared	Comparison perspectives and aspects
			P9.10 Architecture domain P9.11 Analytical approach P9.12 Stakeholder P9.13 Application domain development process
[31]	Tailoring, selecting and adapting EAFs.	ZF TOGAF C4ISR	**P1. Goals** P1.1 Architecture definition and understanding P1.2 Architecture process P1.3 Architecture evolution support P1.8 Standardization P1.9 Architecture knowledge base **P2. Inputs** P2.1 Business drivers P2.2 Technology support **P3. Outcomes** P3.1 Business model P3.10 Transitional design **P9. Miscellaneous** P9.7 Visualization tool P9.14 Conformance

Table 1. A summary of comparison perspectives and goals

2.4 The need for further research on selecting EAF for specific usage

Regardless of the research done by [7] [32] [31][27], further research like the one covered by this chapter is still needed because the systems are becoming more complex and delivering less business value. Focusing on developing better methods of assessing and selecting appropriate EAF to develop EA is critical in enhancing enterprise complexity management, and increasing chances of delivering systems which have more value to the business [27]. Complex systems and EA development requires more specific planning that calls for more comprehensive comparison assessment of the EAFs based on usages we identified, and this will support the comparison and selection of EAF. Most of existing comparisons are limited in scope and usages have not been considered as a basis for EAF selection. For example, only objectives, inputs and outputs perspectives were used [3], [Session 07] selected some criteria for comparison EAF fitness in different applications, [24] used ontology to characterize EAFs, [26] considered EAF contributions, [28] considered only three layers of EAFs, [31] used the same perspective as [27] but with fewer aspects for each, [32] considered contributions each EAF has made towards architecture development support, and [22] used views, abstractions and system development life cycle to compare EAFs. None of these authors considered usages and how EAF support them.

Usages may need to be combined to get the complete architecture design solution and hence the EAFs supporting these usages should be used to get a valuable solution in relation to EA design. Researchers that compared the EAFs in the past did not use weighted comparison criteria except [27]. It is difficult to use non-weighted criteria to compare the EAFs for selection. Although this author used the weighted comparison criteria and talked of blended methodology, he did not provide a step by step process for selecting the best EAF.

Past research reveals that authors used different methods in comparing the EAFs. For example, context of a fictional company having functional operational problems was used as an example of blended methodology by integrating best practices of EAFs [27], [3] used goals inputs and outputs to compare EAFs, [26] used contributions that EAF have made to improve EA effort, [24] used ontology to characterize EAFs, [31] focused on the current state of EAFs, [22] focused on views and aspects in comparing EAFs, [28] focused on EAFs strategic support to IT challenges and decisions, [32] focused on requirements that must be provided by EAFs. However, the assessments conducted in this chapter are special by making use of selected formats that are subjected to all the selected EAFs in order to verify their strengths and weaknesses. The formats used in our assessment include philosophy, dimension of EAF, structure, artifacts, enterprise information system development process, and EAF strengths and weaknesses. We believe that our selection scheme is better compared to the past ones.

This chapter proposes a selection scheme and considers all the perspectives used in the previous comparisons as well as added new perspectives to enhance EAF assessment for more improved and balanced comparisons. A suggestion is given for use of comparison in Table 7, and allowance is given for expanding the table by additional of perspective that can be compared by the user of the chapter or shrinking the table by removing what is not relevant to the user. The scheme we developed has the ability to significantly assess the EAFs and subsequently select the best EAF for each usage we identified in this chapter. The scheme is intended to significantly improve EAF selection. The scheme is used to make use of existing EAFs to avoid developing a new one and to save time and money. Examples are given using some selected usages and perspectives to demonstrate the application. The two cases demonstrated prove that the chapter can be generally used for assessing and selecting EAF for any enterprise.

3. EAFs comparison process steps

There is need to develop tables which are referenced when applying the EAFSS selection scheme in Figure 1. Therefore, this section develops the needed tables for EAFs selection purposes. We identify EAFs to compare, conduct EAFs survey, identify perspective and aspects, determine scaling scheme and finally conduct EAFs comparisons. Below are our steps in achieving the goal. This section identifies EAFs to be compared using some criteria, EAFs assessment criteria and of compares EAFs.

3.1 Selecting EAFs for comparison

It is a fact to say from the literature that ZF, DoDAF, TOGAF, FEAF, and TEAF are the most dominant EAFs and have been used the longest [3]. FEAF is the most complete methodology with ZF-like classification and a TOGAF-like structural design process [2]. FEAF, TEAF, and DoDAF are the common federally sponsored and accepted EAFs [2].

C4ISR was dropped and replaced by DoDAF, GERAM was dropped and replaced by TOGAF because TOGAF is a general EAF and used in any enterprise with modifications [36]. Open Distributed Processing - Reference Model (RM-ODP) was dropped because its commonality with other EAFs is limited.

3.2 Conducting survey on selected EAFs

An enterprise architecture developed for use in developing an enterprise system is the structure or structures of that system, which comprise system elements, the externally visible properties of those elements, and the relationships among them [21]. In this regard, it is necessary to identify the formats that can be used to compare the EAFs in relation to this definition so that we can understand in detail the differences, similarities and the limitations of these EAFs.

3.2.1 Criteria used in conducting survey on EAFs

To present summaries of the major EAFs to be compared, we summarized the following six presentation format items, 1) philosophy, 2) dimension of EAF, 3) structure, 4) artifacts, 5) enterprise Information System (EIS) development process, and 6) EAF strengths and weaknesses.

Details of Presentation Formats

The survey is conducted to understand the relationships, commonalities, dissimilarities, and incompleteness among EAFs, [22]. This will improve EAF selection accuracy, assists to rate EAFs by assigning weights to aspects. This is aimed at saving time and money in developing a new one from scratch. The following six formats were used to evaluate the selected EAFs:

F1) Philosophy: Focuses on the purpose of developing EAFs and goals expected to be achieved; and this may include designing Enterprise System Architecture (ESA), supporting realization of goals, identifying enterprise business potential investment areas, and developing enterprise IT system.

F2) Dimensions of the framework: These are classifications, definitions and presentations of architectural artifacts.

F3) Structure of the framework: This holds basic EAFs items and information about them. It provides theories and outlines performed in business processes and how they are performed.

F4) Artifacts: Final products that describe the enterprise functionalities, interactions and requirements.

F5) Architecture development process: It is a series of steps employed in creating a structural design for an enterprise. The process is followed in planning, analyzing, designing, developing and maintaining the created architecture.

F6) Strengths and weaknesses: EAFs have strengths and weaknesses. The weaknesses limit EAFs usage for achieving certain goals. Strengths enhance its usefulness in achieving expected goals. For summaries of the major EAFs, see [1].

3.2.2 Assessments of EAFs

3.2.2.1 Zachman Framework (ZF)

F1) Philosophy: ZF presents architectural artifacts and focuses on business value and suppleness [13]. It also addresses requirement traceability, builds useful and understandable functionalities, and defines communication among stakeholders [31] [5].

F2) Dimensions of the framework: ZF is divided into two dimensional organizations [13].

The rows are roles for stakeholders, and the columns depict divisions of requests.

F3) Structure of the framework: ZF structure is built on 6 fundamental interactive interrogatives and views as shown in Table 3. The models relate to player groups giving a view of the business being modeled [13]. It has a total of 36 intersecting cells each meeting at a point between a player's perspective and a descriptive focus. A cell is a result of a stakeholder's performed architecture activity on a single system viewpoint.

F4) Artifacts: ZF has 30 outcomes from the 36 intersecting cells, with six views that describe cell items.

F5) Architecture development process: No direct guidance on the step-by-step process in developing the architecture, but the process uses viewpoint of the stakeholders [5]. The process consists of: 1) the individual concerned with the business in an organization 2) business management group 3) the business individuals experts to analyze the business systems 4) the business individuals with design technological knowhow to sort out the business challenges 5) the business individuals to construct the actual system 6) the actual functioning system developed from architectural products.

F6) Strengths and Weaknesses: ZF has been used to create FEAF, DoDAF and TOGAF and classifies architectural products model. It offers a series of views and abstractions and visualization support tools to organize enterprise activities. It identifies various unique stakeholders and provides means of building and reproducing system and enterprise architecture. It has a role for resource and reference structure analysis and is the most comprehensive of the EAFs. It supports traceability from requirements to implementation and is also a basis for reuse optimization.

However, ZF lacks high level abstraction to guide the design and has implicit process without stakeholders' viewpoint for architecture development. It has no decisions on future architecture outcomes and architecture need, as well as governance structure as lacks. ZF lacks a city plan that is suitable for EAF information and is not standard written resulting in lack of uniformity on artifacts. Relation between cells is not defined, and the effects on system component on functionalities and interactions are not addressed [31]. Conformity rules, prescriptions on design justification, quality requirements, architecture advancement and explicit system development process are lacking. Views are not created using order and hence does not follow top-down concept.

3.2.2.2 Department of Defense Architecture Framework (DoDAF)

F1) Philosophy: DoDAF offer guideline on structure breaking to develop products and it is used for enterprise, system, and system of systems architectures [26]. It acts as universal concept for creating systems in DoD to enable the comparison of created systems and supports goals transformation through universal guidance. It supports armed warfare operations, business functions and procedures. It also establishes information sharing architecture for managing data and decision making [3] [6]

F2) Dimensions of the framework: DoDAF is divided into data and presentation levels, and the data level contains data elements and the presentation level contains outcomes and aspects.

F3) Structure of the framework: DoDAF defines four perspectives [DoD Arc. 07]. All views illustrate the architecture designs, span, descriptions, and connections among the other views. While the operational view concentrates on the actions and tasks, the system view concentrates on the system and applications. The technical standards view concentrates on the guidelines, uniformity and controls. It describes products using Core Architecture Data Model (CADM) and architecture products [7]

F4) Artifacts: It describes a set of 26 outputs and 4 views [3][26] [7]. The views are valid to each product with names related to information they document. The 26 products hold details for the architecture from the prerequisite stage to the execution stage.

F5) Architecture development process: It has Architecture Development Process Model (ADPM) that has six steps namely: problem definition, operation and requirements, functions and organizations, information and operation elements and rules, interfaces analysis architecture data, and system performance [26].

F6) Strengths and Weaknesses: It describes outputs and procedures that guarantee uniformity and stress on data for architecture assessments. It provides a common set of items and requirements used by vendors' tools to supply software. It gives a universal group of objects, requirements and architecture elements; and addresses current and target architectures, as well as uses capabilities to measure architectures. It has no unique architecture development, no specialized analysis techniques and offers limited guidance quality attributes. It neither records on architecture rationale nor software evolution method. No information is available on architectural management; and no complete business guidance, financial and technical analysis. All view outputs do not show unique architecture aspects.

3.2.2.3 The Open Group Architecture Framework (TOGAF)

F1) Philosophy: TOGAF is a general architecture development method used for reviewing preparation, architecture completeness checking, etc [36]. It has a common EAF for use by industries to create, maintain and use architectures. It is a structure for planning, assessing and constructing architectures for organization [27].

F2) Dimensions of the framework: TOGAF is divided into four categories namely: business, application, data and technical architectures.

F3) Structure of the framework: TOGAF has Architecture Development Method (ADM) that describes the step-wise activities performed in creating EA [9]. It has a repository with components and tools defining components category outputs. TOGAF consists of business, application architecture, data architecture, technical architecture and communications media programs.

F4) Artifacts: TOFAF has ADM for developing and maintaining business technological structures. It has a repository for describing general or special structural design components and the solutions repository that illustrates actual components implementation. The asset repository has resources, guidelines, templates and background information [31].

F5) Architecture development process: TOGAF process has eight phases that are repeated [27]. The phases include considering vision to be achieved, creating a detailed baseline and target business structure, determining target information and functions; determining the communication media; evaluating implementation possibilities; identifying projects, and evaluating the business opportunity; sorting the projects identified into priority order; and creating architectural stipulations; and modifying the created structure.

F6) Strengths and Weaknesses: It has different levels of abstractions and describes final structure. It has governance structure and offers guidelines for making choice. It describes specific view development method and generates and stresses on basic and structural traceability [36]. It has unique outcomes, and allows modifications and addition of outcomes. It lacks specific products and can be used in different environments. TOGAF can bypass, combine, and transform stages as needed; and guides in the usage of standard classification. It aligns solutions to business using support tools and describes various knowledge bases [35]. It has virtual repository with architectures assets and provides guidance on decision making, resources, and principles. It supports architecture evolution, functions creation, and mismatch risk reduction between business and technology. And it generates value, discovers business transformation opportunities and documents descriptions functions creation.

It does not define generation of EA and implementation of flexibility, as well as offers limited description on document templates. It lacks architecture description structures, models, tools and lacks specific prescription group of EA outcomes. There is limited detail on planning, maintaining, and producing high-quality EA. It does not offer various virtual products and has no descriptions and interactions between products [36].

3.2.2.4 Federal Enterprise Architecture Framework (FEAF)

F1) Philosophy: It is a planning model for improving performance, identifying potential investment areas, supporting goal realization, and providing guidance on segmenting system structure [4]. It also establishes an integrated organization roadmap for achieving objectives and puts agencies' functions under single EA [11][20].

F2) Dimensions of the framework: It has two dimensional organizations. The rows depict perspectives, and the columns portray product abstraction entities, activities and locations.

F3) Structure of the framework: It consists of four tiers defined separately and includes business, data, application and technology structures [11]. The top two rows are the business structures like ZF and the models are in the third, fourth, and fifth rows. The rows represent perspectives and each have a unique goal. It has three columns that represent the what, how, and where respectively. The architectural descriptive representations are formed at the meeting points of perspectives and abstractions. It is organized also into 5 tiers where each tier is dealing with specific issue [4].

F4) Artifacts: It has the business allusion model that gives view of a government's various functions; the component allusion model that gives view of the system supporting business functionality; the technical allusion model that defines tools and standards for building systems; the data allusion model that defines data standard method; and the performance allusion model that defines standard for EA delivered value [11].

F5) Architecture development process: It has four phases that include architectural analysis for defining vision; architectural for defining desired architectural segment state; investment and funding strategy for funding project; and program management for executing projects management.

F6) Strengths and Weaknesses: It is the most complete compared with ZF, TOGAF and GEAF. It offers classification of products like ZF and provides architectural development process like TOGAF [3]. It provides a structure for developing, maintaining, and implementing operating environments. It has principles; and shows movement on vision, strategy and knowledge repository. It defines additional views, perspectives, use of methods, work products and tools. It has a common business definition language and transformation. It segments enterprise for reusability, has best standards practices and open standards for interoperability.

It has no quality prerequisites and has limitedly support on plan validation. It has no design support for modeling and organization standards. It has no presentation guidance on transformation processes, plan, and on stakeholders. It has no organization structures, security guidance, repository, a unit product specification development method.

3.2.2.5 Treasury Enterprise Architecture Framework (TEAF)

F1) Philosophy: It was developed from ZF, FEAF, and DoDAF to organize information, support business strategic direction, harness the integration of treasury offices, facilitate information sharing, common use of requirements and establish common EA structure [8]. It was to establish management foundation structures and assets; identify and achieve objectives; and support managers, business and technical planners [12].

F2) Dimensions of the framework: It has a two dimensional organization matrix having four views on the vertical and four perspectives on the horizontal.

F3) Structure of the framework: It describes views and perspectives comparable to ZF columns and rows [8]. It contains sixteen units, and four perspectives that resemble FEAF and ZF. Its builder combines the builder and subcontractor of ZF and the views match with the columns of FEAF. FEAF data structure matches with TEAF functioning and knowledge structures, and information view. The EA elements are defined with their interrelationships and the structure is built using a set of product guidelines.

F4) Artifacts: TEAF is divided into direction, description, and accomplishment, with products for each of these parts defined [12]. The repository stores all the information.

F5) Architecture development process: TEAF has a nine step development process: planning, analysis, design, implementation, project fusion, functions, assessments, organization and control, and technology advancements.

F6) Strengths and Weaknesses: It describes structures for documenting, modeling EA and creating structure that is aligned with FEAF models and DoDAF products. It defines new perspectives on stakeholder important areas, guides on transition, and offers target description principles. It relates EA to enterprise life cycle, determines enterprise activities issues, addresses configuration management, and delineates modeling techniques. It guides on architecture management roles and responsibilities, and addresses information security and assurance issues [26]. It has standards and investment development; and defines structures and offers governing principles [8]. It defines an EA repository without common department-wide format or mechanism for interchange of structural information [8].

3.3 Determining EAF comparison perspectives and aspects

Perspectives are the comparison criteria that focus on a specific interest on an object and are used to classify content of an object by categorizing them into groups that have related aspects. Aspects are the contents connected to the perspective and can be said to be the attributes of the criteria. Table 2 identifies the perspectives and aspects used in the previous comparison works introduced in Section 2. The last column contains perspectives and aspects, for example, [3] used three perspectives for comparison, i.e. P1, P2, and P3. The P1 perspective has the aspects P1.1, P1.2 and so on. In table 2, when the same perspective or aspect is repeated in the papers, its ID is repeatedly used. Table 2 is referenced in the subsequent sections by quoting their Id.

The chapter identifies several perspectives from past research papers as well as our own newly suggested perspectives to enhance accuracy of selecting EAF. It should be noted that the perspectives and aspects in italic are the ones we suggested hence no reference is indicated. The details on these new perspectives are covered in both sections 3.3 and 3.4.

Paper	Comparison of perspectives/aspects
P1. Goals [3] [31] [24]	P1.1 Architecture definition and understanding P1.2 Architecture development process P1.3 Architecture evolution support P1.4 Architecture analysis P1.5 Architecture models P1.6 Design rationale P1.7 Design tradeoff P1.8 Standardization P1.9 Architecture knowledge base P1.10 Architecture verifiability
P2. Inputs [3] [31]	P2.1 Business drivers P2.2 Technology inputs P2.3 Business requirements P2.4 Information system environments P3.5 Current architecture P2.6 Non functional requirements
P3. Outcomes [3] [31] [24]	P3.1 Business model P3.2 System model P3.3 Information model P3.4 Computation model P3.5 Software configuration model P3.6 Software processing model

Paper	Comparison of perspectives/aspects
	P3.7 Implementation model P3.8 Platforms P3.9 Non functional requirements design P3.10 Transition design P3.11 Design rationale
P4. Views	P4.1 Planner P4.2 Owner P4.3 Designer P4.4 Builder P4.5 Subcontractor P4.6 User
P5. Abstractions [22] [24]	P5.1 What P5.2 How P5.3 Where P5.4 Who P5.5 When P5.6 Why
P6. System development life cycle [22] [24]	P6.1 Planning P6.2 Analysis P6.3 Design P6.4 Implementation P6.5 Maintenance
P7. Guide [32] [27] [26]	P7.1 Meta model P7.2 Procedure model P7.3 Modeling technique P7.4 Role P7.5 Specification document P7.6 Process completeness P7.7 Maturity model P7.8 Reference model guidance P7.9 Practice guidance P7.10 Governance guidance P7.11 Partitioning guidance P7.12 Prescription catalog
	P7.13 Providing guidance architecture descriptions *P7.14 Product definitions* *P7.15 Architecture development* *P7.16 Information reference resources* *P7.17 Tool builders* *P7.18 compliant architecture views* *P7.19 EA development process* *P7.20 Transition strategy and plan* *P7.21 Product and repository issues*
P8. Quality [28] [24] [27]	P8.1 Alignment P8.2 Integration P8.3 Value creation P8.4 Change management P8.5 Compliance

Paper	Comparison of perspectives/aspects
	P8.6 Taxonomy completeness P8.7 Vendor neutrality P8.8 Time to value P8.9 Information availability P8.10 Business focus
P9. Miscellaneous [26][24] [31]	P9.1 Basic organizational approach and views P9.2 Integrated EA product specifications descriptions P9.3 EA strategic vision and goals P9.4 Architecture principles provision P9.5 Product for specifying standards P9.6 Security considerations in EA P9.7 Tool support P9.8 EA repository issues P9.9 Explicit specification P9.10 Architecture domain P9.11 Analytical approach P9.12 Stakeholder P9.13 Application domain development process P9.14 Conformance
P10. Requirements	*P10.1 Supporting methodology domain* *P10.2 Developing interface* *P14.3 Automating EA development and population* *P14.4 Extending and customizing* *P14.5 Analyzing and Manipulating* *P14.6 Providing repository* *P14.7 Deploying architecture* *P14.8 Costing and Vendor Supporting*
P11. Principles	*P11.1 Describing views for integrating enterprise products* *P11.2 Developing organization solutions* *P10.3 Developing physical plant* *P10.4 Developing non-physical plant* *P10.5 Enterprise focus* *P10.6 Performing standard assessments* *P10.7 Assessing products* *P10.8 Assessing new technologies* *P10.9 Tailoring model views* *P10.10 Developing standard profiles* *P10.11 Developing architecture descriptions* *P11.12 Evaluating objectives against requirements* *P10.13 Identifying enterprise problems* *P11.14 Architecture information Repository* *P10.15 Mapping of interfaces and services* *P10.16 Addressing migration issues*

Table 2. Perspectives and aspects compared

3.3.1 The significance and relationships between the selected perspectives and aspects

The numbering of the perspectives for existing and newly suggested perspectives in sections 3.3 and 3.4 is based on their importance in regard to system or architecture building. The perspectives focus on specific interest on an object in question with a set of aspects that are the contents connected to them. Requirements are what the enterprise architecture developed is supposed to satisfy and goals are what are expected to be achieved by the architecture developed. Inputs are to support problem solving so that the gaps in the current system can be identified and worked on to achieve the enterprise set requirements. Outcomes are the expected end results offered by the architecture developed. Data is gathered in order to focus on different stakeholders concerns and to arrive at a solution. More than one level of system abstraction may be needed to mange complexity of the scope of problem coverage.

A system development job is said to be done when quality attributes are fulfilled as stated at the beginning during requirements gathering. To develop a software system from the EA blue prints, we need system development life cycle that guides in the development process. To ensure proper use of the resources at our disposal for both architecture and system creation, we need clear guidelines on how to perform the tasks. Finally, we need the rules which must be adhered to by all concerned to avoid system failure. These rules create consensus and harmony in the created items and so must be followed as stated by the designer who defines the principle.

3.3.2 The significance of the selected perspectives

1) Goals: Specific goals must be identified so that they are accomplished. Identification of goals reveals the specific reasons, purpose or benefits of accomplishing the goals. Identified goals enable establishment of concrete criteria for measuring progress toward the attainment of each set goal and by measuring progress, keeping track of progress, reaching target dates, and realizing motivation gained from previous accomplishments so that future encouragements are possible for achieving future goals. Set goals enables prioritization and allow configuration of means to realize them; and create attitudes, abilities, skills, and financial capacity to accomplish them. Setting goals enable planning and setting of steps wisely, and establishing a time frame for performing the steps. Known goals make it possible to determine whether they are realistic by representing objectives that create willingness and ability to achieve them.

2) Inputs: Inputs of EA are the outline that integrates process and goals in a business enterprise to provide core components of the business process like strategic planning, organizational design, business process reengineering, and systems delivery. Inputs help to effectively exploit the intellectual capital, otherwise, intellectual capital will have no value and meaning without inputs.

3) Outputs: Outputs are like views and models that describe the existing environment and are used to understand the gaps that exist when planning for the future preferred environment. Outputs are like design guidelines and patterns that are used in the activities to govern IT task in the most efficient and shortest path to develop future preferred environment. Lack of output makes it difficult to determine the current status and the path to develop future environment as increases cost of doing so.

4) Views: Views are depictions of the complete architecture that are meaningful to concerned stakeholders in the system. Views allow communication and understanding of architecture by all stakeholders, as well as verification that the system will tackle the concerns.

5) Abstractions: Abstractions enforce a progressive decomposition and maintain traceability from the conceptual design of the architecture to the detailed implementation guidance. It allows the removal of complicating factors by incrementally refining the details to manage the enterprise complexity. Lack of abstractions will result in complex systems that are difficult to manage as risks of systems failure due to inability to efficiently and effectively understand and communicate among concern the stakeholders.

6) System development life cycle: Architecture delivery process allows implementation of a standardized design methodology that consists of well defined artifacts, processes, roles and responsibilities. Implicit process definition fastens design cycles, clears handoffs from organization to organization, and reduces costs.

7) Guide: Guiding process is intended to assist in defining, maintaining, and implementing EAs by providing a disciplined and thorough approach to EA life cycle management. The guide describes EA maintenance, implementation, oversight and control. This guidance is critically important and without it, it is highly unlikely that an organization can effectively produce a complete and enforceable EA for optimizing its systems for value.

8) Quality: Failure to develop good quality software may result in making changes to the software may increase costs in unexpected ways and IT can become unmanageable. Attaining quality attributes are the rightful indication of knowing whether job has been done or not.

9) Miscellaneous: This perspective contains a variety of aspects which cannot fit in other perspectives but are critical for comparing the EAFs. Therefore, it is up to the architect to select the related aspects from this perspective based on the intended usage to be focused on.

3.3.3 New perspectives and aspects

10) Requirements (Should be the top most in the list of perspectives): The requirements are the basis on which consideration of obtaining and applying an inclusive EAF representation begins. With no requirements needing solutions, there will be no motivation towards creating enterprise architecture and hence no need for search for EAF for use. When requirements are identified you are able to anticipate requirements that are critical for use in selecting an EAF. The requirements will enable the focus on the performance that is realized by use of EAF on the key operations required in supporting the EA development activity. Requirements lessen risk and equip an organization enabling it to adjust to unexpected changes, align business operations to evade their failures, and develop integrated business processes in the entire enterprise. It enables achievement of gains in combining information to reduce production, time and cost [33] [34].

11) Principles/rules (No.10 in the list of perspectives): Principles define the fundamental basic rules and guidelines for the use and deployment of all IT resources and assets in the entire enterprise. They reflect a level of consensus between the various elements of the enterprise, and build a foundation for future IT decisions making. Principles are vital decisions that are well-formed and should be explicit with lucid applicability scope [30]. It can be too costly to start enforcement of principles after failure of system due to ignorance. Therefore, each organization should have basic principles used in creating and maintaining the EA and developed system. The aspects are included in Table 2.

Note that the details of the formats used in EAFs survey, the survey results and the detailed explanation of aspects can be found in [1].

3.4 Selecting comparison scales

This section compares comparison scales and selects the best to use. Different comparison scales were used by the different authors. The scale should easily and clearly support visualization, decision making, documentation and clarification of the comparison results. Comparisons of comparison scales used are summarized in Table 3. Rating scale is the easiest way to select EAFs.

Comparison scales	Paper	Advantage	Disadvantage
Mapping other EAFs on the selected reference EAF	[22]	Graphical presentation is more easily understood than text.	Difficult to visualize and decide for several isolated mappings
Using notations to indicate EAF item supporting status	[31] [3]	Comparison items can be displayed on a diagram	Lack of weights makes it difficult to make decision.
Populating table with text on EAF status on item support	[26] [24]	More refined comparison details can be achieved	Complex to document and make decision for large comparisons
Rating the items based on how EAFs addresses it	[27]	Weights are given and so making decision is easy	Rate allocation is justified by EAF survey and related work.
Showing EAF item support status capabilities by legend	[32]	Easy to present and visualize the results	Not easy to make decision because of lack of weighs.
Narrating comparison results of EAF items addressing	[28]	Very refined information results can be achieved	It is very difficult to visualize results given in text form.
Indicating EAF item support status using Yes or No/Blank	[24] [22]	Easy to present, visualize and understand the results	Making decision is difficult because of lack of weights.

Table 3. Comparison of scaling schemes

4. Introducing enterprise architecture framework selection scheme

In this section, we propose EAFSS for selecting the best EAF for each usage listed in Table 5. Figure 2 shows the steps EAFSS uses in the EAFs selection process. The subtotal shows the degree to which EAF addresses each perspective. The total weight for each EAF is how it addresses the aspects. The totals in Table 6 are the scores for each EAF. Rate is the ranking of the EAFs based on the scores.

Enterprise Architecture Framework Selection Scheme
Step 1. Select a usage *U* from the Usages in Table 4, i.e. U1~U9
Step 2. Choose the perspectives and aspects relevant to *U* from Table 6.
Step 3. Assign weights to each aspect chosen in Step 2.
Step 4. Calculate the value of each EAF in Table 7 using the formula:

$$\text{Subtotal}_p = \sum_{i=1}^{n} (w_i \times r(a_i)) \text{ ---------------------------------- (F1)}$$

Step 5. Choose the EAF in Table 6 whose total value is the greatest.

Fig. 2. EAF Selection Example

Table 6 can compare any set of perspectives to select EAFs. We can shrink or expand the number of perspectives, aspects, or EAFs in Table 6. To use Table 7, the following steps need to be performed:

1) remove any unwanted perspectives;
2) add any needed perspectives missing in Table 7;
3) give weights to all the aspects in Table 7;
4) calculate each subtotal using the following formula:
Let $a_1, \ldots, a_n$ be the all the aspects of a perspective p, $r(a_i)$ the rate for the aspect a_i and w_i the weight for a_i. Then

$$\text{Subtotal}_p = \sum_{i=1}^{n} (w_i \times r(a_i)) \text{ ---------------------------------- (F1)}$$

5) sum up all the subtotals to get the grand total and
6) select the best EAF based on the rating totals quality of items that results

The EAFs detailed survey is found in [1]

5. Comparing of enterprise architecture frameworks

5.1 Identifying Usages and Related Perspectives

We identified EAFs usages from literature review for use in application of our proposed scheme. The usages are to be used in selecting the EAFs to be used in a specific EA design. Table 4 shows the usages and perspectives that EAFs should address satisfactorily.

5.1.1 Summary of usages and perspectives

Paper	Perspectives used	Usages
[3]	P1. Goals P2. Inputs P3. Outcomes	U1. Selecting the best EAFs for system or EA development. U2. Tailoring EAF for system or EA development
[26]	P7. Guide P9. Miscellaneous	U1. Selecting an appropriate EAF U2. Incorporating best practices from other EAFs

Paper	Perspectives used	Usages
[24]	P1. Goals P3. Outcomes P5. Abstractions P8. Quality P9. Miscellaneous	U1. Selecting an EAF that fits the task at hand U3. Identifying EAFs features for suitability U4. Identifying similarities between the EAFs
[22]	P4. Views P6. System development life cycle P5. Abstractions	U1. Selecting EAF by determining a best-fit of EAF
[32]	P7. Guide	U3. Determining EAFs capabilities in supporting EA U5. Identifying requirements for developing EA descriptions U6. Developing EA descriptions
[31]	P1. Goals P2. Inputs P3. Outcomes	U1. Selecting best EAF based on the status U2. Tailoring EAF to make sense for specific situation U7. Adapting EAF framework
[28]	P8. Quality	U8. Identifying relationship among the EAFs views U9. Determining EAFs usage growth
[27]	P7. Guide P8. Quality	U1. Selecting the best EAF U2. Developing EAF by blending

Table 4. Review Summary of usages Extracted from Comparisons of EAFs

5.1.2 Usages relevant perspectives and aspects of usages

Different perspectives satisfy different needs in system or EA development. Table 4 above shows the usages and their related perspectives that must be addressed satisfactorily by the EAF that is selected. Table 5 below is developed from Table 4. Letter "U" indicates usage. This table is very significant in that it tells the user the perspectives and aspects that must be satisfied by the EAF to be selected for each usage. The aspects relevant under each perspective and aspects will vary based on usage environment.

Usage	Perspectives and Aspects
U1. Selecting the best EAF for system or EA development	P1. Goals P2. Inputs P3. Outcomes P4. Views P5. Abstractions P6. System development life cycle P7. Guide P8. Quality P9. Miscellaneous P10. Requirements P11. Principles
U2. Tailoring EAF for system or EA development	P1. Goals P2. Inputs

Usage	**Perspectives and Aspects**
	P3. Outcomes P4. Views P5. Abstractions P6. System development life cycle P9. Miscellaneous *P9.4 Architecture principles* *P9.5 Product for specifying standards* *P9.6 Security considerations in EA* *P9.7 Tool support* *P9.8 EA repository issues* *P9.9 Explicit specification* *P9.11 Analytical approach* *P9.12 Stakeholder* *P9.13 Application domain development process* *P9.14 Conformance* P10. Requirements
U3. Identifying EAFs features for suitability	P1. Goals P2. Inputs P3. Outcomes P4. Views P5. Abstractions P6. System development life cycle P9. Miscellaneous *P9.6 Security considerations in EA* *P9.7 Tool support* *P9.8 EA repository issues* *P9.9 Explicit specification* *P9.11 Analytical approach* *P9.12 Stakeholder* *P9.13 Application domain development process* *P9.14 Conformance*
U4. Identifying similarities between the EAFs	P1. Goals P2. Inputs P3. Outcomes P4. Views P5. Abstractions P6. System development life cycle P7. Guide P8. Quality P9. Miscellaneous P11. Principles
U5. Identifying requirements for developing EA descriptions	P1. Goals P2. Inputs P3. Outcomes

Usage	Perspectives and Aspects
	P5. Abstractions P10. Requirements
U6. Developing EA descriptions	P1. Goals P2. Inputs P3. Outcomes P4. Views P5. Abstractions P7. Guide P8. Quality P9. Miscellaneous *P9.6 Security considerations in EA* *P9.7 Tool support* *P9.8 EA repository issues* *P9.10 Architecture domain* *P9.12 Stakeholder* *P10. Requirement*
U7. Adapting an EAF	Goals P1.2 Architecture development process P1.5 Architecture assessment P1.5 Architecture models Inputs P2.1 Business drivers P2.3 Business requirements P3. Outcomes P3.1 The business model P3.2 System model P3.3 The information model P3.4 The computation model P3.6 The processing model P4. Views P4.1 The scope P4.2 The owner P4.3 The designer P4.4 The builder P5. Abstractions P5.1 The what P5.2 The how P5.3 The where P5.4 The who P5.5 The when P5.6 The why P8. Quality P8.1 Alignment P8.2 Integration

Usage	**Perspectives and Aspects**
	P8.3 Value creation P8.6 Taxonomy completeness P8.10 Business focus P9. Miscellaneous *P9.1 Organizational approach and views* P9.3 EA strategic vision and goals P9.7 Tool support P9.10 Analytical approach P9.11Stakeholder
U8. Identifying relationship among the EAFs views	P1. Goals P2. Inputs P3. Outcomes P4. Views P5. Abstractions P10. Requirements
U9. Determining EAFs usage growth	P7. Guide P8. Quality P9. Miscellaneous *P9.3 EA strategic vision and goals* P9.4 Architecture principles *P9.6 Security considerations in EA* *P9.7 Tool support* *P9.8 EA repository issues* *P9.9 Explicit specification* *P9.11 Analytical approach* *P9.12 Stakeholder* *P9.13 Application domain development process* *P9.14 Conformance* P11. Principles

Table 5. Relating Perspectives and Aspects to Usages

U1. Selecting the best EAF for system or EA development: Failures have been evidenced in the past in systems developed using traditional methods [27]. It is like trying to put up a complex construction with no plan. Of course the outcome will not be pleasing and most likely it will be a failure. Likewise, selecting the right EAF based on requirements is one very crucial step in EA development that guarantees creation of the right EA that aligns systems to IT and business needs. This result in a successful system that is build from the right plan developed using the right EAF.

To select appropriate EAF for system or EA development, we have to consider all the perspectives to determine how they are addressed by the EAFs. To start with, the problem must be identified and related requirements gathered towards the solution. A set of goals is needed from which we select what is relevant in solving the problem. Existing inputs to support in solving the problem needs to be identified to point out the gaps to be filled to satisfy the requirements. Outcomes must be known to ensure a complete solution to the problem. Views must be identified that focus on different stakeholders affected by the problem. Based on problem complexity more than one model may be needed and a model may need several levels of abstractions to manage complexity and to enhance understanding and communication among the stakeholders.

Qualities of the products of an EAF that are used to develop system or EA are vital for their proper and correct use. To develop a software system from the EA blue prints, we need system development life cycle that guides the development process. Proper use of the resources for both architecture and system creation requires guidelines on how tasks are performed. Rules/principles are needed that create consensus and harmony in creating and maintaining system or EA. There is need for other additional aspects that are critical for enhancing system or EA effort, which are selected from the miscellaneous perspective.

U2. Tailoring EAF for system or EA development: EAFs are not complete as literature tells and hence no single one in isolation can offer complete solution [31] [12] [19] [3]. Therefore, tailoring becomes a necessity for any selected EAF to enhance EA effort. An EAF may cover most parts of definition but combining them in application can increasingly enhance universal completeness. Also, incorporating best practices from other EAFs and applying them improves the capability of the selected EAF in supporting the building of EA.

To tailor EAF for system or EA development, we have to consider several perspectives that must be fulfilled by the EAF to be selected. To start with, the problem must be identified and related requirements gathered towards its solution. A set of goals is needed from which we select what is relevant in solving the problem. Existing inputs to support in solving the problem needs to be identified to point out the gaps to be filled to satisfy the requirements. Outcomes must be known to ensure a complete solution to the problem. Views are needed that focus on different stakeholders that are affected by the problem. Based on problem complexity, more than one model may be needed that may need several levels of abstractions to manage complexity and enhance understanding and communication among the stakeholders.

To develop a software system from the EA blue prints, we need system development life cycle that guides the development process. There is need for other additional aspects that are critical for enhancing system or EA effort, which are selected from the miscellaneous perspective.

U3. Identifying EAFs features for suitability: Although EAF have many features that are all important at one point in the use of EAF, others are more critical and when they miss they render the EAF unsuitable for use. These very critical features should be identified so that EAFs can be subjected to assessment using them to determine their suitability for application in the different usages.

To identify EAF features for system or EA development, we have to consider several perspectives that must be fulfilled by the EAF to be selected. A set of goals is needed from which we select what is relevant in solving the problem. Existing inputs to support in solving the problem needs to be identified to point out the gaps to be filled to satisfy the requirements. Outcomes must be known to ensure a complete solution to the problem. Views are needed that focus on different stakeholders that are affected by the problem. Based on problem complexity, more than one model may be needed that may need several levels of abstractions to manage complexity and enhance understanding and communication among the stakeholders.

To develop a software system from the EA blue prints, we need system development life cycle that guides the development process. There is need for other additional aspects that are critical for enhancing system or EA effort, which are selected from the miscellaneous perspective.

U4. Identifying similarities between the EAFs: If the similarities in the EAFs can be known, the selection process of the EAF can be reduced tremendously. This is because assessments will only be done on the dissimilarities by assuming that the others are the same. A lot of resource and effort will be saved by lessening the EAF assessment process.

To identify similarities in the different EAFs, we have to consider several perspectives that must be fulfilled by the EAF to be selected. A set of goals is needed from which we select what is relevant in solving the problem. Existing inputs to support in solving the problem needs to be identified to point out the gaps to be filled. Outcomes must be known to ensure a complete solution to the problem. Views are needed that focus on different stakeholders that are affected by the problem. Based on problem complexity, more than one model may be needed that may require several levels of abstractions to manage complexity and enhance understanding and communication among the stakeholders.

Qualities of the products of an EAF that are used to develop system or EA are vital for their proper and correct use. To develop a software system from the EA blue prints, we need system development life cycle that guides the development process. Proper use of the resources for both architecture and system creation require guidelines on how tasks are performed. Rules/principles are needed that create consensus and harmony in creating and maintaining system or EA. There is need for other additional aspects that are critical for enhancing system or EA effort, which are selected from the miscellaneous perspective.

U5. Identifying requirements for developing EA descriptions: Requirements are one of the big problems that most organizations face because they keep on changing with time. If we can imagine of a case where all requirements are identified and set aside for sharing, a lot of problems related to changes can really be reduced. Shared requirements throughout the organization avoid redundancy and system simplifies maintenance process.

In order to identify requirements for developing EA using EAF for system or EA development, we should consider several perspectives. The problem must be identified and related requirements gathered towards its solution. Goals should be set from which we select what is relevant in solving the problem. Existing inputs to support in solving the problem needs to be identified to point out the gaps to be filled to satisfy the requirements. Outcomes must be known to ensure a complete solution to the problem. Views are needed that focus on different stakeholders that are affected by the problem. Based on problem complexity, more than one model may be needed and hence the need for several levels of abstractions.

U6. Developing EA descriptions: EAF are to support the creation of EA which includes the products and their descriptions. Therefore, it is very critical to consider EAF that is capable of creating EA descriptions that covers all stakeholders that have concerns in the system to be developed. Of course, each EAF has products but the extent of coverage in regard to enterprise activities differs and so it is of concern to know which one supports best the development of the needed EA descriptions.

To develop EA descriptions using EAF, we have to consider several perspectives that must be fulfilled by the EAF to be selected. To start with, the problem must be identified and related requirements gathered towards its solution. A set of goals is needed from which we select what is relevant in solving the problem. Existing inputs to support in solving the problem needs to be identified to point out the gaps to be filled to satisfy the requirements. Outcomes must be known to ensure a complete solution to the problem. Views are needed that focus on different stakeholders that are affected by the problem. Based on problem complexity, more than one model may be needed that may require several levels of abstractions to manage complexity and enhance understanding and communication among the stakeholders.

Qualities of the products of an EAF that are used to develop system or EA are vital for their proper and correct use. Proper use of the resources for both architecture and system creation requires guidelines on how tasks are performed. There is need for other additional aspects that are critical for enhancing system or EA effort, which are selected from the miscellaneous perspective.

U7. Adapting an EAF: The task of incorporating best practices from the other EAFs into the best EAF selected can be lessened by adapting an EAF. We have EAFs that can universally be adapted to various requirements. These are the EAFs that are not developed for specific domain. Therefore, time, effort and cost is reduced by avoiding tailoring when adaptation becomes the best option in some situations. Knowing which EAF is best for adapting is of great importance.

To adapt EAF for system or EA development, we have to consider several perspectives that must be fulfilled by the EAF to be selected. A set of goals is needed from which we select what is relevant in solving the problem. Existing inputs to support in solving the problem needs to be identified to point out the gaps to be filled to satisfy the requirements. Outcomes must be known to ensure that complete solution components to the problem are included. Views are needed so that selection is made on views that focus on different stakeholders that are affected by the problem. Based on problem complexity, more than one model may be needed that may require several levels of abstractions to manage complexity and enhance communication among the stakeholders.

Qualities of the products of an EAF that are used to develop system or EA are vital for their proper and correct use. There is need for other additional aspects that are critical for enhancing system or EA effort, which are selected from the miscellaneous perspective.

U8. Identifying relationship among the EAF views: Views are meant to focus on the different stakeholders and to make communication between them possible and best. Lack of enough views means that some stakeholders may not be addressed and the system will not reflect the true status of the enterprise. Therefore, it is critical to identify and relate the views to know the impact of missing them in the EAFs.

To adapt EAF for system or EA development, we have to consider several perspectives that must be fulfilled by the EAF to be selected. To start with, the problem must be identified and related requirements gathered towards its solution. A set of goals is needed from which we select what is relevant in solving the problem. Existing inputs to support in solving the problem needs to be identified to point out the gaps to be filled to satisfy the requirements. Outcomes must be known to ensure a complete solution to the problem. Views are needed that focus on different stakeholders that are affected by the problem. Based on problem complexity, more than one model may be needed that may require several levels of abstractions to manage complexity and enhance understanding and communication among the stakeholders.

U9. Determining EAFs usage growth: As time goes by, systems become more and more complex and managing them without employing EAFs become almost impossible. This is evidenced by the many failures of organization systems which are developed without using EAFs. However, as organizations become aware of the benefits of using EAFs, more and more organizations are motivated to use the EAF, thus the growth in EAFs usage is increasing with time. It is vital to know the EAF usage growth so that organizations are encouraged to use it.

To identify EAF growth for system or EA development, we have to consider several perspectives that may encourage the growth in EAF usage. EAF value creation and benefits through IT infrastructure encourages organizations to adopt it. This calls for addressing quality of items those results in valuable EA development. Proper use of the resources for both EA and system creation reduces cost and time, hence organizations are motivated to use EAF, however, guidelines on how to perform tasks should be available. Additional aspects are needed to enhance system or EA effort, which are selected from the miscellaneous perspectives.

5.2 Comparing selected EAFs

EAFs must be compared because their applications concepts, strengths and weaknesses differ. The user must decide the EAFs based on needs and the paper only guides the user. The weight indicates the degree to which an aspect is addressed. The paper user needs to survey the EAFs, so as to rate and assign appropriate weights to aspects. EAFs differ in concepts and no one is best for any organization. We used perspectives and aspects that we believe are critical in comparing and evaluating EAFs for use. They may not all be relevant to an organization and some may be more critical than others based on needs. We provided a cornerstone to start EAFs evaluation process. Weights are subject to change, and our rates which are fixed may not all be approved because EAFs are continuously being improved. At the end of the comparison process, we should understand the strengths and weaknesses of each EAFs based on needs. As shown in Table 6, "0" indicates that the EAF does not entirely address an aspect. "1" indicates that the EAF does not adequately address an aspect. "2" indicates that the EAF does address an aspect adequately. Using rates like 1 and 4 leaves a big gap that may not give reflective results. Close range of rates gives better results because thorough study is needed for correct EAFs rating. Due to lack of space we used three rates instead of five e.g. 0~4.

Comparison perspectives/Aspects	ZF	DoDAF	TOGAF	FEAF	TEAF
P1. Goals					
P1.1 Architecture definition and understanding	1	2	2	2	2
P1.2 The architecture development process	1	2	2	2	2
P1.3 Architecture transition strategy	0	2	2	1	0
P1.4 Architecture evolution support	0	2	2	2	2
P1.5 Architecture assessment	2	2	2	2	1
P1.5Architecture models	2	2	2	2	2
P1.6 Design tradeoffs	1	2	1	1	1
P1.7 Design rationale	1	1	2	1	1
P1.8 Standardization	0	2	2	1	2
P1.9 The architecture knowledge base	0	2	2	2	2
P1.10 Architecture verifiability	0	0	2	0	0
Subtotal	**8**	**19**	**21**	**16**	**15**
P2. Inputs					
P2.1 Business drivers	1	2	2	2	2
P2.2 Technology inputs	0	2	2	2	2
P2.3 Business requirements	2	2	2	2	2
P2.4 Information system environment	1	2	2	2	2
P2.5 Current architecture	1	2	2	2	2
P2.6 Quality requirements	1	1	2	1	0
Subtotal	**6**	**11**	**12**	**11**	**10**
P3. Outcomes					
P3.1 The business model	2	2	2	2	2
P3.2 System model	2	2	2	2	2
P3.3 The information model	2	2	2	2	2
P3.4 The computation model	2	2	2	2	2
P3.5 The software configuration model	0	0	2	0	0
P3.6 The processing model	2	2	2	2	2
P3.7 The implementation model	1	2	2	1	1
P3.8 The platform	2	2	2	2	2
P3.9 The quality design	1	1	2	1	0
P3.10 The transition design	0	2	2	2	0
P3.11 The design rationale	0	1	1	0	2
Subtotal	**14**	**18**	**21**	**16**	**15**
P4. Views					
P4.1 The scope	2	2	0	2	2
P4.2 The owner	2	2	2	2	2
P4.3 The designer	2	2	2	2	2
P4.4 The builder	2	2		2	2
P4.5 The subcontractor	2	0	0	2	
P4.6 The user	2	0	0	0	0
Subtotal	**12**	**8**	**4**	**10**	**8**

Comparison perspectives/Aspects	ZF	DoDAF	TOGAF	FEAF	TEAF
P5. Abstractions					
P5.1 The what	2	2	0	2	2
P5.2 The how	2	2	1	2	2
P5.3 The where	2	2	0	2	2
P5.4 The who	2	2	1	0	0
P5.5 The when	2	0	0	0	0
P5.6 The why	2	0	0	0	0
Subtotal	**12**	**8**	**2**	**6**	**6**
P6. System development life cycle					
P6.1 Domain identification	1	2	1	2	2
P6.2 Planning	1	2	0	2	2
P6.3 Analysis	1	2	1	2	1
P6.4 Design	1	2	1	2	2
P6.5 Implementation	1	1	1	2	2
P6.6 Maintenance	0	0	1	1	0
Subtotal	**5**	**9**	**5**	**11**	**9**
P7. Guide					
P7.1 Meta model	1	1	0	0	1
P7.2 Procedure model	1	2	2	2	2
P7.3 Modeling Technique	0	2	1	0	1
P7.4 Role	0	1	0	2	2
P7.5 Specification document	2	2	1	2	2
P7.6 Process completeness	1	1	2	1	1
P7.7 Maturity model	0	1	1	1	1
P7.8 Reference model guidance	0	2	1	2	1
P7.9 Practice guidance	0	2	1	1	1
P7.10 Governance guidance	0	0	1	1	1
P7.11 Partitioning guidance	1	1	1	2	1
P7.12 Prescription catalog	1	1	1	2	2
P7.13 Providing guidance on architecture descriptions	*1*	*2*	*2*	*1*	*1*
P7.14 Product definitions	*1*	*2*	*1*	*1*	*1*
P7.15 Architecture development	*2*	*1*	*2*	*0*	*0*
P7.16 Information reference resources	*2*	*0*	*2*	*0*	*0*
P7.17 Tool builders	*1*	*1*	*2*	*1*	*0*
P7.18 compliant architecture views	*0*	*2*	*2*	*0*	*2*
P7.19 EA development process	1	2	2	1	1
P7.20 Transition strategy and plan	0	1	2	1	2
P7.21 Product and repository issues	1	1	0	1	1
Subtotal	**16**	**28**	**27**	**21**	**24**
P8. Quality					
P8.1 Alignment	2	2	2	2	2
P8.2 Integration	2	1	2	2	2
P8.3 Value creation	2	0	2	2	0
P8.4 Change management	2	2	2	1	0

Comparison perspectives/Aspects	ZF	DoDAF	TOGAF	FEAF	TEAF
P8.5 Compliance	1	2	2	2	2
P8.6 Taxonomy completeness	2	1	1	1	1
P8.7 Vendor neutrality	2	2	1	2	1
P8.8 Time to value	1	1	1	2	1
P8.9 Information availability	1	2	2	1	1
P8.10 Business focus	2	1	1	2	2
P8.11 EA focus	2	2	1	2	2
P8.12 Explicit detail of products	1	2	1	1	1
Subtotal	**20**	**18**	**18**	**20**	**15**
P9. Miscellaneous					
P9.1 Basic organizational approach and views	2	1	1	1	1
P9.2 Integrated EA product specifications descriptions	1	2	0	1	1
P9.3 EA strategic vision and goals	2	1	2	2	2
P9.4 Architecture principles	0	1	2	1	1
P9.5 Product specifying standards	0	1	2	0	2
P9.6 EA security issues	0	1	1	0	1
P9.7 Tool support	2	1	1	1	1
P9.8 EA repository issues	0	2	0	1	1
P9.8 Explicit specification	1	2	2	2	1
P9.9 Architecture domain	2	2	1	1	1
P9.10 Analytical approach	2	0	0	2	2
P9.11Stakeholder	2	1	0	2	2
P9.12 Application domain development process	1	2	1	2	2
P9.13 Conformance	0	1	2	1	1
Subtotal	**15**	**18**	**15**	**17**	**19**
P10. Requirements	*0*	*0*	*0*	*0*	*0*
P14.1 Methodology domain supporting	*2*	*2*	*1*	*2*	*2*
P14.2 Developing interface	*1*	*2*	*2*	*1*	*1*
P14.3 Automating EA development and population	*2*	*2*	*2*	*0*	*0*
P14.4 Extending and customizing	*1*	*1*	*2*	*0*	*0*
P14.5 Analyzing and Manipulating	*2*	*2*	*2*	*1*	*1*
P14.6 Providing repository	*0*	*2*	*1*	*0*	*1*
P14.7 Costing and Vendor Supporting	*1*	*2*	*2*	*0*	*0*
Subtotal	***9***	***13***	***12***	***4***	***5***
P11. Principles					
P11.1 Integrating enterprise systems	*2*	*2*	*1*	*2*	*1*
P11.2 Developing organization solutions	*2*	*2*	*1*	*1*	*1*
P11.3 Developing physical plant	*2*	*2*	*2*	*0*	*1*
P11.4 Developing non-physical plant	*1*	*1*	*1*	*2*	*1*
P11.5 Enterprise focus	*2*	*2*	*1*	*1*	*2*
P11.6 Performing standard assessments	*0*	*2*	*2*	*1*	*1*
P11.7 Assessing products	*2*	*0*	*2*	*1*	*1*

Comparison perspectives/Aspects	ZF	DoDAF	TOGAF	FEAF	TEAF
P11.8 Assessing new technologies	*1*	*2*	*2*	*1*	*1*
P11.9 Tailoring model views	*2*	*1*	*2*	*0*	*0*
P11.10 Developing standard profiles	*0*	*2*	*1*	*0*	*0*
P11.11 Developing architecture descriptions	*0*	*0*	*2*	*0*	*0*
P11.12 Evaluating objectives against requirements	*2*	*1*	*2*	*1*	*1*
P11.13 Determining enterprise problems	*2*	*2*	*1*	*2*	*2*
P11.14 Architecture information Repository	*2*	*2*	*1*	*0*	*1*
P11.15 Mapping of interfaces and services	*0*	*2*	*0*	*2*	*0*
P11.16 Addressing migration issues	*0*	*0*	*2*	*0*	*2*
Subtotal	***20***	***23***	***23***	***14***	***15***
Total	**138**	**173**	**158**	**147**	**141**

Not addressed: 0; Partially addressed: 1; Fully addressed: 2

Table 6. Comparison of EAFs

The perspectives used in Table 6 may not be all applicable in all cases; and some may be more critical than the others as dictated by requirements. However, this table serves as a basis on which individual EAF selection evaluation can begin. Comparison of all perspectives is complete in Table 6. Table 6 can compare any set of perspectives to select EAFs. We can shrink or expand the number of perspectives, aspects, or EAFs in Table 6. To use Table 7, the following steps need to be performed:

1) remove any unwanted perspectives;
2) add any needed perspectives missing in Table 7;
3) give weights to all the aspects in Table 7;
4) calculate each subtotal using the following formula:
   Let $a_1, \ldots, a_n$ be the all the aspects of a perspective p, $r(\mathrm{a}_\mathrm{i})$ the rate for the aspect a_i and w_i the weight for a_i. Then

$$\text{Subtotal}_p = \sum_{\mathrm{i}=1}^{\mathrm{n}} (w_\mathrm{i} \mathrm{x} r(\mathrm{a}_i)) \qquad \text{(F1)}$$

5) sum up all the subtotals to get the grand total and
6) select the best EAF based on the rating totals.

Perspectives and aspects serve as a basis on which individual EAF selection assessment can begin. The weight value is how the EAF addresses the aspect. The EAFs survey is found in [1], the result is not presented due to space. All the perspectives and aspects in Table 6 are assumed to have equal importance. Under that assumption, DoDAF leads. However, for specific usages DoDAF may not be the best.

5.3 Comparison results

In Table 6, all the perspectives and aspects were presented as if they have equal importance. In this case, it can be seen from Table 6 that DoDAF is leading. However, there is no consideration made for a specific usage and DoDAF may not be the best when we consider each usage at a time for us to compare the EAFs for selecting the best for that specific usage. Based on the usage chosen by an organization, the architects are to conduct comparison using the relevant perspectives and aspects given in Table 6 and adjust them to fit the situation.

Table 6 can shrink or expand in number of perspectives, aspects and EAFs. The total rate per perspective shows how close or diverse the EAFs are in addressing aspects for each perspective. The closer the rates the better because this shows that there is significance commonality in EAF consideration of those perspectives. The bigger the gap in rates for EAF the worse it is because this shows the commonality is lacking in those perspectives in regard to EAFs.

6. Examples of EAFSS application

In this section, we propose an Enterprise Architecture Framework Selection Scheme (EAFSS) that can be used to identify the best EAF for each usage listed in Table 5. Figure 2 shows the steps of the EAFSS.

Classification of EAFs based on perspectives addressing is possible, and this determines what the different EAFs support in regard to EA. It is possible to assess EAF support for specific usage and its worth towards solving the problem, by ensuring that the selected EAF offers the best solution to the organization. Therefore, in this section we demonstrate how the usages and perspectives can be applied to select the best fit EAF for different usages.

Enterprise Architecture Framework Selection Scheme

Step 1. Select a usage *U* from the Usages in Table 8, i.e. U1~U9

Step.2. Choose the perspectives and aspects relevant to *U* from Table 6.

Step 3. Assign weights to each aspect chosen in Step 2.

Step 4. Calculate the value of each EAF in Table 7 using the formula:

$$\text{Subtotal}_p = \sum_{i=1}^{n} (w_i \times r(a_i))$$

Step 5. Choose the EAF whose value is the greatest.

Figure 3. The EAFSS Steps

EAF is just a planned outline that can be tailored by any organization for a tactical target described by concerned stakeholders. Specifically, EAFs do not indicate the number of levels to model decomposition required to achieve quality of information sufficient for specific objective. The definition of a process to model and guiding principle to abide by are generally not given.

The information we presented in this chapter on EAFs can be used to adapt some of them to different organizations with different needs because information reveals some generality in them. Combination of elements of different EAFs in Table 7 can be performed to satisfy unique development requirements. This enhances speed and accuracy of decision making on development requirements. Incorporation of best practices from other EAFs is performed to develop an integrated EAF that enhances EA effort. Our approach allows the harmonization of tradeoff and recommendation, prior to selecting EAF, by considering EA effort based on the problem to solve, or information needed to solve the problem.

For tailoring of FAFSS, the following tasks need be performed:

1. The user can revise the list of perspectives and aspects based on requirements.
2. The user can give the weights to perspectives aspects according his satisfaction.
3. The user can rate the EAFs based on the allocated weights.

6.1 EAFSS application examples

Here we show two different examples for validating the application of our EAFSS. The first example is the usage for selecting the best EAF for system or EA development, and in this example we considered all the perspectives and aspects in Table 6. This is because for such usage our EAFSS requires to consider all the perspectives and aspects of our selection process. The second example shows how to select the best EAF for determining the EAF usage growth, and in this example we considered relevant certain perspectives and only certain aspects of those relevant considered perspectives.

6.1.1 Selecting the best EAF for system or EA development

This is the usage U1 in Table 5. From Table 6, we can see that all the perspectives are relevant. For this example, we assume w = 1 for all the aspects in the formula (F1) in Section 4.2. This means that all the perspectives and all the aspects are considered to be of equal importance to the assessment and selection of EAF for system or EA development. Therefore, we just add the subtotals to get the total for each EAF and select the best EAF based on the results as shown in Table 7. According to the results in Table 7 DoDAF is the best EAF for U1.

Comparison perspectives/Aspects	ZF	DoDAF	TOGAF	FEAF	TEAF
P1. Goals					
Subtotal	8	19	21	16	15
P2. Inputs					
Subtotal	6	11	12	11	10
P3. Outcomes					
Subtotal	14	18	21	16	15
P4. Views					
Subtotal	12	8	4	10	8
P5. Abstractions					
Subtotal	12	8	2	6	6
P6. System development life cycle					
Subtotal	5	9	5	11	9
P7. Guide					
Subtotal	16	28	27	21	24
P8. Quality					
Subtotal	20	18	18	20	15
P9. Miscellaneous					
Subtotal	15	18	15	17	19
P10. Requirements					
Subtotal	9	13	12	4	5
P11. Principles					
Subtotal	20	23	23	14	15
Total	**138**	**173**	**158**	**147**	**141**

Table 7. Selecting EAF for system or EA development

6.1.2 Adapting an EAF as a tailoring example of EAFSS

For this example we are using U7 and the relevant perspectives to this usage from Table 4 are P1, P2, P3, P4, P5, P8, and P9. We used these seven perspectives with selected relevant aspects only as shown in Table 8.

Let i be the set of all the aspects of a perspectives such that $i = i_1 \cup i_2$

- i_1 : set of relevant aspects
- i_2: set of irrelevant aspects (are ignored because they have a value of zero)

Furthermore the relevant aspects are given weights according to their importance and relevance. The weights are shown in parentheses in the leftmost column of Table 8. For this example, a rating of 1~4 was used.

We are considering an aspect "*a*" and applying weights based on the priority "a" is given in regard to the usage. *For irrelevant aspects their weights are automatically 0 without saying it.*

- $a \in i_1 \Rightarrow w_i = 1\sim4$
- $a \in i_2 \Rightarrow w_i = 0$

The column with WR for weighted rate contains the results of multiplying the weight and the rate of each aspect. Now in Table 8 each subtotal for a perspective is obtained by adding the WRs for the aspects of the perspective and by summing up all the subtotals we get the score for each EAF. The best EAF for the usage is the one with the highest score. In this example ZF is the best choice.

Comparison perspectives/Aspects	ZF		DoDAF		TOGAF		FEAF		TEAF	
	Rate	WR	Rate	WR	Rate	WR	Rate	WR	Rate	WR
P1. Goals										
P1.2 Architecture development process (2)	1	2	2	4	2	4	2	4	2	4
P1.5 Architecture assessment (3)	2	6	2	4	2	4	2	4	1	2
P1.5 Architecture models (4)	2	8	2	4	2	4	2	4	2	4
P2. Inputs										
P2.1 Business drivers (3)	1	3	2	6	2	6	2	6	2	6
P2.3 Business requirements (3)	2	6	2	6	2	6	2	6	2	6
P3. Outcomes										
P3.1 The business model (3)	2	6	2	6	2	6	2	6	2	6
P3.2 System model (3)	2	6	2	6	2	6	2	6	2	6
P3.3 The information model (3)	2	6	2	6	2	6	2	6	2	6

Comparison perspectives/Aspects	ZF		DoDAF		TOGAF		FEAF		TEAF	
P3.4 The computation model (3)	2	6	2	6	2	6	2	6	2	6
P3.6 The processing model (3)	2	6	2	6	2	6	2	6	2	6
P4. Views										
P4.1 The scope (2)	2	4	2	4	0	0	2	4	2	4
P4.2 The owner (3)	2	6	2	6	2	6	2	6	2	6
P4.3 The designer (4)	2	8	2	8	2	8	2	8	2	8
P4.4 The builder (4)	2	8	2	8			2	8	2	8
P5. Abstractions										
P5.1 The what (3)	2	6	2	6	0	0	2	6	2	6
P5.2 The how (3)	2	6	2	6	1	3	2	6	2	6
P5.3 The where (2)	2	4	2	4	0	0	2	4	2	4
P5.4 The who (1)	2	2	2	2	1	1	0	0	0	0
P5.5 The when (2)	2	4	0	0	0	0	0	0	0	0
P5.6 The why (3)	2	6	0	0	0	0	0	0	0	0
P8. Quality										
P8.1 Alignment (4)	2	8	2	8	2	8	2	8	2	8
P8.2 Integration (2)	2	4	1	2	2	4	2	4	2	4
P8.3 Value creation (4)	2	8	0	0	2	8	2	8	0	0
P8.6 Taxonomy completeness (4)	2	8	1	4	1	4	1	4	1	4
P8.10 Business focus (4)	2	8	1	4	1	4	2	8	2	8
P9. Miscellaneous										
P9.1 Organizational approach and views (3)	2	6	1	3	1	3	1	3	1	3
P9.3 EA strategic vision and goals (3)	2	6	1	3	2	6	2	6	2	6
P9.7 Tool support (2)	2	4	1	2	1	2	1	2	1	2
P9.10 Analytical approach (3)	2	6	0	0	0	0	2	6	2	6
P9.11Stakeholder (4)	2	8	1	4	0	0	2	8	2	8
Totals		**175**		**128**		**111**		**153**		**143**

Table 8. Adapting EAF

7. Conclusions

There are a number of already established EAF in use today; some of these EAFs were developed for use in very specific areas, whereas others have broader functionality. In this chapter a review of these EAFs is presented. The chapter conducted a comparative analysis on the basis of previous research. Further, the chapter discussed the importance and background of the selected EAFs. Therefore, the chapter provides a comparison of several EAFs that can then be used for guidance in the selection of an EAF that meets the needed criteria.

The chapter has covered a broad introduction to the field of EAF. As I have shown from the review of EAFs conducted, these methodologies are quite different from each other, both in goals and in approach. This is good and bad news. It is bad news, in that it increases the difficulty for organizations in choosing one single EAF methodology. It is difficult to choose between methodologies that have very little in common. The good news is that these EAFs methodologies can be seen as complementing each other. For many organizations, the best choice is all of these EAFs, blended together in a way that works well within that organization's constraints. The chapter provides a scheme that blends together all the compared EAFs. Therefore, the chapter provides a good starting place for understanding the value of each of these EAFs and how they can complement each other to bring the business side and the technology sides together, so that both can work effectively toward the same goals.

Either route one chooses, we should remember that EAF is a path, and not a destination. EAF has no value unless it delivers real business value in the shortest time possible. The most important goal of any EAF is to bring the business side and the technology sides together, so that both are working effectively toward common goals. In many organizations, there is a culture of distrust between the technology and business folks. There is no EAF methodology that can bridge the divide unless there is a real commitment to change. That commitment must come from the uppermost level of the organization. Methodologies cannot solve people problems; they can only provide a framework in which those problems can be solved. However, as soon as one has that commitment to change, an EAF methodology can be a valuable tool for guiding that change. This change can manifest itself in many ways. The many ways include improvements in using IT to drive business adaptability; closer partnership between business and IT groups; improved focus on organizational goals; improved morale, as more individuals see a direct correlation between their work and the organization's success; reduced numbers of failed IT systems; reduced complexity of existing IT systems; improved agility of new IT systems; and closer alignment between IT deliverables and business requirements.

Due to failures that have been reported in the past as indicated in this chapter [27], it is true that an organization that does well in these key areas will be more successful than the one that doesn't. This is true regardless of whether success is measured with tangibles, such as profitability and return on investment, or intangibles, such as customer satisfaction and employee turnover. The starting point for any EA is some critical self-analysis. These are some of the questions you should ask yourself during the analysis: does your organization spend too much money building IT systems that deliver inadequate business value? Is IT seen as improving or hampering business agility? Is there a growing divide between your business and IT folks? And, lastly, perhaps the most important question of all: is your organization truly committed to solving these problems, and does that commitment come from the highest levels of the organization? If the answer to all of these questions is "yes," EA is your path. It's up to you to take that next step.

Enterprise architects are still stuck in the technology weeds and the resulting lack of connection with business leadership. One cannot make a business case for EA if we do not connect with the business aspects of it. Furthermore, let us highlight the futility of comparing EAFs, because one can admire and maybe express a preference for the architectures of various buildings, however, can we really "compare" EAF in a meaningful way? This is a challenge to us all and that's why for many organizations, the best choice is all of these EAFs, blended together in a way that works well within that organization's constraints. The generic scheme is the best option because it borrows from the other EAFs.

We believe that our approach is better than any of the past approaches. This is supported by the unique information provided on EAFs usages that has not been considered by the past researches. Our scheme can support organizations to systematically select the best EAFs for the usages they envisage to design a desired architecture. The scheme is the best because it borrows perspectives and aspects from all of the major existing EAFs, and blends them together in a way that works well within any organization's constraints. It is the duty of the organization to decide what to include in their blending that best fits the organization constraints.

Tailoring of the selected EAF: Tailoring of selected EAF is agreeable and anticipated because almost all of existing EAFs are not complete to offer support to EA design in isolation. Tailoring is the process of borrowing best practices to fill the gaps identified in the best EAFs based on comparison results. For example, DoDAF is leading in Table 7, however, it is not supporting all the usages and to enhance the EA design effort, tailoring and integration of best practices must be conducted.

8. References

[1] Agnes Owuato Odongo, "E-government system architecture design guided by an e-government development process and an enterprise architecture framework," Master of Science in Engineering Thesis, KAIST, Korea, 2009.

[2] A Practical Guide to Federal Enterprise Architecture, Chief Information Officer Council Version 1.0, 2001.

[3] A. Tang, J. Han, P. Chen, "A Comparative Analysis of Architecture Frameworks", Centre for Component Software and Enterprise Systems, 2004.

[4] Allen Sayles, "Development of Federal Enterprise Architecture Framework using IBM Rational Unified Process and the Unified Modeling Language", Rational Brand Services, IBM Software Group, 2003.

[5] David C. Hay, "The Zachman Framework," Essential Strategies, Inc., 2000.

[6] Department of Defense, "DoD Architecture Framework Version 1.5: Volume I: Definitions and Guidelines," 2007.

[7] Department of Defense, "DoD Architecture Framework Version 1.5: Volume II: Product Descriptions," 2007.

[8] Department of Treasury, Chief Information Officer Council, Treasury Enterprise Architecture Framework, Version 1, 2001.

[9] Fatma Dandashi, Rolf Siegers, Judith Jones, Terry Blevins, "The Open Group Architecture Framework and the US Department of Defense Architecture Framework", Published by the Open Group, 2006.

[10] Federal Enterprise Architecture Program Management Office (2007). FEA Practice Guidance.

[11] Federal Enterprise Architecture, Chief Information Officer Council, Version 1.0, 2001.

[12] Frank Goethals, "An Overview of Enterprise Architecture Framework Deliverables", Information Systems Frontiers, Volume 8, Number 2, pp. 67-79(13), 2006.

[13] J. A. Zachman, "The Zachman Framework For Enterprise Architecture: Primer for Enterprise Engineering and Manufacturing", 2003.

[14] J. A. Zachman, Viewing and Communicating Information Infrastructure: Enterprise Architecture (EA), 1987.

[15] J. Schekkerman, "Trends in Enterprise Architecture", Institute for Enterprise Architecture, Report on the Third Measurements, 2005.

[16] John Wu, "Frameworks and Models: The Myth" EA Consultant, 2006. [Wu 06]

[17] John Zachman's: Foundations for Enterprise Architecture, A two-day briefing for business and IT executives, 2008.

[18] Jon Siegel and the OMG Staff Strategy Group, "Developing in OMG's Model-Driven Architecture", Object Management Group White Paper, Revision 2.6, 2001.

[19] K. Langenberg, A. Wegmann, "Enterprise Architecture: What Aspects is Current Research Targeting?" Technical Report, EPFL, 2004.

[20] Lee Deidre, James Flyzik, Federal Enterprise Architecture Framework Version 1.1, 1999.

[21] L. Bass et al. "Software Architecture in Practice", Addison Wesley, Boston, MA, USA, 2nd edition, 2003. [Bass et al. 03]

[22] L. Urbaczewski, "A comparison of Enterprise Architecture Frameworks", Issues in Information Systems, Vol. 7, No. 2, 2006.

[23] M. Ekstedt, P. Johnson, A. Lindstrom, M. Gammelgard, E. Johansson, L. Plazaola, E. Silva, J. Liliesköld, "Consistent Enterprise Software System Architecture for the CIO - A Utility-Cost Based Approach", 2004.

[24] Oddmn Pauline Ohren, "An Ontological Approach to Characterizing Enterprise Architecture Frameworks", ICEIMT, 2004.

[25] Osvalds, Gundars "Manuscript Instructions/Template for 2001", Proceedings of the 6th International Symposium, INCOSE 1996. ... [Osv01], 2001.

[26] Paula J. Hagan, "Guide to the (Evolving) Enterprise Architecture Body of Knowledge", MITRE Corporation. 2004.

[27] R. Sessions, "Comparison of the top Four Enterprise Architecture Methodologies" EA Comparison ObjectWatch, Inc., 2007.

[28] Richard V. McCarthy, "Toward a Unified Enterprise Architecture Framework: an Analytical Evaluation", Issues in Information Systems, Vol. 7, No. 2, 2006.

[29] Rob Thomas, Raymond A. Beamer, Paula K. SowellCivilian Application of the DOD C4ISR Architecture Framework: A Treasury Department Case Study.

[30] Ruth Malan and Dana Bredemeyer, "Guiding Principles for Enterprise Architects" Architecture Discipline, 2004.

[31] S. Abdallah, G. H. Galal-Edeen, "Towards a Framework for Enterprise Architecture Frameworks Comparison and Selection", Fourth Int'l Conf. on Informatics and Systems, 2006.

[32] S. Leist, .G. Zellner, "Evaluation of Current Architecture Frameworks", SAC'06, April, 23-27, Dijon, France, 2006.

[33] Schekkerman Jaap., "How to survive in the jungle of Enterprise Architecture Frameworks: Creating or Choosing an Enterprise Architecture Framework", Third Edition, Trafford, 2006. [34] Schekkerman Jaap., "The Economic Benefits of Enterprise Architecture, How to quantify and Manage the economic Value of Enterprise Architecture". Trafford Publishing, Canada, 2005.

[34] The Open Group Architecture Framework Version 8, Enterprise Edition, 2002.

[35] The Open Group Architecture Framework Version 8.1.1, Enterprise Edition, 2006.